The Life & Lines of Brandon Block

by Matt Trollope

Copyright © 2011: Block & Troll Ltd

All rights reserved.

ISBN: 1467923400
ISBN-13: 978-1467923408

Art Direction: Jimmy P
Interior formatting/layout: Matt Trollope
Front cover image: Alexis Maryon
Back cover image: JaxEtta

No reproduction without permission

Every reasonable effort has been made to contact copyright holders in this book. If any have been inadvertently been overlooked, the author would be glad to hear from them and make good in the future editions any errors or admissions brought to his attention.

brandonblock.com
matttrollope.com

Hi, I'm Brandon Block, and this is my story...

...well, what I can remember so far, at least.

Every time I read through this book the more of my crazy adventures come to mind, but we have had to draw the 'line' somewhere, at least for this volume anyway.

It's taken quite some time and the patience of a saint... in fact, Matt Trollope is Roger Moore and Val Kilmer rolled into one!

Now it's finally here, though - my labour of love, and hopefully a little insight into what has been an extremely enjoyable, albeit occasionally dangerous journey.

Fortunately I made it through, via the odd near death experience, loads of adversity and despite tonnes of 'wallop'.

With any luck, some of you out there can even take heed and realise that there is always a way back.

It's been emotional...very!

I dedicate this book to my mum Viv, my dad Harvey, daughter Lily, sister Emma, Aunt Arlene and Uncle Clifford, cousins Adam and Elliott and grandparents Goldie Sklar and Joe Block. Thank you for being the best family anyone could ask for and for all your unwavering support throughout my life. You all deserve medals!

And thanks to Dr William Shanahan for showing me the way back.

Blocko x

CONTENTS

1	ON HIS WAY TO WEMBLEY	9
2	LYON DANCING	23
3	THE ACID TEST	35
4	THIRSTY WORK	49
5	MILKING IT	63
6	FLYING SOLO	77
7	WATCH THIS SPACE	93
8	PASS THE DUTCH 'E'	111
9	GOA, GOING, GONE	127
10	BAGGY'S TROUSERED	141
11	NOT ALL GIRLS A LOUD	149
12	CANER GET A WITNESS	169
13	IT'S A WRAP	183
14	CARRY ON UP THE BYPASS	193
15	OUT OF HIS BOX	209
16	A QUICK DRIVE ROUND THE BLOCKSTER	227
17	WE WANNA PARTY LIKE IT'S £19.99	239
18	BRITS & IN PIECES	251
19	I'M GETTING TROLLIED IN THE MORNING	271
20	A WHOLE NEW BALL GAME	295
21	BACK TO BLOCK	313
22	LIVING ON A PRAYER	321
23	YOUR STORIES	333
24	DEDICATIONS	343
25	ACKNOWLEDGEMENTS	347

FOREWORD BY MATT TROLLOPE

It was a summer, the like of which we will never see again. Lots of smiley faces, loads of great tunes, one big party and, in all, two or three months of sheer hedonism.

But this wasn't the summer of love in 1969, or the so-called second summers of love in '88 or '89, this was the summer of 2011, and what I'm calling, the 'Summer Of Bruv'.

It was the final push for The Life & Lines Of Brandon Block as, after several years of sifting through my subject's fragile memory, we attempted to complete the final draft.

However, spend any amount of time with Brandon Block and you'll be vying for air time with the multitude of phone calls coming and going his way. He has more than 800 'bruvs' in the address book of his iPhone, and dozens check in each day..."hello mate"...."all right bruv?"... "right maaaaaaaaate"... "you there bruv?"... "that you bruv?"... "you alright, son?".

As summer jobs go, though, 'working' for Brandon Block is surely as good as it gets. A more colourful 'boss' you would be hard pushed to find. One minute you are getting ticked off for being late, the next you've been whisked off for a round of golf. Or it's suddenly a case of downing tools for a compulsory stint in the hot tub, with my Blackberry recording and perched precariously on the side.

And just when I thought it was time to break up, when this (old) school was out...there was a compulsory field trip to undertake.

"I'm sorry, Matt, but if we're going to do this properly, we've got to go to Ibiza. We're going to Ibiza, whether you like it or not."

The overall result? Well, like any key player/infamous era...Brandon was there, but struggles to remember it all. And it's not just the stuff that Brandon can't remember, it's that, for the most part, he couldn't remember what he had already told me either!

The bare bones of this fascinating story, however, quickly came to the surface.

Brandon, the joker in the pack, the Ibiza 'nutter', the party animal who single-handedly created the Caner Of The Year category, was literally lying on his death bed.

And despite the chronic situation that he found himself in, with drips attached to his ravaged body as he battled jaundice and tuberculosis, he was still trying his hardest to shovel as much cocaine as possible up that famous hooter of his!

The result of a spiralling drug habit which, at its peak, saw him take an ounce of coke a day for almost a year (that's a mind-boggling 28 grams a day) was his bewildered doctor telling him that he would die within two weeks if he didn't stop pronto.

But that wasn't going to deter our Brandon. No chance!

He pleaded with friends to bring coke to the hospital and they duly, if reluctantly, obliged. If he was on his way out, then he was going out on a high, at least that was the twisted and warped way he looked at it. However, by then he had to take so much of the stuff for it to actually register that it almost defeated the object.

Clubland had snorted him up one nostril and blown him out of the other. A haunting shadow of the livewire DJ who leapt on to the house music scene in the late '80s, Brandon somehow managed to drag himself out of the mire and lived to tell the tale.

With his astronomical coke habit - and the complex network of dealers who fuelled it - now fortunately in the past, he is able to look back (through somewhat hazy spectacles) on a 25-year-career which spans the highest highs and lowest lows.

His own success and turmoil has weaved in and out of the so-called acid house generation and seen Blocko, like no other DJ, crossover into mainstream celebrity too.

Six million Google images of him - compared to 1,500,000 of global superstar Carl Cox - tells its own story. While his pioneering residency with Alex P on the Space terrace in Ibiza in the early '90s took club life in Ibiza and throughout the world to a whole new dimension.

Meanwhile, away from the edgy world of underground dance music, he famously stormed the Brits stage, scrapping with Rolling Stone Ronnie Wood, ending up splashed across the front of the tabloids the next day, with Richard and Judy appealing for his whereabouts later that night!

He talked about coke addiction on national television and later celebrity detoxed in Thailand, among a whole host of other reality TV show appearances. He's presented (for MTV/Channel 4/Kiss 100) and produced (a No 3 UK hit as Blockster).

These days his bookings diary is still full and his love of DJing remains, but you'll also find him down the gym three times a week, or playing badminton with pals. Sure he still likes a drink, but insists he hasn't touched the white stuff since 1996.

In this amazing account we look back at the career of this cheeky-chappie-made-good, a DJ who was there from the very start of the modern-day club movement, who had grafted as a pub and mobile DJ during the mid-'80s, a few years later finding himself in a prime position when, like many others, he discovered the drug ecstasy and house music quickly followed a love of disco, soul, jazz funk and hip-hop.

This rollercoaster of a ride charts how that underground dance music scene became a national and global phenomenon and how Brandon was intrinsically linked to it all, headlining an era that changed the lives of millions, but also becoming a symbol for its excess.

We witness the meteoric rise of a cocky Jewish schoolboy from Wembley who became an Ibiza legend along the way. And how he and his suburban peers led a recklessly hedonistic lifestyle that was the envy of their generation.

We see how the odd cheeky half here and there led to more cocaine than you can shake a rolled-up bank note at.

It's messy, murky, mental and memorable and often takes no prisoners.

I can't quite remember when I first met Brandon Block, and I can guarantee he cannot either. I had come across him loads in our native London, but in earnest, I probably got to know him better in Ibiza (if that's possible?) - the island where he made his name.

Like in 1993, when I was writing for DJ Magazine, at the Tahiti in Playa D'en Bossa, the after-party beachside bar opposite Space, which hosted many a lively daytime session, and where he and Alex P plied their trade after another busy stint on the now world-famous terrace over the road, and where each year I made more lifetime friends in the space of a week than I will ever again.

Or the following year at the Aqualandia Water Park party in Ibiza, when Alex, Brandon and his sidekick Baggy Baxter launched their own short-lived venture Sac Le Nez - French/cockney translation for nosebag!

The dynamic trio were staying in an apartment above the Café Del Mar, with Sac Le Nez posters everywhere, showing a cartoon of a horse with his schnozzle in a bag of sugar. The boys were grinning inanely, but then Brandon was always grinning inanely.

My articles on the Tahiti bar, Sac Le Nez and when he posed in a hard hat with Nicky Holloway as the latter prepared to open Velvet Underground in Charing Cross Road, London, stuck in Brandon's mind.

I won't claim to have been a close friend of Brandon's over the years, or even to have possessed his mobile phone number since those heady Ibiza days of the early '90s…but, through my articles at that time, and his sheer showmanship, a mutual respect has always existed between us. And it has been impossible to ignore his colourful career ever since!

Over recent times the idea of writing his memoirs came up intermittently. Five years ago, after the Notting Hill Carnival, I found him rolling around the garden of The Lodge, a bar I co-owned in his native north west London, and he mumbled something about it. A couple of years later he officially asked me to write his life story. And it's been one hell of a journey.

Naturally, spending hours upon hours with Brandon, going through his 44 years on this planet was essential. We've lunched numerous times in his favourite Italian restaurant in Park Royal, but most time has been spent at his large bungalow in Ruislip. Either in his front room, while Corrie, The Sopranos or Man v. Food is on; in his office, while eBay and Facebook are both active; or flicking through photos in his poker room when we needed to jog that battered memory of his.

During one stint at the house, with Mr Block Snr relocating to America the next day, we conducted a whole afternoon's interviewing while attempting to sell his dad's S-Type Jaguar. At one point, Brandon and I were both in the running, until his friend snapped it up.

Then there were the online chats, which were hilarious to say the least! Once Brandon worked out that the noise caused by my other half shuffling around our flat was not, in fact, someone breaking into his house, we were OK. Although, he did spend that whole Skype session armed with a baseball bat…just in case.

Delving back in time for most of us, at the best of times, is an arduous task. Childhoods can often be easier to remember than teens, twenties and thirties, and the fact alcohol comes into play during those phases of most of our lives is surely no coincidence. Add buckets-full of white powder - or Man v. Cocaine - and the task in hand becomes even more painstaking.

Up until Brandon leaving school and starting out on his frivolous social life presented no major obstacles, but when we entered the so-called acid house years everything suddenly got increasingly blurry.

The classic Morecambe and Wise sketch with Andre Previn springs to mind. Morecambe takes to the piano to impress Previn, and after the resulting disastrous performance, he utters the immortal line…. "I'm playing all the right notes, not necessarily in the right order". And that just about sums up Brandon's recollection of everything between 1989 and 1996… "not necessarily in the right order".

Fortunately, the fact that I had kept every issue of leading dance music publication MixMag (1990 – 2003) in my dad's cellar was finally not wasted. See Dad, I told you they would come in useful one day! And no, this doesn't mean you can now take them to the dump!

By leafing through every issue, I was able to chart Brandon's career, fortunately played out each month on the various full-page adverts and random, yet extensive, column inches that dance music journos devoted to their favourite party animal.

Securing the medical and psychological 'ins and outs' from consultant psychiatrist Bill Shanahan, the man who treated Brandon, was invaluable.

Speaking to the various cohorts (friends, DJs and music business associates alike) that Brandon has partied, worked and generally hung out with along the way, has also been enlightening, although very few had an encyclopedic memory of anything either.

But we got there in the end. So here it is - The Life & Lines of Mr Brandon Block! Snorts and all.

THE LIFE & LINES OF BRANDON BLOCK

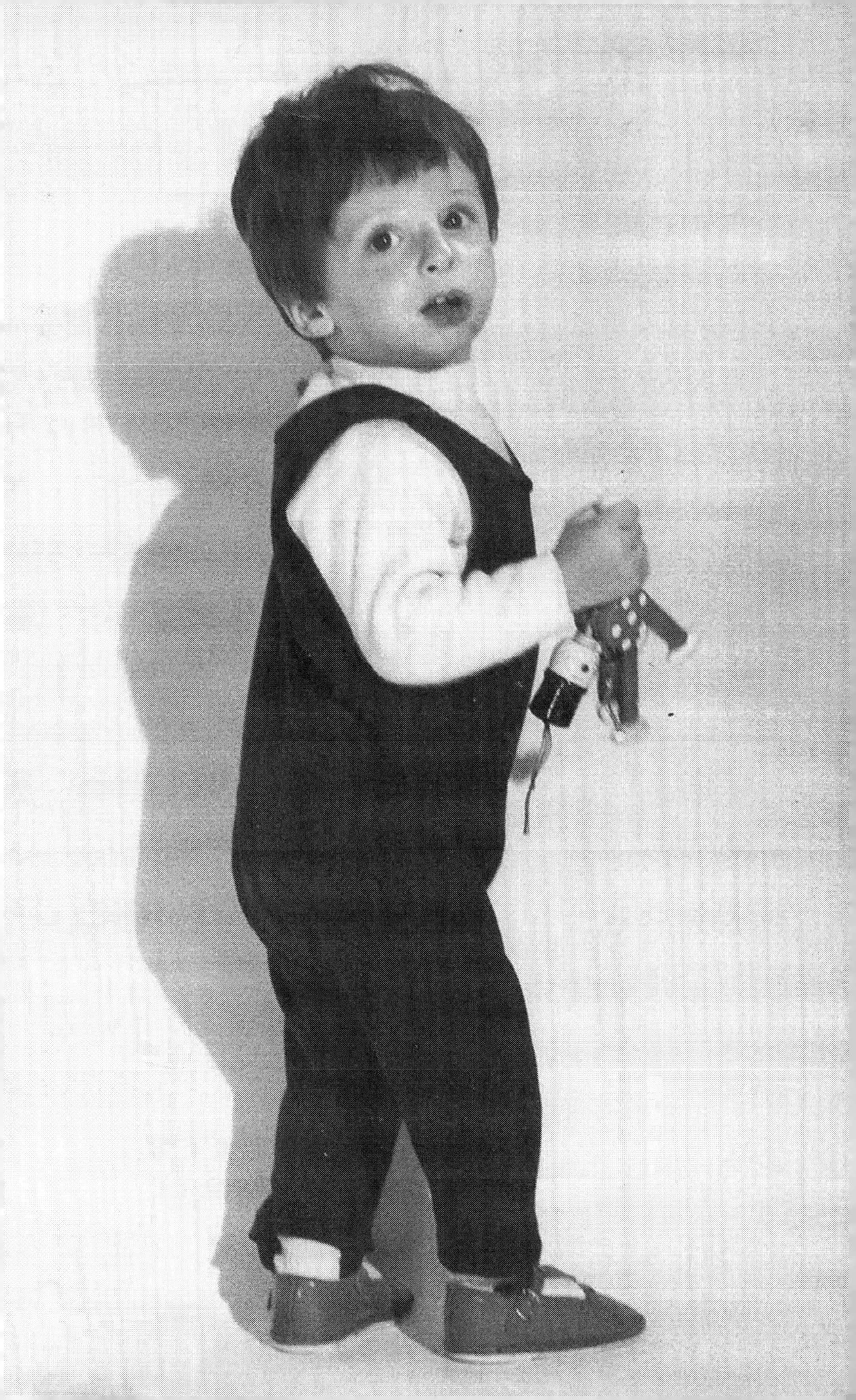

THE LIFE & LINES OF BRANDON BLOCK

ON HIS WAY TO WEMBLEY

Dad driving home through our affluent north-west London cul-de-sac in a brand, spanking new Aston Martin DB7 in the summer of 1973, is one of my earliest memories. All the other parents came out of their houses and were shouting "oi, oi, Harve". The old man was lapping it up. It was a lovely car - black with gold trim... beautiful.

I was born on March 8 in Hackney six years earlier, and we had left east London at the end of the 1960s, settling in Sudbury Croft, in the heart of the Wembley suburbs in a modern new-build three-floored town house.

We lived alongside other Jewish families, including many colourful characters. Two doors away, were my Aunt Arlene and Uncle Cliff, and my two younger cousins Adam and Elliott. My auntie played a major role in my upbringing, often picking me up from nursery if mum was late from work, and superbly handling the daily difficult task of getting me to eat my greens and beans.

One family friend and neighbour was then Top Of The Pops producer Brian Whitehouse and his glamorous job made a quick and early impression on me.

Shortly after the DB7 became the latest addition to the family, only child Brandon, his clothing entrepreneur dad Harvey and mum Vivienne moved again, driving the short distance to Nathans Road, in nearby South Kenton, just north of Wembley, where they remained until the couple divorced when Brandon was 13.

Nathans Road was on a lovely little estate. It was very communal, family-orientated and half the Parent Teachers' Association lived there. I joined my primary school, Byron Court, when I was six so, in old money, that was the first year infants. The school backed on to our house and I used to climb over the fence to get home. I can't even remember being at school before that.

And I possessed one hell of a trump card – rows of horse chestnut trees, which separated the family house and the school

playing fields. I was the toast of the school every morning in October when I turned up with my pockets full of conkers. And this was long before conkers were banned for Health & Safety reasons, when conkers was about as much fun as you could have in the playground, long before Gameboys and iPhones ruled.

My best and first mate there was Lee Birch, who was in my class. My other close mate, Phil Ember, was seven and in the year above. I'm still close to Phil to this day, while Lee started DJing with me when I first began playing out. The three of us went to cubs together and I stayed there long enough to be a 'sixer'. In fact, between the three of us we had more badges than a TGI Fridays waitress. Sixer is the highest achievable rank in the cub scout regime...the governor, only second to Akela really. I had a go at scouts too, but I don't think that was for me...starting at the bottom again, and all that.

The three of us knocked around the South Kenton area of Wembley and played for the same football teams - the usual Saturday morning under-10s and 11s stuff, I guess. I played up front and I was quite sporty as a child. I won a competition at Wembley Tennis Centre, and also swam for the London Borough of Brent too. All those pursuits came to an abrupt halt when I was briefly diagnosed asthmatic at the age of 12.

And it was at junior school that I first surrounded myself with pretty girls, the 'Charlie's (or Brandon's) Angels' of Byron Court, in fact - namely Laura Kirk, Tina Simpson and Tracey Tyler, who frequently came to visit me at home. The girls were quickly befriended by my mum, who would take us all swimming. We were just friends, though - no petting!

Like any regular kid of the late 1970s and early '80s, Brandon progressed effortlessly from Raleigh Chopper to Raleigh Grifter, via skateboard, but mostly rollerskates, culminating in him forming the dubiously-titled South Kenton Skate Patrol.

Still in touch today with many of the friends he made at Byron Court, a whole gang of them later moved on to Wembley High School in East Lane. One of few Jews at 'big' school, Brandon quickly tapped into some 'older kid' contacts, and was promptly encouraged to bunk off on his first day with a certain second year called Ember!

The skate patrol was later followed by the effervescent and all-singing, all-dancing South Kenton Soul Patrol. In fact, at this point in our lives we were highly affiliated with many so-called local action groups. Others included the South Kenton Thunderbird Patrol, named not after the successful TV series, but the popular and affordable street tipple of the day.

Phil took me into the West End on my first day at secondary school, and when we were milling around he pointed to a shop and asked me to get him 20 Lambert & Butler. Next thing I knew I was in Ann Summers on Tottenham Court Road - this little runt in a blazer, being chased in and out of the dildos by the staff. And this was when these shops weren't as acceptable as they are now. Needless to say, I was quickly and unceremoniously escorted from the premises. It was my first experience of the West End, and little did I know, there were many more good vibrations to come!

To be honest, going to secondary school was actually quite a harrowing experience. I was easily influenced and because I was hanging around with older kids, people like Baggy Baxter, John Arts and Bowlsy, I was always going to get led astray eventually.

At the start, though, I was the Jewish kid with the briefcase and I got picked on loads. And because I was Jewish, I got it from all the skinheads. It was a kids' thing, they were just going with the fashion at the time. Unfortunately, the fashion at the time was to flush the head (and briefcase) of any unsuspecting Yiddo down the toilet at any given moment.

This meant I had to try and avoid the one joint entrance and exit to the school, not ideal to say the least. I would hug the fence on the opposite side of the road where the skinheads would congregate. It was head down and fingers-crossed that I wasn't spotted or, hopefully, that something else had distracted them. It doesn't sound or seem that serious now, and it was only for the first few months, but at the time it was very unpleasant, like any form of bullying, I suppose. Fortunately at Wembley High the skinhead movement at that time soon passed, everybody got into funk and soul and things were much more about the music from then on.

Our house was on the Wembley High cross-country run, which went through the streets and straight past my front door. Me and my mates would slowly drop to the back of the pack, slip inside, brew up, spark up fags, and then rejoin the group when they ran back past half an hour later, usually at the front and always cutting our otherwise awful laps down to quite competitive times.

I was quickly into my mischief-making stride, and I can remember my first cigarette vividly. I could only have been about 13 and I did try and resist for a year or so. Then one night I had a fag and promptly coughed my guts up. The next morning I bought a pack of 10 Lambert & Butler, which I think was the first brand to start doing 10s in those days. And strangely, my asthma seemed to disappear at that point.

I was a tearaway, but I wasn't violent, just very, very naughty. Not like now. Kids these days have slightly more devious agendas. Back then the teachers hit us, now it's the other way round. I didn't play truant that often at Wembley High because I was too busy having fun. In fact, I took not concentrating to another level, and was asked to stand outside the class a hell of a lot, which I enjoyed because it gave me time to conjure up the plot to my next fun-packed lesson. And I always felt that I found the lessons much more rewarding than any of the teachers did.

Around that time, I hosted the one and only house party most teenagers got away with...like those in the classic '80s Yellow Pages advert and cult British movies Party Party and Quadrophenia all rolled into one. It was carnage. My mum came home and people had climbed over the neighbours' gardens and were causing mayhem. There were empty cans of beer and Watney's Party 7s everywhere and everyone was hammered. What a mess!

Brandon can refer back to the textbook 'could do better if he concentrated' school reports, but there has been little improvement over the years.

When interviewing him for his book, What Kind Of House Party Is This: History Of A Music Revolution, in 1995, Jonathan Fleming noted *"trying to get the man to be serious for one minute was a hard task"* and *"his brain was elsewhere, his answers were monosyllabic"*, before concluding *"he had completely forgotten I was there"*.

And I, for one, can vouch for this...one laptop (loaded with Facebook and eBay) and a phone constantly buzzing with texts is bad enough, but Brandon constantly flits between two of each, and an iPad, and when he isn't bickering with his big white cat Charlie (an apt name, to say the least!) he is making or answering a call. On one occasion he actually fell asleep as I was interviewing him. The job in hand is a hilarious one, and the patience of a saint is certainly required. I have every sympathy for those Wembley High teachers in the late '70s/early '80s.

With a few second years and several fourth years soon on side, the final piece in my Wembley High security jigsaw was a fifth year called Yemi Abedewali. And importantly, Yemi ruled the roost at the Thursdays lunchtime disco sessions.

Yemi was the biggest kid in the school. He was also the master robotic dancer and he used to smuggle me into the disco under his blazer. We must have looked like the odd couple, but we bonded through a love of funk music.

The discos were only meant to be for fourth and fifth years, but they always got me in. I remember it well, every Thursday lunchtime in the Norfolk house room. The fourth years were the trendy lot, they'd wear the jeans with the piping and soul belts, baggy sweatshirts and college loafers, sourced from Ravel - who supplied the must-have footwear for any discerning 'funkateer' of the early '80s. They'd listen to Greg Edwards' Soul Spectrum show on Capital FM, and later it became waffle trousers, Gabicci tops with penny loafers.

Wembley High, and in particular the lunchtime disco, was where the name Blocko was cemented, and by one particular fourth year, who, himself, would go on to have a nickname of some repute.

Paul 'the birds' Avery was so-called for obvious reasons. However, in more recent times, it must be said, he is better known as Paul 'not so many birds' Avery.

One day Paul was walking down the corridor at school and felt a tug on the back of his blazer. He looked behind and I said "pleased to meet you, I'm Brandon Block". Paul said he wanted to give me a slap, but didn't because I had so much front for a first year.

After school sometimes, me, Phil Ember and Lee Birch would ride down to Northwick Park where Paul and the rest of the other jazz funkers would be playing football, and stand at the sidelines watching them, doing our apprenticeships, so to speak. What great days, and what a laugh! I had such fun and I was determined it wasn't going to end.

Paul and his mates had formed a crew called The Funky Plumbers, and their thing was these leather plumbers' bags. The lunchtime disco itself became a weekly AGM for anyone into jazz funk, with various groups of 'soul heads', like our South Kenton Soul Patrol, who in later years were sub-contracted out to various under-18 events and roller-discos in the area, and became affiliated to other local enthusiasts like the Harrow Breeders.

The school disco session was where I also met a lot of the other guys I'd go on to spend my early drinking days with, including Baker, Duff, Sam, Mick, Harry Boy, Roy and Steve Cloak, Panos and the Culver brothers (Chris, Tim, Paul and Dave)...thanks for the memories, lads.

Another haunt of the local jazz funkateers, as we called them, ie the cooler kids, was the disco at St Cuthbert's Church in Wembley every Thursday night. This is where I first met my good friend Ali, who I would begin my DJ career with, and get into all sorts of personal and professional scrapes with. Also Fran Sidoli, who would later become an integral part of my first music production, Power Of Love, as FUBAR, and also one third of Blockster. Rick Williamson, another long-standing friend, was also a regular at Cuthbert's and and my mentor where the development of my jazz shuffle was concerned. To this day Fran and Rick are the best white jazz dancers I've ever seen. Although, Tommy Mac comes in a close second.

St Cuthbert's was one of those typical church-run midweek evening youth clubs of that era for all kids in the surrounding area, and naturally lots of pals from my school attended. It also doubled as the local fighting arena, our own little Madison Square

(clockwise) * Brandon, aged 5
* With dad Harvey Block in Cannes
* With Harvey Block and grandfather Joe Block in 1981
* Uncle Cliff and Auntie Arleen
* With Jason Griffin, girlfriends and mum Vivienne at Harrow Road in 1982

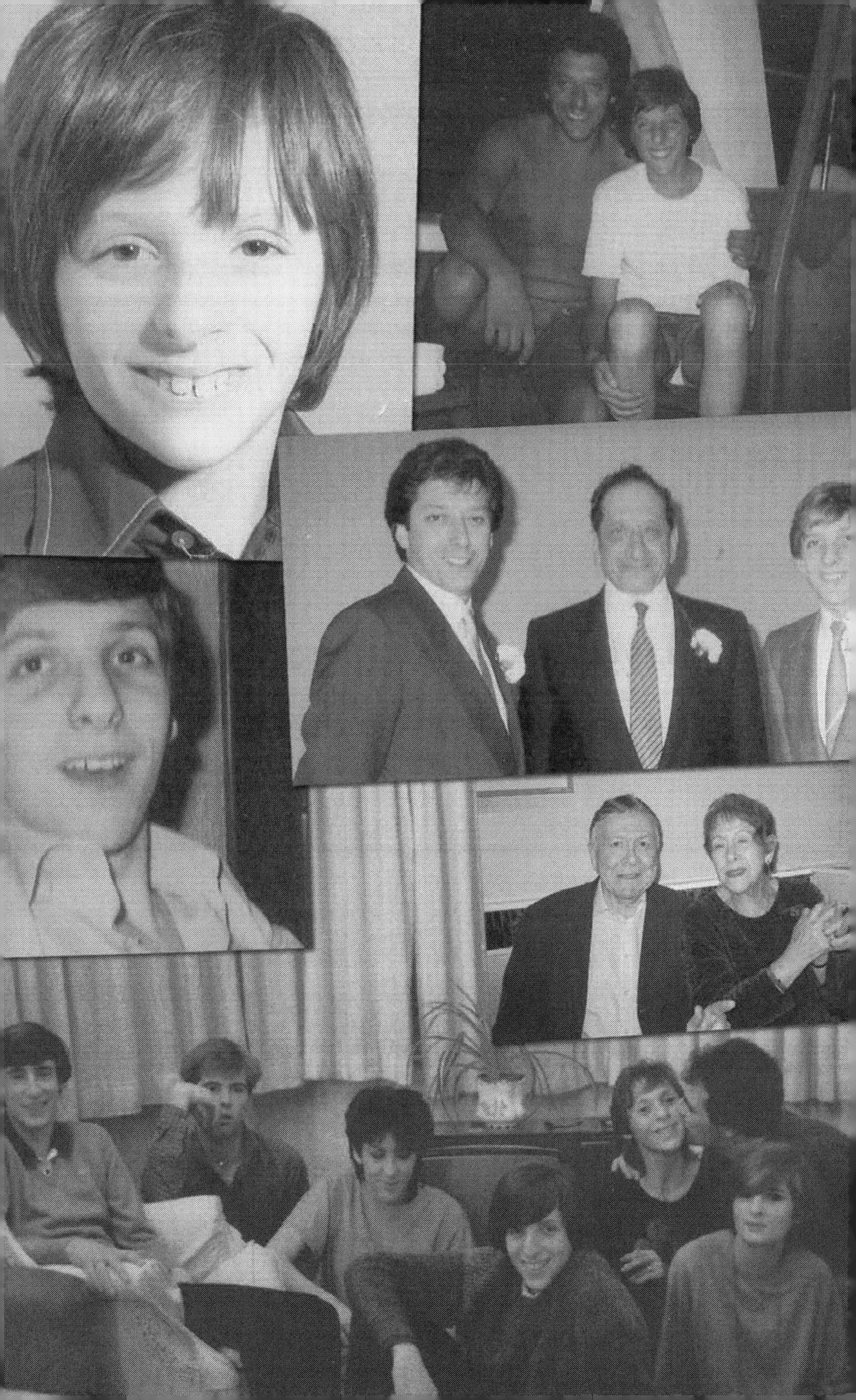

Gardens. Fights with rival gangs and between local hard men were arranged on a weekly basis and days in advance, so there was never a dull moment, and much anticipation in the lead-up to Cuthbert's.

The bouts were arranged for around 5pm, so as not to interfere with the rest of the evening's dancing. The trademark cries of "fight, fight, fight" would ring around the church courtyard, and the victor/victors would usually be in sooner or later to show us a few celebratory knee spins. The fights never used to last much longer than a minute, and were overseen by The Almighty to ensure there were no underhand tactics.

Rick Williamson would later become a nemesis of mine for a year or so after he stitched me up when we were at a house party in Sudbury. I had arranged to go and meet Laura Kirk, who was THE fittest girl in our year at the time - it was probably the fourth year, so we would have been about 14 or 15. Rick said he would come along with me to get Laura, so I gave him a 'backie' down to her house. I suddenly realised the three of us would not get back on the bike, so Rick kindly and sneakily offered to accompany Laura to the party on the 245 bus, knowing full well I would need to cycle back alone. I'm not quite sure how I expected a young lady of Laura's calibre to climb on to the back of a Raleigh Racer at 10pm anyway. Oh well, Rick and Laura's relationship only lasted for a couple years. I was tailing the bus, peddling frantically and Rick was on the back seat with one arm already around Laura and the other giving me a V-sign.

At least Rick and Fran had already shown Brandon the art of that ageless shuffle, and various other tricks like knee spins, windmills and all the other moves associated with jazz dancing and the jazz funk scene.

One 'older kid' who wasn't around in 1978 was a certain Baggy Baxter, who had been carted off to Borstal, the Government's youth prison, intended, according to its Wikipedia page, to "reform seriously delinquent young people" and to be "highly regulated", with a "focus on routine, discipline and authority".

The Criminal Justice Act 1982 abolished the Borstal system in the UK, and while both Baggy and Brandon would be routinely high for many years to come, focus, discipline and authority would not be their strong points. Baggy explains:-

I was in the same year and class as 'Aves' [Paul Avery], and was sent to Borstal in the fourth year. It was meant to be a short, sharp, shock for young offenders, and it was horrific. I was only a child really, 15-years-old, but there were kids in there younger than me. I never went back to school, and while Brandon and the jazz funkers were still doing the school and church discos, me and the older lot were going to places like the 100 Club in the West End.

But although Brandon was still having to ply his trade locally, and on a juvenile level, his record collection was quickly becoming older than his years.

It was at this time that I really discovered my love of all things disco and jazz funk. Tracks like Space Base by Slick, Fat Larry's Band's Looking For Love and Act Like You Know, Francine McGee's Delerium, Shame by Evelyn Champagne King, Shalamar's Take That To The Bank, Roberta Flack and Donnie Hathaway's Back Together Again, George Benson's Give Me The Night, Funkadelic's One Nation Under The Groove, and, of course, Sugarhill Gang's Rapper's Delight, to name but a few, were favourites, and all played on one of those large cassette players you would always find in a school hall or music room in the '70s and '80s. I owned a Sharp GF777, which was a twin-cassette, six speaker suitcase, a classic to this day.

Away from school life, my parents held a bar mitzvah for me when I was 13, but shortly afterwards their differences saw them split. My dad had been in the schmutter (or clothing) trade all his life. He had factories in the Turnpike Lane and Manor House areas of north London, manufacturing men's suits. Mum was a secretary in Baker Street.

My folks were quite liberal and as I entered my teens they were going through a very rough time and weren't forcing me to do anything really, they had too many issues of their own to deal with.

Also at this time, when I used to live in South Kenton, there was a railway bridge which separated two sides of South Kenton, and some of us used to travel across to the other side - to the

Windermere Estate, where we became part of a very close-knit gang, who used to rollerskate, smoke, drink, pinch motorbikes and talk about the possibility of shagging someone.

I was dragged along where joyriding motorbikes was concerned. I admit that I took the odd one, but we always used to try and put them back. I was 14 and my parents were mid-divorce so I did a few stupid things during that period, but I think I was happier sitting in nearby Northwick Park drinking and smoking while all the other kids tore around on the bikes.

Models like the Fantic Caballero, FS1E Yamaha and the Honda step-through were all classics of the time. Lovely bikes.

Fortunately, as soon as those mates hit (not so sweet) 16, they either bought a bike of their own, or started saving for a car, which they could drive legally a year later.

They loved cars more than their bikes, so they didn't want to risk not being able to drive by still messing around with the bikes. Now they'd left school it was all about getting a job and a decent motor, which would become their pride and joy.

And they had some great cars too, iconic looking back now - like the Ford Escort Mexico Mk II, in colours like signal orange and peppermint green, or the Sunbeam Lotus, which was a rally version of the Talbot Sunbeam, one of which was owned by Fran Sidoli.

Also various Ford Escorts, including the Mark 1 Lotus Twin Cam and the RS1800 Mark II (BDA), the Lotus Cortina Mark II, the Triumph Dolomite Sprint and Triumph TC 2000, the RS 3.1 X-Pack Ford Capri, and the very rare Aston Martin Tickford Capri (if anyone was lucky enough to be able to afford one). Sorry to be such a train (or car) spotter, but I'm sure many of you appreciate what status symbols these motors were at the time.

Looking back, I certainly don't remember having an unhappy childhood. In fact, despite all the mad times I've had over the past 20 years or so and what I've achieved since, I always look back at those years directly after the divorce most fondly of all - the late '70s/early '80s, growing up, discovering dance music, hanging around with my mates, starting boozing and going to house parties for the first time.

I don't know where the later anger and self-loathing came from. I guess the obvious thing is to say it was because of the repercussions from the divorce. Mum and Dad remained friends throughout, and still are, and I remember finding that confusing, and thinking, like most kids would at that time, "why can't they still be together?"

After the divorce Mum and Dad bought separate houses. I'd stay at my dad's place in Wembley, round the corner from my mum, and he'd have all this crumpet coming over, always a stunning bird in tow, and I remember thinking, "I wish that was me". And if I was at home with Mum, who had now moved to Harrow Road in Sudbury, I'd row with her boyfriend, who was trying to play 'dad', and who I ended up resenting and constantly falling out with. One day I chased him around the kitchen with a walking stick and actually whacked him with it, cutting him and drawing blood. Funnily enough the walking stick was an inventive design of the time, and would have been a winner on Dragon's Den today. Inside it was a test tube where you could keep a shot or two, of which mine was Bacardi, and it was never empty.

Vivienne Block had a delicate situation on her hands.

When that particular partner of mine was there, that did affect Brandon, and I remember he threw a coffee table at him once. The guy was trying to be a father figure, but it wasn't working, and I thought "I don't want this, I'm not going to be in the middle of this", so that partner left.

I'm sure the break up of the marriage did affect Brandon enormously, but you just don't realise at the time how much, because you're in the middle of it all. But I think Brandon was fortunate to have two parents who did get on, despite the split. Although we couldn't live together, at least there was never that terrible animosity.

I think it was difficult because Brandon was an only child, and if he'd had any brothers or sisters, then he would have had siblings who he could have expressed his feelings to.

He certainly made up for it with the amazing amount of friends he had. In fact, there were always mates of his at Harrow Road after me and his dad split. I would retreat to my bedroom when I got home most nights, simply because I couldn't get in the front room.

Throughout all this madness, one of the things that kept me fairly on the straight and narrow was my love of rollerskating. At the age of 13 or 14, a group of us, called the Medway Marauders, including Phil Ember, Lee Birch and my new rollerskating buddy Matthew Donegan, used to go to rollerdiscos every Friday night at Harrow Leisure Centre. Matt would years later book me to DJ at the Brits' after-parties, and be a close mate throughout my career.

And bombing around the Harrow Road area on rollerskates was a far cry from being bombed out of The Brits. Donegan remembers:-

I already knew Brandon from school, but not that well, even though we were in the same year. Then I bumped into him on the Harrow Road in Sudbury, and he said he'd moved from north Wembley, just around the corner to me. Through our love of rollerskating we became inseparable for the next few years. As the Medway Marauders, we had a street hockey team at the leisure centre. A few other groups started to form too, with the Sudbury lot, and kids from Harlesden and Stonebridge. We all used to nut around on rollerskates and later came the whole casual thing.

A perennial daydreamer and underachiever where schoolwork was concerned, Brandon's academic chances came and went.

I only turned up for three exams, one O-level and two CSEs. I was thrown out of one after I wrote my name on the gymnasium floor and jumped out of the school hall window halfway through another; concluding my studies with A+ in 'eating your own still life subject', namely a fresh, juicy Granny Smith apple. A novel take on proceedings to say the least, but typical Blocko all the same.
One thing I did want to learn about, though - like many of my peers - was dance music. And I set about building a funk, soul and hip-hop collection, mostly acquired from the legendary record stall at Wembley Market, run by Daddy Ernie, these days a respected presenter on London's Choice FM.

By the time I left school in 1983, my record collection was growing nicely – pride of place were tunes like Level 42's Wings Of Love, Azymuth's Jazz Carnival, Funkmasters' Love Money, Original Concept's Can You Feel It, all of Morgan Khan's Streetsounds albums and tracks by acts like Mantronix and Whodini, and nearly every early hip-hop import. My musical tastes widened at this point as those early hip-hop, rap, and b-boy influences started to filter through to the discos.

No education or not, Brandon knew he would need a job to help fund these records, as well as his interest in fashion which, naturally, was increasingly playing a bigger part in his life.

And because, like many teens of his age he had managed to blag his way into local pubs while he was still 15, there were rounds of drinks to be paid for too. Importantly alcohol was still Brandon's only poison.

LYON DANCING

I'd been given my first joint at the age of 14 but also had a bad experience smoking sensimilla around that time too. It was horrendous, but for any fledgling puffer, 'sensi' probably wasn't the best thing to start off with.

A couple of years later I discovered the highs and lows of getting stoned with mates in car parks all night. This, thank God, didn't become a habit and I quickly retreated to the safe confines of The John Lyon pub, where pints of snakebite and whiskey chasers were much more easy to handle.

But it wasn't until the age of 16, at a very posh Jewish family wedding, for which I'd shaved my hair off in an act of rebellion, that with Mum, Dad and his new wife, all happily getting on, my horrible drunken alter-ego Harry The Bastard first reared his ugly head.

This function was being held at the Regent's Suite at London Zoo (also the venue of various Special Branch parties) and halfway through the night I somehow managed to scale the perimeter fence of the zoo, and smash every information sign in my sight.

Found in a drunken stupor, to all of the guests' dismay, I was coaxed back by my father, quickly shuffled off to the 'Beema', and courtesy of one of his associates, also in attendance, was given my first line of cocaine to straighten me out, which it did immediately. I was so naive that I had no idea what I was taking.

Harvey Block is philosophical at just how much 'coaxing' he had done that night.

That was scary because it was the first time that my son had approached me and I thought he might actually hit me. He was pissed out of his head, standing there with a glass of champagne in each hand. He suddenly went loopy, threw one of his glasses at a mirror, took off his rented dinner jacket and tried to rip it to shreds, and then proceeded to smash up a sign directing people to various parts of the zoo. It was pouring with rain and he was soaking wet, and he was risking getting electrocuted as he tried to dismantle the lights on the sign as well. I dragged him off and he said he was going to hit me. He put his hands up, and then flung his arms round me and told me he loved me. I was saying "Brandon, you need to straighten yourself out", but he was all over the place. It was chucking it down, so we put him in the car, and my mate said "whack that up your hooter", and, let's just say, it straightened him out. And that was that, the first time, as far as I know, that he had indulged in any of that wicked powder, so I suppose you could say I was the one who set him on the road to rack and ruin.

Now 16, and following in the family menswear tradition, Brandon managed to secure an apprenticeship at Burtons in the West End, first on a YTS scheme, working in sales on the shop floor, and later as a window dresser.

Already a local at The John Lyon in Harrow when he started at Burtons, he soon hooked up with some familiar faces at the pub.

It was now that I cemented friendships with some of the funkateers - Paul 'the birds' Avery, Duff, Ali and other lads like Alan Baker. I'd managed to blag it into The John Lyon before my 16th birthday, and a lot of the fourth years who had looked after me when I started at Wembley High now drank in there regularly.

So when I started going to the pub it was natural for me to hang around with them. Later we all bonded further on various coach trips to soul haunts like the Goldmine in Canvey Island, Zero 6, Flicks in Dartford and Caister Weekenders.

Our little crew, Birchey, Jason Griffin and myself, were like the 'under fives' - we could dance, we were 'dressers', all the young girls in the pub loved us, but we eventually shagged all the older birds too. We'd drink 'Pils 'n' arf', so you would get more than a pint, and it was cheaper than a pint.

Also in our little gang were some lifelong female friends. Selina and Jane, who were also John Lyon regulars (love always, girls...). Selina remains one of my closest friends to this day. She worked in Rivaz, the trendiest fashion boutique Wembley High Street had to offer so we were always kitted out in the latest fashion trends.

I was a cheeky little so and so, a real jack the lad. It was 1983 and I'd done the casual thing by now, the Fila, the Tacchini, Ellesse, Kappa, Lacoste designer sportswear, etc, and not forgetting Benetton rugby shirts. The casual years were great, every Saturday evening myself, Lee, Jason, Bowlsy, Matty D, Shaun Griffiths, Darren Ruddock and Paul Smith, and the Perivale casuals, would head up further into town to the ice rink at Queensway, via Shepherd's Bush, where we would meet up with the QPR boys, including Chalky White, who went on to become a well-respected MC.

With fashion ever-changing, sportswear was replaced by high-end designer labels so we'd save as much money as we could for clobber like Armani, Fiorucci Jeans, FUs, Lois Jeans and Nike Waffle trainers, and, perversely, now looking back, Fruit Of The Loom sweatshirts.

By this time we ran our lives totally around the opening hours of The John Lyon and, on Saturdays, the nearby Carlton Lodge (for those in the know…).

Originally, The John Lyon was being run by Den and Edie, a lovely couple who became our second parents. We used to have lock-ins, lock-outs, knock-ins and knock-outs. Textbook pub life for anyone growing up in the early '80s, I guess.

I don't know a bunch of people whose pub was so important to their lives. Those were great days, we'd be sitting at the pub on a Saturday, all tanked up, and then suddenly decide to go to a soul all-dayer somewhere - Bournemouth, or the Royalty in Southgate - just on the spur of the moment. In fact, one trip to the Bournemouth Soul Weekender resulted in my first brush with the law at the now legendary Longs bar.

This point in my life was also my first experience of how not to manage money. After my first month of full-time wages I found to my dismay that I had been summoned by the bank manager, with my account already seriously overdrawn, and him asking me how he was going to cash all the cheques he now had in his possession made payable to The John Lyon pub. To which I replied "Den and Edie are all right". The bank manager snapped back, "I'm sure Den and Edie are all right, Mr Block…it's not Den and Edie I'm worried about. It's your total disregard for money."

One epic night when the resident DJ at The John Lyon didn't show up, it was a classic case of "come on lads, go and get your records" as Den and Edie gave Brandon one of his first big breaks in the DJ world.

That night I was with Ali and Birchy-boy. We all went home and came back with our records in crates and it went off in there. All the older kids from school were going mad so the resident was sacked and we were given the gig. We were paid £30 between us every Friday night, and when the pub closed around 11pm, we had enough money to get a cab up to a club in the West End called Hombres, where special offers could mean drinks were as cheap as 25p a pop.

Hombres was in Wells Street, just off Oxford Street, and a couple of weeks we actually went every night it was open. Monday was cocktail night, Tuesday was 25p a drink night, another night cocktails would be 50p at midnight, and so on. Basically, every night you could get paralytic and your cab home for a tenner. And the crumpet that we'd try and pull in Hombres was amazing. It was quite incestuous, though, with a lot of inter-relationship shagging going on, so to speak.

And as I was now a fledging DJ from a suburban pub the first thing I did at a big West End club was introduce myself to the resident DJ there.

Hombres' resident was a guy called Johnny Norman who is a friend to this day, and who tried to book me to play at a pub in Acton only the other week.

Back then there was also Bananas in Wardour Street, where it was £10 to get in and then drink what you want. You'd literally be stepping over people at the end of night where lots of punters had collapsed, or sharing the floor with them.

Back at base, The John Lyon was part of the Pub 80 chain, and one of the first to break away from the style of a traditional London boozer. It had white decor, with a decent sound system and proper disco lights in what was a designated DJ room called JLs, which held around 100 people, and featured Baggy Baxter as a bouncer!

Elder statesman Paul Avery witnessed a sudden increase in numbers at the pub.

Before the boys started DJing at The John Lyon, there was just us lot down there, but then various other groups of people started coming down. People came from everywhere, from loads of different manors.

But not everyone was a massive John Lyon fan. Matthew Donegan was preferring to make inroads further into central London.

I was more interested in smoking dope, hanging around Portobello Road and discovering so-called London clubs. Later I started DJing, but I really have no idea how I ended up doing that. I literally fell into it by accident, when through some mates I was asked to play at The Trip, in The Keith Moon Bar at The Astoria. It was my first gig and I was playing alongside Fabi Paras, Andrew Weatherall and Terry Farley, doing my thing in central London. Me and Brandon were both still living at home with parents, just moving in different circles.

Brandon, meanwhile, was still DJing in his local pub. And being based at Burtons in Tottenham Court Road was giving him a daily taste of the West End.

When he progressed to window dresser, flitting between that store, the Oxford Circus branch and the surrounding Soho area meant he was surrounded by bars and clubs.

And having a close friend and DJ partner who was a tube driver made Brandon's daily commute from Sudbury Town on the Piccadilly Line that little bit easier.

Around that time Ali was driving a train, and I used to climb in the front with him at Sudbury. Ali would stop just before the platform on the way in, and I would jump in the cabin, and then he would bring the rest of the train in. It was hilarious, I would jump on the Tannoy, and make announcements, looking through the spy hole in the driver's door, scaring people by saying things like "you in the blue, wake up" or "if you look to the right, you'll see..."...etc...etc.

I don't think I was actually at Burtons for that long, probably less than a year. I used to get a staff discount, but was only allowed

so many items, so I'd pinch a load of extra shirts, so that our little crew were all kitted out. We all wore the same T-Shirts, just different colours - pink, yellow, sky blue, etc. We'd be ringing each other up to check who was wearing each colour so we didn't clash, and sometimes people would have to go home and get changed if there was a mix-up . Then I got everyone chinos, the first beige chinos that came out, in fact.

I was sacked over a Sony Walkman (the iPod of the day, for you youngsters out there) which was intended as a prop for a dummy in one of my shop windows. I pinched the Walkman from one store successfully, but it was the batteries, which I nicked from the Regents Street store that resulted in the termination of my employment. I don't know what I was more annoyed about - getting the sack or having to buy a new pack of Duracells. But enough of this bunny.

Out of work all the same, Brandon's mates came to his rescue with a series of unlikely roles, assisting in the various trades they had attempted to take up. Step forward a certain Paul Avery.

It was ironic after all of the stuff that he had out of Burtons that he got done for two batteries, but we were all in the building trade, or at least having a go at being in the building trade, so as his mates, we all helped him out, so he could earn a few bob until he found something.

The first job with me was roofing in Harrow On The Hill. It was a lovely day and the view was great. We were up top, and Brandon said to me, "what shall I do mate?". It was boiling hot and I said, "enjoy the view pal, and from time to time bang that hammer on the roof". Which he did very well with a big grin on his face.

His dexterity with the hammer was quite something, so why would I doubt his ability to take on another minor task, involving a roll of

(clockwise) * Window dressing at Burtons, 1983
* Quids in at The John Lyon in 1984 with landlady Edie
* At The John Lyon with Panos, Steve Cloak and Tom Baker
* At The John Lyon with Paul Avery and Lee Birch
* With 'the boys' in 1985, from left to right.
(back row) Brandon, Chris Dimmock, Paul Avery, Roy Cloak, Bill Cloak, Gary Cloak, Paul Duffy, Mick Parker
(leaning/kneeling) Chris Culver, Steve Simmons, Steve Cloak

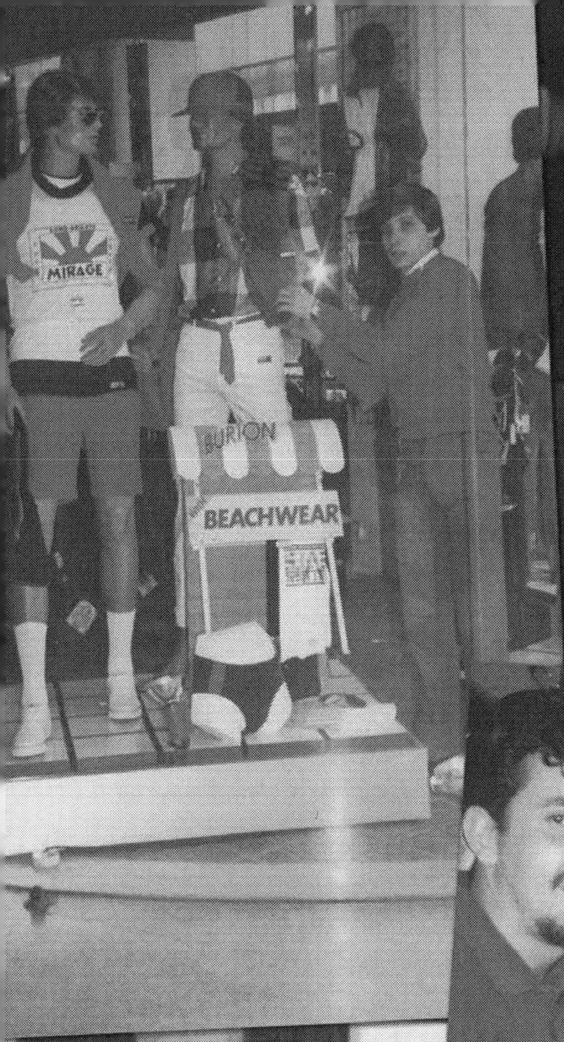
MIRAGE
BEACHWEAR

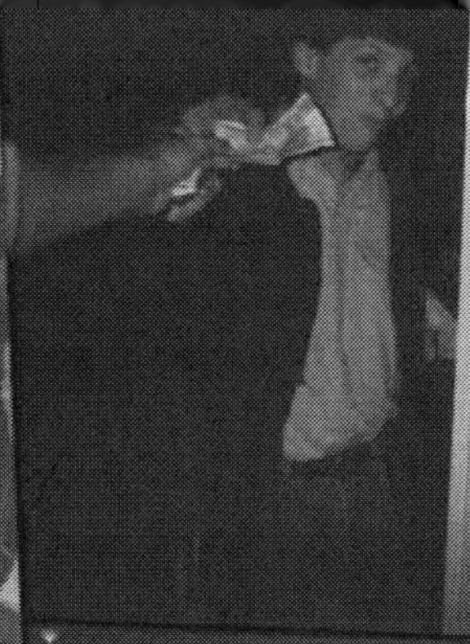

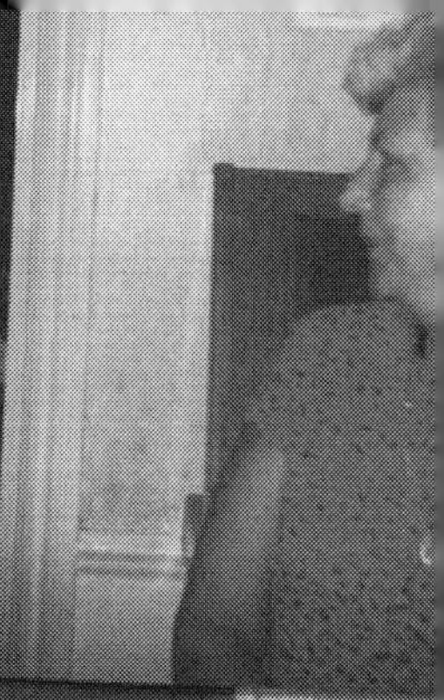

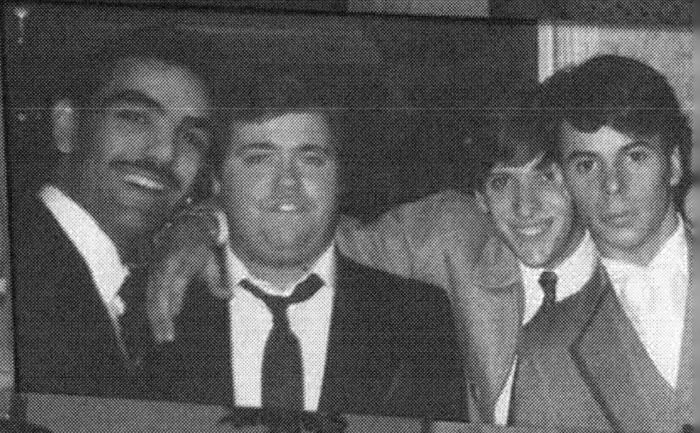

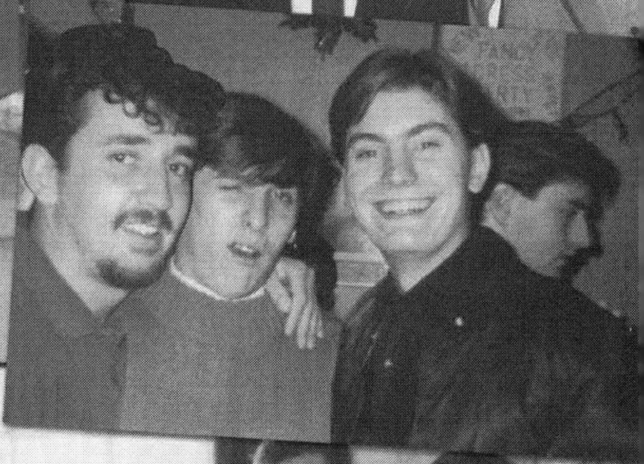

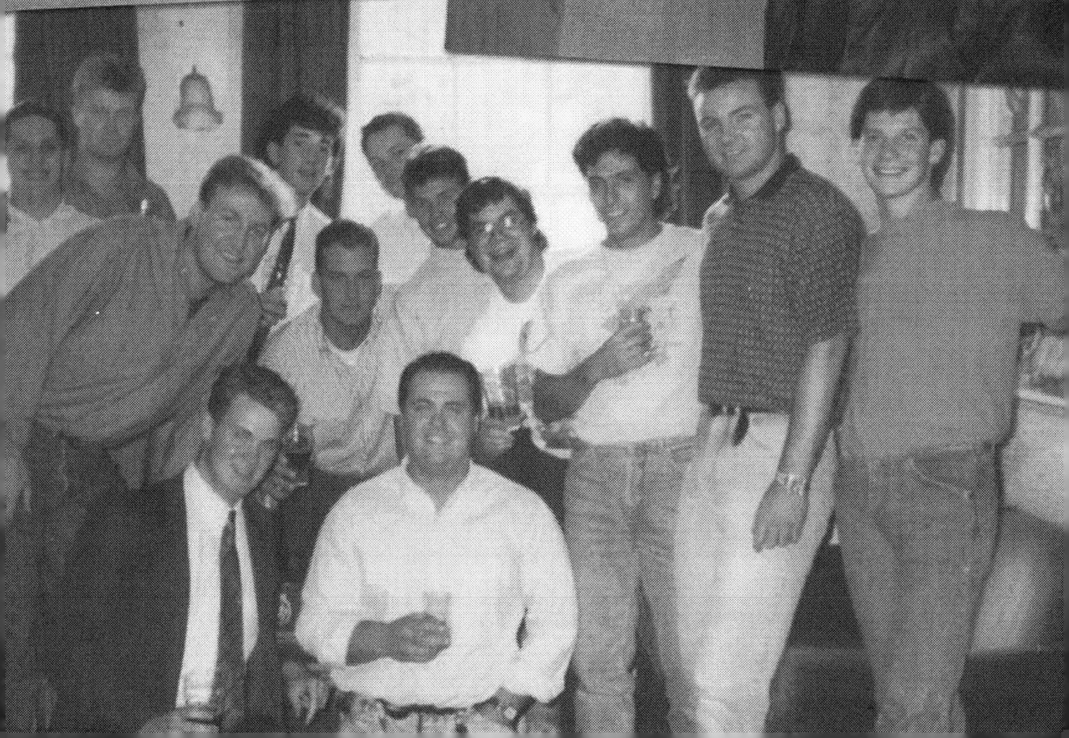

flashband and a cracked valley, or in layman's terms a huge band aid, which seals, with the aid of hot tar, a hole in the roof. The result is a short-term fix for a long-term problem, but Brandon's problem when I got back was that he had not only managed to wrap himself up in the flashband, but he was also stuck to the roof. Only Brandon!

I also had a short stint helping Jason Griffin - who had become an electrician - when he was rewiring the house of a local headmistress. Jason asked for £500 for materials, spent £300 on those, and then we went out and spent the other £200 on a slap-up night at Hombres and other haunts in the West End.

We turned up for the job absolutely paralytic...the headmistress left five minutes after that and we literally climbed into her still warm, unmade bed, and slept until five minutes before she returned, explaining that we'd been busy rewiring in the loft all day.

Paul Avery remembers his waistline expanding over this boozy period.

During that time Brandon was out of work we put on a hell of a lot of weight, meeting up most lunchtimes for drinking sessions. At least three nights a week we'd have a curry, and we must have put on two or three stone over a twelve month period. Later the drugs kicked in, and that was the best diet in the world.

In between jobs, a few months after getting sacked, I was in the pub getting pissed and I bumped into a mate of mine, Mick, whose girlfriend worked at a recruitment agency. I didn't even know what one was! She arrived later and suggested that I'd be good as an interviewer, but again, I didn't have a clue what that was either.

Lo and behold, within days, she hooked me up, and I was the newest addition to a predominantly female company (waheey, here we go!) in Ealing called Atlas Staff Bureau.

And I did really well there. After a few stints at various other branches, I progressed to the role of senior interviewer at their office in Wembley, where I stayed for a couple of years. It was good

money too and, along with my DJ fees, I spunked the lot on records, booze and clothes.

Brandon Block the DJ was on his way, albeit I hadn't got much further than the Harrow Road yet. And it soon became obvious that some serious equipment was needed to take my budding career further afield than The John Lyon pub.

The natural progression was to launch my own mobile set-up, which I did with Ali. We headed for our local Tandy store - like you did, in those days - for what would be my first, and certainly not my last, taste of hire purchase credit!

We couldn't afford Technics 1200s - no way! They were about £700 each back then, so me and Ali invested in a set of new belt-driven decks. I got myself a personal Tandy account, complete with a store card. We bought an amp, a pair of speakers and the decks, which we quickly learned how to speed up and slow down.

All that was needed now was a second hand van, in this case an old BT Commer, which was emblazoned with the duo's new name - Ecstasy Disco…ironic to say the least, particularly as this was 1985 and the drug ecstasy wouldn't be passing through north west London for a few years yet. Meanwhile, Brandon's celebrity was growing at The John Lyon and he managed to lose his virginity at the grand old age of 17.

I guess I lost it pretty late, considering I'd been hanging around the pub for a couple of years with loads of dollies. In the end it was in the back of an Escort Mark 1 in a nearby builder's yard, with a barmaid from The John Lyon, some heavy metal chick. It must have lasted about two seconds, and I remember her saying, "ah, never mind", and then me replying "how wasn't it for you?"

Then after popping my cherry I managed to procure my first ever love, who also used to work at The John Lyon, and was actually the best barmaid the pub ever had. She was sought after by many, and especially me.

I'd never been happier. A 17 year-old in love with a 28-year-old blonde bombshell…it doesn't get much better…until, of course, your young heart gets broken.

That summer I'd experienced my first boys' holiday. With Jason Griffin, Birchey and another of my old school mates Vince Buckeridge, I enjoyed one of the best weeks of my life, thus far, in the Spanish resort of Lloret De Mar. We never really made it much further than the disco in the basement of our hotel and I managed to add a rather large Scottish lady to my relatively small list of conquests.

I remember showing my romantic side by offering to walk my new Glaswegian friend to the beach for some romantic respite. Showing early signs of OCD, I folded my clothes neatly and found a safe place among the rocks to store them, before heading into the sea for some 'och aye the nude' and my first attempt at saltwater shagging. When we returned to shore, to my dismay and embarrassment a large wave had washed up my clobber and left it strewn all over the beach.

And now I had those holiday guilts and couldn't wait to get back and see my current squeeze back home. Ali picked us up from the airport, and all I could ask was "how's my baby?" However, I was dumped soon after, so maybe word had got around about my holiday romance.

The John Lyon closed in late 1985, but I had already begun to spread my wings by then, and the more I got about the more DJ contacts I made, although I found one particular cohort somewhat closer to home.

My mum's hairdresser Heather was round at our house one day and started talking about her boyfriend, saying how he was also a DJ, and that I'd get on well with him. And that's how I met Dean Thatcher.

I went to one of his parties where he used to play rare groove, Motown and northern soul 7s. We got pissed together, I danced my nuts off and we've been great mates ever since.

Thatcher, who has been married to Heather since 1992, was in good company at his modest promotion, as many of the people who played for him would go on to become major players in the dance music scene. He remembers:-

I had this night at a place called The Villa in Uxbridge, that I used to do with Simon Dunmore. It was a soul night. Gilles Peterson and Nicky Holloway used to play there, that sort of vibe. This was around 1986, pre acid house. I had called it Flying, after the Beatles record of the same name.

Then acid house quickly took over and we started playing house, and at that time it just turned everything on its head. You could say it went tits up from there, I guess. Me and Brandon had just clicked and we quickly became 'partners in crime'. Brandon was always the life and soul of the party, and if he hadn't become a DJ then he could have definitely been a stand-up comedian….no problems.

Socially, with The John Lyon no more, between 1985 and 1987, Brandon broadened his horizons and the move to The Mitre pub, a quarter of a mile up the road, was effortless. He also started attending the so-called trendier and more underground soul and funk parties in central London and the Home Counties, including the Special Branch presents Doo At The…parties, held at venues like London Zoo (the scene of his wedding crime), Lord's cricket ground, Hammersmith Palais and The Royal Oak in SE1, all run by Nicky Holloway, and with a music policy of funk, rare groove, hip-hop and "some house".

For many years The Middlesex & Herts Country Club would also be a favourite haunt of the north west London clubbing fraternity.

DJ-wise, 1986 was one of those years where we were just doing our time. Myself and Ali were doing the pub circuit with our mobile disco, while I was also working at Atlas, where now my manageress was no less than Karen Dunn (girlfriend of hairdresser Tony Chester, back then Hayes' answer to Vidal Sassoon). Karen would go on to become my DJ agent, launching one of the house scene's leading agencies, Unlimited DJs, while her other half would go on to become Charlie Chester…again, more of him later.

Together with the other staff from Atlas we'd meet up regularly after work at various local pubs and drink until closing time, in those days only 11pm. Karen and I often used to continue drinking at Mum's house in the Harrow Road. The three of us would all sit in the front room on the sofa bed drinking until the early hours.

Karen Dunn remembers:-

Brandon was the best fun at work, everybody loved him! He was always chatting up a girl on the phone and he'd say "I'm going to have her later". And sure enough, later that evening, we'd be back at someone's house after the pub, and he'd be sitting there with some girl I didn't know, and it would be the one he'd been canvassing for leads earlier that day.

Seriously, though, it was a tough job that Brandon had, but he was very good at it. He had the gift of the gab, charmed everyone and earned loads of commission.

So Brandon was on a roll where both his private and professional lives were concerned, and feeling fairly invincible after a general upturn in his sexual fortunes, he quickly looked to build on his new found success where the ladies were concerned.

And at Atlas you couldn't fail. I was one of only two guys working there with scores of women. I didn't only try and shag everything walking around the office, but most females that walked into it too!

As interviewers we would arrange company visits to speak to various personnel officers, and after lengthy conversations you may even arrange a drink after work with them. One evening, after the whole office overheard my flirting, I'd arranged a meeting with a woman from the clothing company Sonnetti called Pat, who seemed particularly up for it. To me this was no more than a blind date, and hopefully, a pulling formality.

I arranged to meet Pat at the pub where Karen and Chester were waiting for a drink after work, The Fusilier in Wembley. This woman turned up, to my shock, looking like Mavis from Coronation Street…flowery dress, blue rinse, the lot. When she walked in, we all ignored her, assuming she was the pub cleaner. After she introduced herself, I spent the rest of the evening trying to fob her off politely. Fortunately, on this occasion I still got the business, without having to part with the goods. And at least there were many more fruitful encounters with work colleagues more my age.

THE ACID TEST

A world away from the heady heights of recruitment, in August 1987, Nicky Holloway, Paul Oakenfold, Danny Rampling, Trevor Fung and Johnnie Walker famously embarked on their infamous trip to Ibiza, stumbling across Alfredo's pioneering sessions at Amnesia and sampling the drug ecstasy for the first time.

Inspired by the heady mix of Balearic tunes, acid house and ecstasy, the group returned and set about trying to recreate that magic in the capital. Within weeks London's clubland was literally buzzing.

In November of that year Rampling launched Shoom (at The Fitness Centre in Southwark), and in the same month Oakenfold held Future parties in the back room of Heaven in Charing Cross Road. Soon after in January 1988, Oakenfold started The Project Club in Streatham to cater for his London-based Ibiza following.

In February the first Hedonism illegal warehouse party was held in the Hanger Lane area. Oakey went on to open Spectrum at Heaven in April of that year, on a Monday night too, and Holloway launched The Trip at The Astoria in Shaftesbury Avenue at the end of May on an initial 12-week run, returning later that year to continue as Sin.

The same year public school-educated Tony Colston-Hayter, reportedly reacting to an increasingly more exclusive door policy at Shoom, put on his own rave events at Wembley Studios called Apocalypse Now.

Brandon would go on to be a regular at all these nights, but wasn't one of the first to try ecstasy. One of his close friends, who preferred to remain anonymous for this particular anecdote, had formed close links to the police.

I was learning electronics at college, and had been put on a paid scheme, which included work placements as a civilian at a garage where all the police vehicles came to get serviced. Someone gave me my first ecstasy tablet at college around the summer of 1987 when I was 18 or 19, and all that time I was living the student life and getting paid by the 'Old Bill'. I was taking E at the weekends, and then coming into work on a Monday, wearing pink tinted glasses, with a top-knot in my hair, servicing all the radios the police had used to raid warehouse parties at the weekend.

In the queue at Apocalypse Now as the doors were forced open by the crowds, I had the good fortune of meeting another clubland legend, by the name of Dizzi. We both stood out from the crowd with ponytails on our heads, wearing dungarees and baggy jumpers. More later about Dizzi, who would become a founder member of 'The Goat Club'.

I remember around this time, when people had started doing pills, and I hadn't yet partaken, Paul Avery had a flat in Preston Road, north Wembley with six bedrooms. His grandparents had moved out and left him to rule the roost, which he did with the help of Baggy, Larry, Rocket, Stiggers, and whoever else needed a room for the night.

However, it put years on Aves. He was in this one armchair all day, in his dressing gown, endlessly puffing. He had his long curly hair, and you'd go around there and say "all right Aves?", and he'd just raise his eyebrows and nod, in a haze of smoke. He'd turned into Rigsby overnight. I remember him and Baggy cooked us magic mushrooms for Christmas dinner that year, in a unique take on quirky late night food recycling TV show Get Stuffed.

But before that, one historic night the boys went to this illegal acid house do at Staples Corner, near Brent Cross. They all took ecstasy that night while I stayed back at Paul's expansive flat, drinking. They all said they were going to this warehouse party, and I said "no, I don't think that's for me, no, fuck that, I'll stay here". That's how anti-drugs I was at the time.

When my mates returned later with jibbering jaws they kept talking about "the bells, the bells". I later discovered this was the infamous acid house anthem Dance With The Devil by Paul Oakenfold as The Project Club, with the bells chiming throughout and because they'd been doing Es they just couldn't get it out of their heads.

The very next evening I finally succumbed at a house party in Frognall Road, Harrow… Phil Baxter (Baggy's older brother) and Debbie Mania's place (a couple soon to be married at Wembley Conference Centre, with me and Ali DJing, and playing Todd

Terry's Can You Feel It as their first dance at what must surely have been the first acid house wedding).

It was at this fateful (although, I could also use the words "absolutely wonderful") party in Harrow that I shared my first ecstasy tablet with my good friend Matthew Donegan. It was funny, a few years earlier we had all shared this love of funk music, but before the acid house thing hit, some of the cooler London lot, who now included Matty D, didn't want to be seen with our pub crew.

Then acid house took over the world, and suddenly it didn't matter because everybody was at it, the rule book was thrown out. Matt had said "come to this party with me, and try one of these", and before long we were inseparable again! I just thought "fuck it, let's see what this is all about". I took half a pill, a little yellow burger, I think it was, and ended up dancing on the garden shed roof until 4pm the next afternoon…on my own! Everyone else had gone home.

1988 would be a seminal year, to say the least, with more and more illegal raves popping up in warehouse spaces in and around the Wembley area, including more Hedonism events. One in April on Alperton Way, W5, boasted Soul II Soul, House Specialists and Colin Faver on the bill.

Also that month Fun City began at Shaftesbury's in Harrow, with DJs Frankie, Andy Weatherall, Trevor Fung, Andy Nicholls and Colin Hudd all on the first line-up.

I was going to these parties and hearing all this acid music, stuff made on the 303, and thought "bang on". However, it seems mad looking back now that initially I had been anti-drugs and although my mates were doing pills at those parties, I had refused to try it.

Now I couldn't get enough of this and the night after Phil and Debbie's party, with no sleep, I was out again, searching for the music and, of course, this amazing feeling from ecstasy. I didn't have to look far and a party everyone was talking about was in a house, on the Chalkhill estate (R.I.P). There was a queue going up the stairs to Bowlsy, who was in one of the bedrooms with the pills. He'd literally just arrived and had been herded to the top of the stairs so the madding crowd below could form a not so orderly queue. I was straight in again, pushed my way to the front and necked one whole.

That was it, that next week, after I'd done my first Es, I went straight to The Record & Disco Centre in Rayner's Lane and bought a whole new acid house record collection. The 'R&D', as we called it, was situated in the basement of a video rental shop, owned by Jon Jules, who at the time, and to this day, was and is my mentor as a DJ. I worked at the shop at one point, along with Dean Thatcher and Simon Dunmore, who in the late '90s went on to become head of the UK's leading dance label Defected Records.

Jon Jules has a remarkable memory for dates and reflects.

I'm a year older than Brandon and I first him when I was 15, through rollerskating. I wasn't in his South Kenton Skate Patrol but I was in another crew and we used to see them down at Harrow Leisure Centre. We had lots of mutual friends at the time, and he always used to be in the middle of whatever was going on, making everyone laugh. He's always been nuts, so nothing has changed.

I used to go down to Crackers on a Friday, bunk off school, and then go to the 100 Club on a Saturday, between midday and 3pm, because, although we were underage we could get in there on a Saturday afternoon.

Brandon used to go there too, as did a lot of the Wembley lot. We all used to listen to the same pirate radio stations too. Then I started going to clubs like The Royalty in Southgate and The Goldmine, where DJs like Froggy, Tom Holland, Chris Brown and a very young Pete Tong used to play.

My first job was working for Tesco, in the Home & Ware section, and I joined purely because they sold records. Then I got an assistant manager's job at Our Price and from there started working at The R & D for then owner Andy Mann in June 1986. It was right at the forefront of house music, with the first records coming through from the States on Trax.

On March 30, 1988, I bought the shop from Andy Mann. They were crazy times. Working there midweek was me, Simon Dunmore, Glenn Gunner and a guy called Jerry Green. Then on a Saturday there would be Brandon, Darren Rock (aka Rocky), Ian Baker, who was in Jesus Jones and guy called Wayne. Charlie Chester, who was a cabbie then, was in there all the time too.

Paul Oakenfold was working in A & R at Champion Records. He was always in the shop, as was James Hamilton from Record Mirror, who we did a chart for, and Andy Thompson who was A & R for Pete Tong at London Records and people from Cooltempo as well.

Between late 1987 and 1990 it was madness. We were hyping loads of people's records, getting boxes of promos from the various labels and making sure they got to the right people. Those three years are a bit of a blur, actually. On a Friday night we'd all go down to Oakey's night Ziggy in Streatham and hang out there, and most of the staff started DJing out.

Brandon worked at The R & D on a Saturday there between '87 and '89, and even if he didn't come in for the whole day, he'd come in for a couple of hours, and I'd pay him in records most of the time. I used to go and hear him DJ down at The John Lyon playing funk and disco, and then I'd got a gig as resident at Zig Zag at Broadway Boulevard for Alan Warman and Carl Pearson, and Brandon would be badgering them for a house set and I used to say "let him play, he'll be good".

I'd always bought the odd house record, stuff like the Mike Pickering track, T-Coy by Carino, but now I had to get kitted out properly. Tracks like Rhythm Is Rhythm's Strings Of Life, loads of Todd Terry and Derrick May stuff, all the Trax records, the Balearic Beats album (a must for any aspiring house head in those days), DJ Pierre's Fantasy Club, Adonis' No Way Back and Kenny Jammin Jason's Can You Dance, to name but a very few.

I had been DJing out quite a bit by then, doing my funk sets still. Then I went to the Baxters' house party, and these acid house albums were playing back to back, tracks by people like Spank Spank, Mike Dunn, Lidell Townsell - real pioneers of their time. The music was literally entrancing....the sound that the all-new 303 machine made. Everyone was doing pills, and from then on recreational drugs became unavoidable.

I have amazing memories of working and hanging around The R & D. I later did a couple of days a week at the world famous Blackmarket Records in D'Arbly Street, Soho. I was behind the

counter with long-time friend Ashley Beedle, one of London's finest DJs and later famed for being one of X-Press 2, one of the UK's best-known dance acts. I've always had a lot of time for Ashley.

We had cubbyholes in the back office for all the leading DJs, and myself and Ashley had to make sure they all got the best promos out at the time.

I was eventually asked to leave by then owner Dave Piccioni because of continual absences and not always being compos mentis, but there was no ill feeling, because he was right. Dave has done well for himself since, with Azuli Records, and now owns the Armante Beach Club in Ibiza, so big respect to him.

Armed with this new record collection and a thirst for acid house and ecstasy, Brandon successfully managed to persuade Zig Zag promoters Warman and Pearson to give him a residency at Broadway Boulevard in Ealing, where he would play alongside Jon Jules, and at other promotions the pair were putting on in the area, including at Shaftesbury's and Lucky's, also in Ealing.

The Boulevard played host to a lot of the local pioneering acid house DJs and cohorts at the time, who I had the pleasure to meet. Phil Perry and Fiona, Trevor Fung, Paul Oakenfold, Martin The Poet and Mark Haggerty, to name but a few. It was here that I cemented a lifelong friendship with Kevin Swain, later of D.O.P fame, who remembers me saying to him, "fuck me, I'll die on this gear". A case, almost, of "never a truer word said in jest".

It was also at The Boulevard as a punter just before I started DJing there that I had my first ecstasy epiphany, when I tried my first California Sunrise pill (known as 'callies'). I had three (nothing by halves anymore).

(clockwise) * Brandon 'calls it acieeed'
* 'Starring' in Chemical Generation
* Apocalypse Now/Sunrise artwork
* Hand drawn Sunrise flyer
* Russell McKensie helps decorate the Baxter's infamous acid house 'house' party, all 1988

You are invited to:
10pm - 10am · 20k turbosound · UV lights · lasers
Burn it up at sunrise

You Tube — Search
Old rave video (spot brandon block in the pink)
mclean1979 5 videos Subscribe
TCR 00:03:22:07
0:13 / 0:26
Like Add to Share

THE TODD TERRY
"BANGO"
(TO THE BATMOBILE)
(T. Terry, A. Russell)
1. CLUB BANG   5:27
2. BONUS BANG 3:47
33 1/3 RPM
FRE-SR117X
Produced & Mixed by Todd Terry For Nine Pr
Mastered by Herb "Big Bang" Powers of Frank
New York Style Music—Kiln Muka-
FRESH
RECORDS
1674 Broadway

Inside Info
FROM THE PEOPLE WHO BROUGHT YOU
Apocalypse Now
AT WEMBLEY
NOW BRING YOU
SUNRISE
ULTIMATE AFTERHOURS
FOR LOCATION DETA
AND INVITED PHONE

GET UP

And it was that night, after the TV cameras had been let in to film at the Boulevard, that I famously ended up in the World In Action documentary Chemical Generation which exposed our new acid house scene to the nation.

see youtube link 'old rave video (spot Brandon Block in the pink)'

Also that night, a girl called Karen, who worked with my mum at the Middlesex & Herts Country Club and who I had fancied for many years, turned up. Little did I know, she had the hots for me and had come to The Boulevard especially to see me and mainly because my mum had told her I'd be there. Thanks Mum!

There I was, off my nut, on the stage and this bird is suddenly standing in front of me. I was rushing like a madman on these 'callies', not knowing what they were doing to me, and falling more and more in love with her by the minute.

We ended up going back to my mum's, but Karen had no idea I had taken ecstasy. We were getting down to business on the bed, but I kept coming up on the pills. I had the Todd Terry Project/ Back To The Beat 12 inch on repeat on my record deck, and intermittently, as the rushing intensified, I had to jump up and have a little dance around the room, before getting back to the action. The look on the poor girl's face was an absolute picture.

Outside of the weird and wonderful world of his 'box room', Brandon was keen to check out as many nearby haunts and other local DJs as possible, including Mark Fenton who ran a 'midweek acid house night' at The Game Bird in Watford. Swainy points out:-

Back then it was still a very small scene, and there were only a few clubs throughout London playing that sort of music. I'd been going to Shoom and Spectrum and The Boulevard was one of the only clubs outside of those two that I'd been to, in terms of a full-on acid house night. I met that bloody nutter there and that was it, it was all over. The Boulevard was a funny one, it was a proper mad old gaff and, looking back, it's pretty amazing they had an acid house night there.

Brandon's DJ fee had increased from the £30 that he, Ali and Lee shared at The John Lyon, to maybe £100 if he and Dean played together or around £75 on his own, and he was often billed as 'DJ Brandon' or 'Brandon'. But it was still as much about clubbing and experimenting with recreational drugs, than simply DJing.

It was the jump from pub to club, I guess. The club owners could see that certain DJs would bring people and that they could use the DJ's name to promote the night and thus pay us more. But this had already been going on for a long time in the soul scene. DJs like Froggy (RIP), Steve Walsh (RIP), Chris Hill, Greg Edwards, Sean French, Bob Masters, Bob Jones and Norman Jay, to name but a few, were already heroes and inspirations to us through our various soul trips and had been commanding much bigger fees for some time. Most of those soul jocks from the '70s had been regulars at Special Branch parties too.

Another seminal moment for me around the summer of '88 was a party I went to in Acton called Destination Moon, with Rampling, Steve Proctor and Boy's Own co-founder Terry Farley all on the bill. It was there that I met pioneering rave promoter Tony Colston-Hayter, the man behind the event, and the night I tried my first line of cocaine since that 'straightener' at the family wedding!

I remember vividly leaving Destination Moon at 8am the next day, and the cry of "acieeeed"...had changed to "two Es and a nutnut"... nutnut being the strongest acid around at that time.

I wasn't playing at the likes of Spectrum or Shoom, but I did get a gig at later Club Sunrise events, after selling a coach full of tickets for the first ever Sunrise rave, famously promoted by Colston-Hayter, who The Sun newspaper quickly hailed as the 'King Of Acid House'.

Destination Moon had been my first big night out at an event like that and my first line of coke in that sort of environment. The pills were the best ever so far too. I'd got talking to Colston-Hayter, and I blagged him that I knew loads of people and I'd sell tickets for him.

At that point I felt I'd found my niche, whether it was selling myself as a DJ or an actual event, or both. Then the combination of the music and the drugs and getting people together for a party became my way of life. The first Sunrise, in October 1988, was stopped by the police and never happened. But it was rescheduled

for November, tickets for which I sold from The Dog & Duck pub in north Wembley, now our favourite combined ticket and drug outlet. The pub was later to be the first venue for myself and Swainy's notorious Under The Pool Table Club, which involved running the gauntlet down East Lane, at great speed, straight into the pub, diving under the pool table, where we would try and remain for the rest of the day, sniffing gear and drinking beer.

For the new Sunrise party I remember we all had to meet in this car park in Shepherd's Bush, where the Westfield Shopping Centre now is, and there were loads of coaches from all around the country, with signs saying where they'd come from in the front windows, like Bournemouth, Portsmouth, Manchester, Sheffield, Leeds, etc. And there was me and 50 of my mates in our coach with a big sign saying BRANDON. There were loads of club faces on there, including Matty D, who would soon start putting on his own parties.

The party was famously at an equestrian centre, and was affectionately known as the 'mystery tour', which was the first of many to come. The coach journey was eventful to say the least. As soon as we left; joints, pills, coke and acid, even bongs, all came out. Someone also brought a huge bag of mushrooms, and one guy called Eddie helped himself to too much. He ended up dancing naked around the bouncy castle all night. The next day he moved to India, changed his name, lived in an ashram, and wasn't seen for at least two years! And honestly, it happened that quickly.

Meanwhile, the poor coach driver had to pull over several times because of his (not so) passive intake of smoke fumes, eventually leaving us all a mile short of the venue, and because he couldn't drive any further, we had to walk through a forest to the rave.

This was an epic journey, to say the least. As a somewhat bedraggled coach party negotiated our way through the deepest darkest woods of Aylesbury, like a mirage, with strobe lights and billowing smoke, the equestrian centre appeared in a valley of love, so to speak. It was here that my first true smoke-filled, mind-bending laser extravaganza took place.

I vividly remember Steve Proctor following Paul Trouble Anderson, to rapturous applause. Picture the scene, a vast room filled with smoke, a layer of dry ice settled at just below head height to the dramatic and overwhelming sounds of Space Odyssey, coupled with the laser set at sweeping mode, and leaving a sea of heads above the scanning green light. A truly unforgettable moment.

As a fun-packed evening drew to a close, the party continued in the car park, with various car stereos being pumped to the full, and a familiar figure of Anton The Pirate conducting proceedings from the roof of a Range Rover. Fascinating video footage of this scene, long before video phones, can be found on YouTube, with me gurning/grinning at the end.

see YouTube - 'Acid House Sunrise 1988 Part 4 posted 23 March 2008'

Paul Avery was one such Sunriser.

About twenty cars were following the coach to the equestrian centre, and going through red lights because they didn't want to lose the coach, because nobody actually knew where they were going, not even the coaches.When we got off the coach, it was like Star Wars, with all the Ewoks scampering through the forest moon of Endor. The effort that both the promoters and the people going to the parties went to in those days was something else.

Meanwhile, Brandon's time in the recruitment business was gradually coming to an end. Atlas had let him go when a move to a different branch hadn't worked out. That same evening, after being asked to leave, he popped into a small employment agency in Wembley called Travail and asked for some work.

A wonderful woman there called Claire Bowman took me under her wing, God rest her soul - a lovely lady - and I did quite well, getting all my mates work in the process, in jobs they didn't have a clue about.
I'd say they were fully qualified for the role, they'd turn up and blag it within an hour and end up staying for months. One such person was Paul Avery, who had never seen a computer in his life, but I got him a senior job at B.A.S.F as a technician.

And because me and these friends all worked locally every day, and I was back in Wembley, we'd meet up in the pub every day for lunch and later for drinks after work.

It was 1988 and alcohol still played a major role, but, like many, ecstasy quickly became part and parcel of my life too.

I had by now managed to afford a pair of Technics decks and with the Ecstasy van on its way out as more and more guest DJ bookings at clubs came through, a lorry load of Es were about to be consumed.

Myself and Ali had found ourselves following slightly different paths, and as my DJ bookings were becoming more regular on the club circuit we decided to sell the van and Ecstasy Disco ceased trading as the world of mobile DJing gave way to something a lot less strenuous and a lot more fun.

As I carried on with the music, Ali went in more of a promotion and security direction. We were still sparring partners though, and had some memorable scrapes.

One that particularly springs to mind is an ill-fated acid-house roadtrip to a Boy's Own party in Brighton straight from the aforementioned 'first acid house wedding'.

We made it there in one piece, thank God, but on the return journey, to our dismay, we found ourselves stranded on the middle of a roundabout in East Grinstead, which is where we had to lay Ali's Peugeot to rest…and leg it!

Thankfully, a thoughtful passer-by did his duty for the day and gave us both a lift to Gatwick. Without him, we quite possibly could have been there for days, because pre-Motorola, the chances of getting hold of a cab at this un-Godly hour was very slim.

Ali looks back on those scrapes with Brandon fondly.

I was playing my jazz funk, doing my thing, as we had been, and I also had this radio show on a pirate station based in Harlesden, just down the road in north west London, called Girls FM.

They had given me a new Saturday morning show, which started at 8am, and I would take over from the tapes running through the night. Me and Brandon were going to this boat party with a fancy dress theme the night before and ironically, I guess, we'd gone as pirates.

Someone had dropped the key off at my house while I was at the party, and given me directions to the studio in this flat above a chemist in Harlesden, No 96, and I was sure I knew where it was, so we rushed back to my place from the party, the worse for wear, to say the least, at about 6.30am, grabbed the key and headed down to Harlesden.

We got to the chemist, put the key in the door next to it, and went in. It was pitch black so we fumbled around and turned the front room light on and this guy on the sofa nearly jumped out of his skin. He was screaming at us, and I said, "it's no problem mate, just tell us where the studio is", but he was still screaming, saying he was going to call the police.

Turned out we were in the wrong flat. We were meant to be above the chemist at the other end of Harlesden High Street, by the Jubilee Clock, but by chance, the key had worked in this other No 96, also above a chemist. What were the chances of that?

When I finally started the show, Brandon jumped on the mic and said "well, you're not going to believe what just happened to us".

Brandon was becoming less and less employable, but really didn't care. He was holding out for the vacancy of full-time party animal, a position he took up not long after, and held for some years at managing director level.

I left Travail after a year, and had another job as a computer recruitment consultant at a firm called Computer Help. I stayed there for about three months, but eventually got the sack for "non-attendance over consecutive weeks". Time spent much more wisely, I thought, off my head, going to clubs like Spectrum on a Monday and carrying on partying through the week...more drugs and drinking like a fish too.

I ended up working for my dad - he had his own printing firm now, doing all the stationery for bankers Merrill Lynch. I was his warehouse manager for a short while, which was laughable. If I wasn't falling asleep in the factory, I was doing lines of coke in his office. It got to the point when the old man said "this isn't fair on anyone else working here, son".

And that was my last proper job, if you can call it that.

More than 20 years later and Brandon hasn't had a 'proper job' since, well not unless you count his three-week stint on the BBC's Celebrity Scissorhands in 2007!

THIRSTY WORK

As 1988 drew to a close, my new DJ career had taken me by surprise, and if you had told me that 20 years later I would be working in a televised hair salon as part of a BBC TV show for charity fundraiser Children In Need I would have laughed in your face.

While myself and Dean had bonded through the new acid house coming through, Ali was not so sure. I played him some early acid house, and he said "nah, I really can't be playing that stuff", and then as DJs we kind of drifted apart musically, I guess. Ali couldn't get his head around acid house, certainly the first lot of records we were hearing.

And I can see where Ali was coming from. The first batch of acid house that came out was dominated by the Roland 303 bass synthesizer and the Roland 909 drum machine. It was hard for a lot of the jazz funk crew to grasp it, especially as lot of us weren't doing drugs when the first tracks came out, and hadn't been in an '808 State' yet.

So musically, not everyone was keen on playing the acid house that was driving the scene forward at such a frightening pace. But Brandon had another idea for Ali.

Brandon came to me, and said about me doing the door at this new night he and Dean were going to be doing at Queen's, and I thought to myself, "you know, I think I could do that". I'd never done it before, and you didn't need your doormen's badge or licence or anything in those days. And so I did it, and then it can only have been a matter of weeks and people were coming to me and asking me to do their doors, as more and more house music nights popped up. We did a few raves at the time, but it was mainly clubs.

My door teams were popular because we were still just ourselves, and I made sure that the people who were working for me were clubbers as well. I was always mindful that the last thing people wanted when they were going to a club was to get pissed off at the door before they'd even got in the place.

Suddenly it just went mad, and everybody wanted me on their door. This soon took over the DJing side of things and work was coming in thick and fast. Unlike other more old school doormen at the time, we were able to appreciate the clubbing revolution that was taking place. Our main priority was that people inside the venue were safe and we weren't taking advantage of the situation, by confiscating clubbers' personal gear, for instance, and then selling it in the club, or controlling what was sold in the club, which obviously happened a lot.

The odd rave that we did do, we ended up working alongside other teams who weren't as understanding as us, so we concentrated on the smaller clubs, the people we knew. I went on to do the Boy's Own parties and Full Circle every Sunday.

Like many of his peers at that time, Brandon was going with the flow, as DJ work started to come in on a regular basis. A house music night of his own was next on the agenda and teaming up with Dean Thatcher was a no-brainer.

Since the April of 1988 Phil Perry had been putting on weekly Sunday all-dayers at Queen's in Colnbrook, near Slough, a 25 minute drive down the M4 from Wembley, set on the Queen Mother's Reservoir in Berkshire.

Queen's was the epitome of after-hours clubbing at that point, bringing people from all over the country for a Sunday afternoon frolic in the Royal county of Berkshire. Yippee fuckin' aye-yay! The most amazing day out there was, which led perfectly into the rest of the week of debauchery and fun. I played there once or twice, and Baggy had somehow managed to blag a spot of guest list work there alongside London legend Dave Courtney and his door team. There was simply no stopping clubland at that time, with nights springing up everywhere and many different options after Queen's on a Sunday too.

Dean and I wanted to do a midweek night at Queen's and the manager gave us a Tuesday at the end of January, 1989. Dean asked me if I minded his mate Charlie Chester getting involved, saying he'd be useful with the promoting side of things. I knew

Charlie, of course, because his other half Karen had been my boss at Atlas.

It made sense for Charlie to help out, and for us to use the name Flying, from Dean's night at The Villa, literally because we were always 'flying' - we were all high as kites. The first one was actually called Flying presents The Batman Party, which was probably something to do with the then popular LSD Batman blotters. Me, Dean and 'special guest' Phil Perry were on that first line-up. I might have done the warm-up, but I'm not sure. I don't think Charlie was that keen on me playing. The politics were starting already.

We went on to do it every Tuesday for months and although I wasn't playing there much, we were earning good money, splitting the door take three ways and getting up to 600 people in. Ali was no longer spinning tunes as I quickly installed him as Flying's Head Of Security. Other local DJs Terry Farley and Rocky & Diesel would guest regularly. And the fact that it was on a Tuesday didn't seem to matter because people started going out every night of the week.

We were each coming away on a Tuesday night with £300 or £400, and then I was earning at least another £100 to £150 DJing at the weekends.

One early flyer for Tuesday February 28, 1989, read:-

Charlie, Dean & Brandon invite you to FLYING, Dex: Mark Ravenhill, Dean Thatcher, Brandon Block and special guest Andy Weatherall (Shoom), visuals by Pop (Trip, Sin), admission: £4.

Thatcher remembers he and Brandon were more than happy being the musical faces of the night, even if Brandon was being booked to play less than Dean.

When we got the night at Queen's we couldn't for the life of us think of a name, so I said let's call it Flying. I'd already got some artwork done of this geezer playing a sax, by some rockabilly guy known as Rockin' Harry, so it made sense to use that. Later Dave Little would update it to become the famous Flying logo that is now synonymous with that era, but it was always based on Harry's version.

Charlie was my best mate at the time, and he always used to come to our night at The Villa, and because me and Brandon wanted to concentrate on the music, and Charlie wanted to get involved, we left him to do all the organising, which in those days meant getting lots of mailing lists together and physically posting people flyers because there was obviously no emailing or texting then.

It was actually very hard work, that side of it, and Charlie was very good at it and certainly stepped up our operation pretty quickly.

And it wasn't long before Charlie took over and became the face of Flying. I worked alongside him on everything, and I guess Brandon did get left out in the cold at some point, but I'm not even sure why. When Flying moved to the Soho Theatre Club on a Saturday, Brandon rarely played at that, but he always came down after wherever else he'd been playing. Then we'd all end up back at mine or Charlie's and party through the rest of the weekend.

It was never really brought up why Brandon wasn't as involved, not even by Brandon really. We were all too busy enjoying ourselves.

A week after Flying launched, Brandon embarked on a new weekly Sunday night residency at Haven Stables, not a stables at all, but the old Lucky's bar in Ealing, west London, where he had been a regular DJ, and which had now been refurbished.

Boulevard promoters Carl Pearson and Alan Warman were launching a new Sunday-nighter at Haven called A-zee K-zee, and I jumped at the opportunity. It was, after all, for me another night out, playing music and getting my name out there.

It was a roaring success for everyone involved, myself included, even though I was only paid the princely sum of £50 for the night. I undertook the residency on my lonesome initially and had usually been to Queen's earlier in the day.

The Haven Stables sessions were becoming more and more fruity too, with so many girls trying to woo me, three or four birds constantly around the DJ booth at one time, throughout the six or so hours I was there. Ooh to be a DJ, the spin-offs were becoming more and more apparent!

Record bar takes at Haven Stables meant I was quickly on great terms with the owners Dave and Geoff, and soon I pretty much

had the run of the place. I was even entrusted with the use of the club after it had closed most Sunday nights.

Step forward Swainy, and other close friends, plus whichever ladies had decided to stay that night. Out would come the green and yellow 12ft throw from the back of my Metro, my mode of transport back then, and which had a LET'S TAKE THE METRO BATMAN sticker in the back window. And with copious amounts of whatever was needed to continue the frolicking and a free run of the bar, we cracked on. We just had to leave a note, saying what we'd had from the bar. Wayhay!

Sometimes the management actually used to lock us in and let us stay until the cleaners turned up in the morning.

Meanwhile, one guest DJ at Haven Stables would go on to play a major part Brandon's life and career.

The venue was a long thin club, and you could see right down into it, with the bar area as you walked in, and the dancefloor and DJ booth at the back. One week Alex P was playing and mid-mix, all of a sudden, as he tells the story, he could see a massive kerfuffle at the entrance to the club, with a mixture of arms and record boxes up in the air, people shouting "Blocko, Blocko". I finally plonked my record boxes down in the booth, shook his hand, sprinkled a load of gear on the record he was mixing in, put a rolled up note on the mixer and said "nice to meet you, my name's Brandon Block".

At the time DJing was becoming more about perfection in mixing and professionalism, but when Alex had managed to complete his last mix, I ran his final record to the end, playing the scratching noise of the needle over the speakers. Then I put a fresh record on the other turntable and jumped up on to the other deck, arms aloft, shouting "oi, oi, let's have it". I then bent down to press the cue button, and to rapturous applause Third World's Now That We've Found Love kicked in. A magic moment!

And soon after Brandon was very popular now that he'd found an unassuming black leather pouch in a west London club.

I looked inside this small bag and quickly realised that this was the best find since The Mary Rose.

It was amazing…there was a jar of little yellow burgers, around 50 of them, and about 35 grams of charlie, plus some solid and weed. It was worth a fortune. We went back to my house, and were like proverbial kids in a sweet shop, saying to each other "well, we don't want the puff so we'll pass that on, and we'll have some of that, a bit of that, and we'll try that later".

But by the next weekend there was nothing left! We'd gone to Venus in Nottingham the following night, and during that week, with the help of others, we'd done the lot.

By this time I had several tricks up my sleeve where the procuring of narcotics was concerned. One blag at house parties was to pinch a mirror from the bathroom and tape it just next to the decks. Anyone wanting to rack up a line of coke on the mirror would be obliged to do the decent thing and offer the DJ one... "oh, OK, go on then".

However, there were soon less and less house parties to attend, and more and more nightclubs to visit. One Flying session at Queen's resulted in my first road trip to Manchester, which back then boasted the legendary Hacienda nightclub among its ranks and, as far as many northerners at the very least are concerned, was and is the UK's spiritual home of house music. As this particular Tuesday drew to a close at Queen's, at around 2am, it was time to divvy up the door money, but a certain Mr Chester was nowhere to be seen.

Charlie had said at the start of the night that he was going up to Manchester straight after the party because the Hacienda were opening a bar up there. It was the soon-to-be infamous Dry Bar.

Around 1am, me and Dean looked around for him and he'd only fucked off up there with all the cash. I said to Dean, "c'mon mate, let's go up there after him" and a couple of our friends Justin and Brad, volunteered to drive us, like you do in the early hours of a Wednesday morning. But then people were up for anything like that at the drop of a hat in those days.

I had never set foot in Manchester, but I was already known by many there through my involvement with Sunrise.

Three hours later and we were strolling around Manchester City Centre looking for Chester and the Dry Bar. It was hilarious. We didn't know the fuck where we were, but we turned the corner and literally bumped into him. His face was a picture.

Me and the others ended up in this B & B for the night, and then spent the next day getting pissed in the Dry Bar, with me and Dean later playing some records there too.

Then it was off to the Hacienda for the Wednesday night Void session, which I remember Graeme Park was playing at - some amazing stuff too. Tracks like Stetsasonic's Talking All That Jazz mixed into De La Soul. Pure DJ mastery, and Graeme has remained as one of my DJ heroes from that time on. And if I'm not mistaken, there was another young chap DJing that night, by the name of Pickering. Mike went on to huge success with his band M-People. Big up yaself Michael!!!

We had a great time in the Hacienda. It was 1989 and the club's heyday and to experience it first hand was amazing. I was fortunate enough to play the 'Hac' on numerous occasions over the years - a truly iconic venue.

Dean Thatcher remembers the London – Manchester connection fondly.

Queen's was great and, regularly, we'd leave there in the early hours of Tuesday morning, go back to Charlie's place, stay up all night, then have a few pints in a nearby pub on Wednesday lunchtime before driving up to Manchester. We'd hang out in the Dry Bar, then go to the 'Hac' and get home Thursday evening, just in time for the weekend. That was the life.

Acid house had ensured London's clubland was expanding at a frightening pace and in the spring of '89, Brandon was booked by school pal Matthew Donegan to play at a party at Didcot Railway Centre in Oxfordshire. It would be his first encounter with Lisa Loud, or more like Lisa's first encounter with Brandon.

Matthew was putting on this party under the Respect Presents name with Chris King and his (eventual) wife Mandy, and Mark

THE LIFE & LINES OF BRANDON BLOCK

Archer (aka Tenerife Mark)…all very prolific faces at the time. I got a spot in the VIP room, and the likes of Trevor Fung, Oakey, Farley and Lisa were all playing in the main room, which was in the actual museum itself, so it was an important booking for me.

After his accidental DJ spots at Trip, which people at the time, and even now, would have given their right mixing arm for, Donegan had chanced his other arm at promoting parties in unusual spaces, first in February 1989 with a party called Winter Roses in a building in Wardour Street owned by The British Library, and then a month later at Bray Film Studios, near Windsor. Next up in May was an ambitious party, supposedly a record company event, for 3,000 people at Didcot. Donegan reflects:-

I hadn't booked Brandon for the previous two parties, but I did for Didcot. It was a railway museum, and we put flooring down in the engine shed, and had smoke and lights coming out of all of the engines. The police kept paying us visits at the entrance to the museum, telling us to turn the music down.

Then suddenly, with me at my wits end, I saw two more Old Bill coming down the tracks. I was getting angry now, and very frustrated. But I knew these policemen were on the premises, so that meant they were probably now going to try and shut us down. As they got nearer, I realised it was actually this guy I knew called Dean and his mate, who had turned up in fancy dress. I was about to throttle them, when I decided to lead them in, that it would be a great chance to wind everybody up.

I led them into the chill-out area, and people were throwing their gear everywhere. I then took these two 'coppers' in to the VIP area, and through to the engine shed. The DJs there had left the decks as panic spread throughout the venue, but I ushered our 'boys in blue' up on to a big podium in the middle of the dancefloor. I grabbed Brandon, who was none the wiser too, and told him to put a record on.

*(clockwise) * In the box room at Harrow Road*
* Brandon and co off to a flyer (various) in 1990
* The pioneering Roland TB-303 synthesizer
* With Ashley Beedle at his Pimps & Hustlers birthday fancy dress party, early '90s

DJ's Don't Mind If I Do
New Year's Night
1st January 1990

Broadway Boulevard
NIGHT CLUB
10 High Street, Ealing W5
Telephone: 01-840 0616

- JON JULES
- DON BLOCK
- DEAN THATCHER
- KY & DIESEL

9pm – 3am

Admission £5 before 11pm — £6 after

Code: Smart Casual
Denims acceptable
Trainers or Mountain Boots

FLYING
eens HORTON RD
COLNBROOK BERKS

invite you to
FLYING
SDAY 28th FEB
K: MARK RAVENHILL
EAN THATCHER
RANDON BLOCK
AL GUEST
WEATHERALL

THIRD WORLD
WIP 6457
WIP 6457-A
℗ 1978 Island Records Ltd
Carlin Music Corp
Time: 3.55

NOW THAT WE'VE FOUND LOVE
(Gamble-Huff)

PRODUCED BY ALEX SADKIN & THIRD WORLD
EXECUTIVE PRODUCER
CHRIS BLACKWELL

GIVE ME SOME SUBSTANCE

CARL PEARSON & ALAN
INVITE YOU TO
A-ZEE K-ZEE CL
AT
HAVEN STABLE

SUNDAY 3rd DE
DJ'S
JOHNNIE WALKER
ALEX PEDRIDES
8pm–1am

SUNDAY 10th DE
DJ'S
FABIO, DJ SHORTY
RICHARD NEUTRON
8pm–1am

SUNDAY 17th DE
DJ'S
MARVIN (RENEGADE)
BRANDON BLOCK
8pm–1am

XMAS EVE PAR
DJ'S
FAT TONY
&
ALEX PEDRIDES
9pm–2.30am
MEMBERS £10
NON MEMBERS £12.50

NEW YEARS EVE PA
DJ'S
GROOVE RIDER
BRANDON BLOCK
9pm–2.30am
MEMBERS £10
NON MEMBERS £12.50

Roland TB-303 Computer Controlled

The policemen were standing on the podium, shining their torches down on all the startled clubbers. Brandon dropped the Sylvester classic Mighty Real, and our police officers broke out into a John Travolta-style arm waving dance, ripping their uniforms off and tossing them into the crowd. The place just erupted, and went absolutely mental, with loads of people coming up on their Es at the time. Pulling off that party in the first place was the scam upon scams and our two 'policemen' really topped it off.

Didcot was a mad mad party, and, in general, Matthew's parties, because they were at venues not always associated with clubbing, and because they attracted the trendier lot he'd been hanging around with further into central London, were events where people would dress up a bit more. Looking back I think they were a forerunner for events like Puscha, which took one-off parties on to the next level in the early to mid-90s. Those times and those Respect parties always remind me of hanging out with the Wilson brothers, Alan, Paul and Brains - three of the biggest clubland legends of that era.

And Didcot also gave me a chance to introduce myself to Lisa Loud, who I'd wanted to meet since she had put on the Loud Noise parties a year earlier with Nancy Noise, and because she'd played at Future. Our paths had never really crossed socially, but at Didcot I went up to the decks when she was playing, said hello and added something embarrassing like "Fuck me, you're gorgeous". What a prick! What a shit chat up line!

But in true Brandon-style he did leave a lasting impression and would have plenty more opportunities to try and impress Lisa Loud over the coming years.

Loud remembers driving there in a "beaten up" Peugeot 205, belonging to her then boyfriend, Paul Oakenfold.

It was a mad party in a mad venue, surely one of the best ever used to this day, in fact. If I remember rightly I think the Peugeot broke down on the way too. Those were the days, huh? I do remember Brandon coming up to the decks. How funny?

The Haven Stables evening sessions were going so well, that Brandon asked Dean if he fancied starting a daytime session there, which had particular advantages.

I had worked out that rather than making the hazardous journey to Queen's every Sunday lunchtime from Wembley, and back to Haven Stables in Ealing again in the evening, me and Dean could do our own Sunday brunch session at Haven Stables and therefore hang around in the same area all day.

We came up with the name Thirst, and this new daytime session would run at the same time as Queen's, with Matty D on the door. I must stress that the party at Queen's was still the daddy of afternoon raving at this early stage in the extreme clubbing stakes, and was still going strong, hosted by Phil Perry, his other half Fiona and Martin The Poet.

Haven Stables in Ealing was only ten minutes from our base in the Wembley area, as opposed to a good hour there and back from Wembley to Colnbrook where Queen's was…so for those of us who were too incoherent to drive that far after the rest of the weekend's shenanigans a bit of stability, if you can call it that, was much needed. Haven Stability, in fact!

We launched in the summer of 1989 and Thirst would start at midday and run until 6pm. Then they'd shut the venue, clean it up and reopen at 8pm for Carl and Alan's night. However, they found it harder and harder to get me out of the pub across the road during the changeover, but I did get back there eventually, often via other local watering holes.

A lot of people would roll on from Saturday night, and loads of our mates were inside the venue before we even opened. Then there would be queues, literally around the block from midday. Haven Stables was a great day (and night) out and Harvey Block was often in attendance – not a surprise with all the ladies about!

And Harvey Block soon got a taste for club life.

I wasn't really there from the start of his DJ career. I did go to The John Lyon on one occasion, but then because Brandon never really got on with my second wife and I was off doing other things, I didn't really witness the start of his DJ career, as such. When I spoke to him, he always seemed to be playing at "a friend's party", so it didn't really seem like a career to me. The first time I was aware of it developing into something bigger was when he invited me down Haven Stables, and that's when I first witnessed what was going on. It was a New Year's Day, and he'd done a whole load of gigs the night before. That was the first time I'd seen him DJ, other than The John Lyon, and I realised how good he was. I was very proud of him, and I suppose I became an old aged groupie from that point on.

The first indication I had that he was into disco or dance music had been when he went to Harrow Leisure Centre for the rollerskating. He was brilliant on the skates, with all the tricks he could do, and he actually became a bit of a celebrity down there, long before the DJing.

Later in the '90s, I'd go with him to places like The Gardening Club, and other gigs too. I'd often carry his boxes in there for him, and the one thing I was proud of was that he would always introduce me to everyone and say "this is my dad", and I loved that. I'm not saying that there wasn't, shall we say, certain side effects that weren't very enjoyable, that I didn't also see the benefits of. Too much booze and all the other stuff, I guess, but I used to have a great time.

I went up to Leeds with him when he played at Up Yer Ronson for Tony and Adam, and we had an absolute riot...it was madness, what I can remember of it. We had some great times. I went to Ibiza with him, and had some amazing times there too. He took me to Dubai with him, and we had a ball. I was just full of pride, wherever we went.

One kid came up to me in Es Paradis in Ibiza when Brandon was playing up in the gantry, and asked if he could shake my hand and I said no problem, and he added "I'm just blown away that boy there is the fruit of your loins".

I was treated like royalty everywhere I went. Another time I turned up at The Camden Palace, and on Brandon's instructions, told the long-haired bloke standing there with the clipboard that I was Brandon Block's dad. There was a massive queue halfway down the road, and this bloke said "oh, yes, yes", and I was whisked straight in. Those are the sort of things that you don't forget.

Then there was the Christmas Eve that I'd invited him round to my flat in West Hampstead for a festive dinner with all the trimmings, because he had a gig, actually on Christmas Day night, and wouldn't be around then. He turned up 12-handed, and invited loads of people on the phone during the night. We ended up with Sasha and his girlfriend Marie, Seb Fontaine, Jimmy Mitchell, and various other people. Some guy called Achilles, who was a mate of Sasha's, turned up with green hair, and Brandon joked "Achilles hairdresser". That party was madness, and I eventually slung everybody out late on Christmas Day, because there were loads of people we didn't know, and I had a party of people coming round for Boxing Day dinner. I think Brandon stayed, and missed his booking that night in the end.

During a later stint at Haven Stables for promoter and clubland face Dave Mahoney, Brandon wasn't best pleased one Sunday when told an up-and-coming musician would be accompanying him while he was DJing.

Dave said to me one night "I've got this kid who plays keyboards, do you mind if he plays tonight while you're on?". I reluctantly said "OK, I'll give him a go", but when I saw my so-called support slot, he looked like an up-and-coming Adamski. He seemed about 12-years-old, so I said to him "if you're going do this, then you need to play along with what I'm doing". He started doing his own thing and I said "get him off, get him off, and do me a favour, someone brush his hair on the way out". And that's how I famously threw Jamiroquai out of Haven Stables, obviously unaware that Jay would become not only Britain's finest modern day soul star, but also a friend. In fact, years later, ironically, myself and Alex warmed up for him at one of his concerts. Fortunately, he didn't return the compliment.

As the '80s, an eventful decade for dance music, drew to a close, and with both Haven Stables Sunday sessions in full swing, Brandon was picking up DJ bookings left, right and centre.

September '89, saw him line-up alongside Evil Eddie Richards, Paul Anderson, Phil Perry, Carl Cox, Phil & Ben and Jumping Jack Frost for Club Sunrise at Heaven in Charing Cross, and he was also on rotation every Sunday at Ronnie Scott's, with the likes of Farley, Proctor and Weatherall.

He wrapped up this iconic year playing alongside Alex P and Grooverider for A-Zee K-Zee at Haven Stables, and also for an

Independence Christmas party at Regals in Uxbridge with Fat Tony and Kevin Hurry, and then began 1990, with an A-Zee K-Zee New Year's All-Dayer at the Stables, alongside Alex, Mark Doyle and Richard Neutron, followed by a spot the same night at Don't Mind If I Do at the Broadway Boulevard with old muckers Jon Jules, Dean Thatcher and Rocky.

Brandon's notoriety was increasing all the time, and 1990 would become a defining year in many ways for the 23-year-old from Wembley.

Ever since he could remember he had been drinking, partying and generally having the time of his life, but now it looked like he could make a decent career out of it all, and this phenomenon called acid house didn't seem to be slowing down, or at least not its spirit.

MILKING IT

Somehow I had become a fully-fledged DJ and it was beginning to look like I would't be confined to the four walls of an office for quite some time.

As 1990 unfolded, Flying was now cementing a new Saturday reputation at Soho Theatre Club, just along from The Astoria, in London's West End.

I was more and more in demand elsewhere, though, with Fridays and Saturdays starting to get booked out well in advance, and Haven Stables all-day on a Sunday providing reliable work towards the end of the weekend.

Flying was continuing to build throughout England and beyond. The rolling out of the brand throughout the UK, linking up with the best club nights and DJs from each main city, was built on the same philosophy as Flying's new central London base, which ensured that the cream of the UK's house jocks guested each week in the capital alongside Thatcher and, when he was asked, Brandon.

Regular Friday work for Brandon included The Brain in Wardour Street with the likes of Judge Jules, and on Saturdays The Menace at Starlights in Paddington, with Fabi Paras and Steve Proctor.

Even Thursdays were busy, with bookings at the dubiously-titled Shagaramas at The Reflex Club in Putney, where one week Brandon would be on with Weatherall, and another, with Ibiza out of season, you could find Amnesia legend Alfredo alongside Steve Savva.

Another new and important addition and house music option for London's West End had been orchestrated by Nicky Holloway, who, with Sin still thriving at The Astoria, in April of 1990, opened his own much smaller and more intimate venue across the road on Sutton Row. The Milk Bar had a capacity of just 200, and quickly became one of THE places to hear house music in London and would go on to provide another Sunday home for Brandon.

But before that, the spring of 1990 would give him his first taste of an island, which in turn provided a platform to take his DJ career to so many more levels.

I had heard all the stories about Ibiza and witnessed first hand how its influence had transformed clubbing in London, but now it was time to check it out for myself.

Charlie Chester had the idea to take a load of us out there, put on some parties, basically an extension of what we were doing in and around London, and so he asked me and Scott Braithwaite, another Flying DJ, to go out there with him on a 'recce' before the start of the season. The three of us headed out there at the end of May, pitched up in San Antonio, and booked into a hotel at the back of the West End.

The guy we first met was called Jose Luis. He owned Ibiza's first upfront record shop, called Disco Galleria, so we hung around there and me and Scott got to play a couple of times at the F.B.I Bar, on the main road in to San An. It's changed name a few times since then, it's the one next to Hyper Centro and is now a washing machine repair shop!

Someone had the idea to hide a sheet of trips underneath the stickers on my record box. Thanks for that! Class, eh? Or should I say, class A.

What a gaff, though? First time to Ibiza and as soon as I stepped off the plane, at what was then a tiny airport, at the back end of nowhere, the feeling came over me and it has never changed to this day, drugs or no drugs.

I'd been getting through the trips, which were Strawberries, as if they were one of our five a day...so I took five a day. While Charlie was off talking to club owners to see what he could arrange, I hooked up with some other pals from London and decided that we would invent the game of football with no ball, around the streets of San Antonio, which was a right laugh until we accidentally kicked our imaginary ball through a local tapas bar window. Tripping off my head I ran, apologetically, to a very bemused innkeeper, who obviously could see no ball, let alone a broken window. He was even more confused when I offered to buy a round of drinks by way of compensation.

At this time there were no UK or international promoters on the island, as such. Charlie was going to be that pioneer and credit where credit is due, he did it, and convinced all the superclubs to put on nights, which he would promote and fill with the first big wave of British clubbers.

Sure, the likes of Oakenfold, Rampling, Holloway, Fung, Walker and, no doubt a few others, had done the pilgrimage for a few years previously, but this would be the first big promoter-led trip from the UK.

I vaguely remember 'monkey-walking' through Pacha on the A-frame that used to stretch the length of the dancefloor, kicking people in the head as I swung. I know they were all pilled up but I bet they loved me, eh? Although, I didn't 'hang' around to find out!

The group returned to London, and while Chester set about organising an early season trip to Ibiza he was approached by a Channel 4 film crew planning to make a documentary about club culture in Ibiza.

The project would become the critically-acclaimed A Short Film About Chilling and fledgling director Angus Cameron, who went on to work with Guy Ritchie on Lock Stock And Two Smoking Barrels, and various production assistants, including a young Jo Whiley, would film the motley crew of more than 500 people who followed pied piper Chester to Ibiza.

But Brandon was not one of them.

Charlie wouldn't even put me on the line-up for the actual Ibiza trip and it really pissed me off, so I didn't bother going. I'd been playing less and less at the Tuesday night Flying party at Queen's, and that's why I had been keen to start my own thing, Thirst, with Dean.

The Ibiza trip proper took place to legendary effect with The Farm and The Beloved playing at Ku (…later renamed Privilege), A Man Called Adam playing Pacha and 808 State doing the Amnesia night. Flying sold tickets including flight, accommodation and club passes for around £300 and the likes of Terry Farley, Danny Rampling, Andrew Weatherall, Rocky & Diesel and Clive Henry all joined local hero Alfredo behind the decks over the various nights.

Back in London and fresh from his success in Ibiza, Charlie Chester was at his entrepreneurial best and in his element as a wave of clubland optimism swept over London and the suburbs. Chester set about opening the Flying record shop in the Kensington Indoor Market on Kensington High Street, an iconic myriad of independent stores and units and, alas, long given way to developers.

Like many jocks that Chester knew at the time, Brandon and Dean - who had both worked at R&D in some capacity - also worked part-time at the Flying record shop, as did Clive Henry, later of DC10/Circo Loco fame. And Flying quickly became one of THE places to hang out and buy house records in central London. Thatcher picks up the story:-

Flying had quickly gone from being mine and Brandon's baby to Charlie's thing, and the shop followed, and then his label, Cowboy Records. I managed the shop for a while, and then later spent more time in Hayes where the offices for Cowboy were above a HHS hire shop.

Charlie and Brandon had always been great drinking buddies, but something went wrong between them, and I've never been able to put my finger on it. Along the way various things got bitter and twisted, as they always do when mates are working together and there's money involved, but I was always fine with Charlie taking the Flying brand on. I was too busy having a good time, DJing all over the place. It was just a bonkers time for all concerned.

Some days me and Brandon would be working in the shop together with Lofty (aka Steve Harper) and we'd just look at each other and say "pub", and then spend the whole day in one of our locals, leaving Lofty, the manager, and Clive to run the shop. Charlie would come in and go mad at us. And all we could do was laugh...because we were all just mates really.

My band The Aloof was originally signed to Cowboy, and our track Never Get Out Of The Boat quickly became a Balearic anthem. I was working at Cowboy more and more and Brandon was off doing what he was doing, getting booked everywhere by now, and by then me and him were taking totally different musical paths. I was more on the left side of things, embracing trip-hop and techno, while Brandon was playing the peak-time, big room stuff that the larger club brands were starting to want, so we were on a completely different circuit, although still within the same scene.

There was loads of us from our area that became DJs, and gradually we all went off and did our own thing, as dance music genres started to splinter off. Weatherall in particular went more underground, and the Weatherall fans were always loyal to wherever he played.

Then in 1994 I got offered a record deal by Warner Brothers for The Aloof. I had felt something would happen for some time with the band, and the offer of making music and touring the world, compared with working in an office in Hayes was too good to turn down. We may not have been that successful, but we were signed to Warner for seven years and getting paid to party round the world and make music full-time for all those years is something I will never forget.

These days I'm a music consultant for River Island, compiling the music for all their stores, and also compile the Zzub Chart for Update/ www.dmcworld.com, a spin on the old Buzz chart. And away from music, I also work part-time as a postman, which I really enjoy. That gets me out of the house and also ensures a bit of guaranteed money.

As Dean has said, it was a time of discovery and the acid house scene opened so many doors - those parties in small sweaty clubs in south London and north London, and wherever else, a music scene and different genres that we later took for granted. It also reinvented indie rock music and Oakey was a big part of that with his remixes of Happy Mondays and Massive Attack, and later U2. Acid house became techno, techno became house, house became garage and garage became grime, and that's without even mentioning rave, hardcore, jungle and ragga.

As people started making records and producing new sounds, particularly with machines like the Roland 303, over the years house music evolved and things slowly began to start going in different directions. Look at The Prodigy in the early '90s, with Charly Says. That was groundbreaking, to say the least, but where the fuck did that come from? As The Prodigy said in their track Out Of Space, the different genres really did start to "take your brain to another dimension". And in turn that stuff led on to happy hardcore and drum and bass.

Great pioneers at that time in those scenes were Ratpack, Slipmatt and Lime (aka SL2), Mickey Finn, Nicky Blackmarket, DJ Hype, Kenny Ken, Jumpin Jack Frost and Fabio & Grooverider, to name but a few. Also Goldie with his innovative Metalheadz project. Over the years I've had the good fortune to work and hang out with DJs, artists and producers from various genres of music, for all of whom I have the utmost respect.

Despite his Ibiza snub, Brandon's bookings diary was healthy, and in the summer of 1990 he was asked to play at a new party called Gosh, co-promoted by Rocky and Clive Henry.

The first in July featured usual suspects Thatcher, Perry, Gunner, Paras, Braithwaite, Brandon and Clive, with the next one in August at Dingwalls in Camden headlined by DeeeLite from New York (live), with Brandon joined by Weatherall, Thatcher and Bob Jones.

In October 1990, Phil Perry, who by now had finished his Sunday session at Queen's, after one too many complaints by boating people in the area, launched his new and soon-to-be legendary project, Full Circle.

Then Flying visited Venus in Nottingham in November and Ibiza stars The Farm headlined a Flying Presents gig at The Astoria in Shaftesbury Avenue at the end of December. Brandon was involved in neither party, with Thatcher playing at both. Other DJ guests across those two events included Weatherall, Farley, Rocky & Diesel, Phil Perry, Lofty, Glenn Gunner and Stripey.

Phil moved to The Greyhound because they were getting complaints from the people who sailed their boats on the Queen's Reservoir. They hadn't taken too kindly to dungaree-wearing, ecstasy-chomping, acid house-loving nutters spreading their word.

So Phil went to the nearby Greyhound in Colnbrook, going on to achieve massive success there with Full Circle and the rest, as they say, is clubland history.

There was no animosity between me and Dean. We were doing Thirst together and he was doing his thing with Charlie. He was Charlie's good mate, but later when Haven Stables had run its course I went off and did other stuff myself. It was never an issue between me and Dean, never has been.

It was at that Farm gig at The Astoria that I was to come across Lisa Loud again, this time with good pal Lisa Horan by her side. I also managed to find myself on stage with The Farm's frontman Peter Hooton during one of the band's anthems, Altogether Now.

I bumped into Lisa and Lisa, who were always together then, and set about trying to charm them. I managed to do just that and me, Paul Avery and Baggy ended up back at Loudy's flat in Elgin Avenue, Paddington later that night, but not before I went back stage and Hoots beckoned me to join him because I was 'dad dancing' to the side. I ended up right next to him singing Altogether Now in front of a packed house in a really bad northern accent.

Back at the flat in Paddington, I remembered feeling honuored to have gone back to Lisa Loud's place. It seems silly now, as we became, and still are, the best of friends. We stayed there for about three or four days, getting smashed and drinking blue label Smirnoff vodka, which was the strongest vodka you could get in those days. We'd drink that by the gallon and go down and restock from the corner shop near her flat. We'd go down there at all times of the day, in all modes of transport – shopping trolleys, all sorts.

Lisa Loud admits that she quickly became the *"hostess with the mostess"*.

Everyone was always at my place, it was all laid on, and me and Lisa Horan were always the "let's get everybody up for Full Circle" brigade. Me and Lisa would sneak off for little sleeps here and there, but Brandon and the boys would just keep going.

And I remember that we always ran out of the vodka, and the boys used to go down to my local shop, in wheely bins, naked with saucepans on their heads, and pester the poor little man who used to see me in there every day. But those were the days when, no matter what time of the day, we used to manage to buy some vodka which, looking back, I find hard to believe because in 2011 in my little sleepy Richmond village, when I'm trying to get a bottle of Rioja at five to eleven in the morning, they just won't serve me.

THE LIFE & LINES OF BRANDON BLOCK

Back then there was an endless supply of vodka, morning, noon and night, although there might been a few brown paper bags and inflated prices involved.

We all bonded over those couple of days and with the two Lisas, Dean Scratcher, Baggy, Swainy and a few other fellow loons, ie Pat and Paul Rogers and Bill Cathcart, we inadvertently started putting together our own little club of likeminded 'have-it-as-long-as-you-can' nutters.

We started going out together, to places like Shoom at The Park in Kensington, before it went on to the Milk Bar and became Glam, and the two Lisas also started spending more time with us in the west London suburbs.

Around that time my ecstasy intake was huge, often consuming pils by the dozen over a 24-hour period. And so much wallop too, now my official name for it. By this time I was never without at least an eighth of an ounce on me, so around three or four grams.

After his stint for me at Thirst, Matty D also went on to do the door at Ronnie Scotts in Soho. I remember he was working there one night, and he rang me up and said the act due to perform that night were driving him mad for some gear. Matt said "can't you see me and sort something out". I said, "ok, let's do it", and took a load up there for him. I was in Sudbury, so a good half an hour away, but it was all right because my mate was driving, so I said "my bruv will bring us back together". The band got tucked in as soon as we got there. The drummer had coke all over his face, and I remember Matty telling him that he looked like a nun. The guy asked what he meant, and he added "you're wearing your habit". That was a great line... literally.

Pills and, more and more, the coke were part and parcel of it all for me. A pal of mine Tom had this huge flat in Maida Vale and I remember me, him and my mate Trevor went back there one night. We'd got this ounce rock of coke between us and put it in

(clockwise) * with 'the boys' at Soho Theatre Club
(l to r) With Prim, Avery, Scratcher, Pat R, Bill C, Paul R
* Gosh at Dingwalls flyer * Brain club flyer, 1990
* The Under The Pool Table Club at The Mitre

at the BRAIN
11 Wardour St London W1
DAYS 10-3am

GLEN GUNNER plus
Jan JUDGE JULES · MFI
Feb PHIL PERRY · Queens
Feb ALFREDO · Amnesia Ibiza
Feb MARK · Freedom
rd Feb BRANDON BLOCK ·
            Haven Stables

GOSH! MONTHLY

7 MEMBERS 8

WHAT'S THE CRACK AT DRY THIS MONTH!
I DRY
FOR INSTANCE WE HAVE
WITH DJ'S
BRANDON BLO

LIVE FROM NEW YORK
Deeelite
FRIDAY AUGUST 17th
DOORS OPEN 9:30 TILL 4:00
DINGWALLS
ANDY WEATHER
DEAN
PLUS SPECIAL GUEST J

ART: DAVE LITTLE

the middle of this large glass coffee table, crushing it down into one massive line, which must have been about six foot, basically the length of the table. With a straw each, me and Tom started from each end and after, a short break, eventually met in the middle. All that was left was this average-sized line and I said to Trevor, "help yourself mate".

Looking back, the late '80s and early '90s were mental. My drug intake was astronomical and I can now see that the addiction developed at a rapid pace. I was DJing all over the West End of London and for a lot of friends.

I had first met Paul Dennis in the early days at clubs like Cheeky Pete's, Gulliver's and The Wag. He was also a regular at Haven Stables and Queen's, and I played for Paul at Legends in Old Burlington Street, at his Club Trick parties around 1988, '89, and then for him at The World at The Limelight, Paul's weekly promotion with Gary Haisman. Paul was a man-about-town, doing all sorts of events, Beastie Boys after-parties, loads of music industry stuff.

Paul, who later went on to promote loads in Ibiza, including hosting the Privilege opening party in 1995, was also my co-driver in one famous journey from Space to Cafe Mambo. Much to the dismay of the two girls we'd just met, and Mambo resident DJ Roberto, I did the gears and Paul did the steering....from the back seat of our hire car. All 16 kilometres, and that was when the roads from Playa D'en Bossa to San Antonio weren't half as good as they are today. The other three were nervous wrecks by the time they actually got out of the car at Mambo.

Paul is a larger than life character who has been a clubland legend since year dot. I was delighted in the summer of 2011 when I was able to play at his 50th birthday party in Ibiza, and so glad he even made it that far.

Another longstanding friend of Brandon's, Simon 'Johnboy', was a bonafide Shoom regular and 'Sunriser', who has his own theory about the sudden emergence of cocaine in clubland in the early '90s.

Personally, in the late '80s/early '90s, I think it must have been very very scary for whoever was in power, especially in Britain, where you have such a class divide, when suddenly there were huge gatherings of people from the very darkest criminal elements, all the way up to the people who are studying at Eton and Marlborough, Cambridge and Oxford.

For the first time ever in British history these different factions were mixing in fields, among crowds of 30 - 40,000 other people, talking about social, political and economic issues, for hours on end, without fighting or arguing.

The year before that, if you had Chelsea Headhunters and Millwall Bushwackers in the same city they would hunt each other down like rabid dogs, but now they were sitting there complimenting each other on the scars they gave each other the year before at London Bridge station.

You had these decision makers and some of the biggest gangsters in England, not talking about how to cause problems, but how to solve problems.

Ecstasy was very powerful stuff back then. So are drugs bad? Well, it depends how they're taken. I personally feel that it's very coincidental that cocaine suddenly reared its ugly head, a drug known to be very egotistical and which separates people, as opposed to an empathetic drug like ecstasy/MDMA.

MDMA has been known to be given to people in therapy sessions, because it brings people together. Cocaine isn't used in therapy sessions for people with marriage problems, for instance. Never has and never will be. Pure MDMA lasts. There is no comedown. It really is a deep drug and people come out of their shells on it.

I put it to Simon that everyone loves a conspiracy theory, but he was quick to argue:-

It's not a conspiracy theory, it's a chess game and one they've been playing with us since time immemorial, since the days of Babylon. They've always kept the minions and the people at the top of the pyramid away from each other.

As 1991 got under way, Brandon was at the top of his own particular game, but probably still felt like one of the minions too. Haven Stables was still wrapping up his weekends and ensuring he was partying through until silly-o-clock on Monday.

My involvement in Flying events was now patchy, to say the least. However, my personal DJ bookings were relentless, as myself and Baggy partied harder and harder with the two Lisas.

One day I saw the film Tango & Cash, and they used the phrase FUBAR... "he's FUBAR man"... which famously stands for 'Fucked Up Beyond All Recognition'. It just described me perfectly. At my insistence we quickly adopted the name for our group. We travelled countrywide as a group to our gigs, which myself and Lisa were getting booked for more and more, and even had T-shirts with Terry Fuckwit from Viz magazine printed on the front. Later Viz introduced a cartoon strip called Ravey, Davey, Gravey, with the tagline "he's like Brandon Block on acid...on acid"...which, of course, I often was.

Also in tow was our mascot, the revered clubland legend The Guv'nor. Now, The Guv'nor was procured from The Horse & Barge pub in Harefield after one such FUBAR Full Circle outing. On our travels back from The Greyhound one evening we happened upon this pub and above the fireplace was a portrait, quite obviously of the boss of the pub, complete with a plaque saying 'The Guv'nor'.

Naturally we wanted The Guv'nor in our group and quickly signed him up, somehow smuggling him out of this boozer. He became part of clubland history too and was always on the guest list, often appearing in the DJ booth alongside whoever was DJing. He used to have his own seat on coach trips and in people's cars.

One night in Nottingham, though, the The Guv'nor was kidnapped, never to be seen again. There was a substantial ransom offered but, alas, we heard nothing. Then a few years later, after moving to Ruislip, me and Paul Avery stumbled across The Horse & Barge again on a Sunday night pub crawl. A barman overheard me and Aves giggling about The Guv'nor, and revealed himself as The Guv'nor's son and told us how, after the picture had disappeared, they'd heard of the old man's clubland escapades when someone showed them a copy of an article about him in MixMag.

He then proceeded to introduce us to The Guv'nor himself in person, who was enjoying a Sunday evening cigar upstairs. It was both surreal and a real pleasure to meet the man who had become such a legend. What a great sport, so much so that he brought down a polystyrene bust of himself, which he'd had made when the painting was pinched, for me and Aves to spend the rest of the evening drinking with.

THE LIFE & LINES OF BRANDON BLOCK

FLYING SOLO

My time behind the counter at Flying Records came to an abrupt end at the start of 1991 and it really was classic Charlie Chester.

I was out on the piss with him one night and it got to about five or six in the morning and I was due at the Flying shop to start work at 10am, but Chester told me not to bother going in, saying it was cool, no worries. So I didn't turn up, and then he sacked me. That, coupled with the Ibiza snub and less and less involvement in actual DJing at Flying events, meant it was time to go out on my own.

Even though I was essentially one of the founders of Flying, I never really felt part of it. Maybe, I wasn't cool enough. I remember finding the whole thing at that time very cliquey. I did get booked for more Flying parties a year or so later, but I think that was mostly after I'd done my first season at Space.

Following various excursions to the Hacienda in Manchester, and to Venus in Nottingham, where he had played at a Flying party in February '91 alongside Justin Robertson, Brandon had continued to spread his clubbing wings outside of London, whether he was booked to DJ or not, and found a kindred spirit at a party soon after - a promoter from Leeds called Tony Hannan.

Both Pisceans, with addictive personalities, the pair hit it off immediately and years later Brandon would be best man at Tony's wedding. Hannan picks up the story:-

I'd been at an event where Sasha had been DJing, and I'd ended up at the after-party and literally bumped into Brandon. We both had sunglasses on, and lifted them up at the same time, as if to say "you'll do for me".

I had been putting on some events called Kaos in Leeds at a small club called Ricky's. The manager there had given me a Bank Holiday Sunday, as a lot of the club owners did then because they were unsure about house nights, and when I'd filled that a few times, I started to do a monthly Tuesday at a much bigger venue called The Warehouse. I was soon doing weekly Saturdays at Ricky's, and I asked Brandon to come up and play at one of the Warehouse events, and I think that was one of his first club bookings outside of London. That night I also booked Sasha and Dave Dorrell.

A few months later I had booked M-People to play a gig at The Warehouse with Mike Pickering DJing too, and after we were all at my house in Headingley having a 'back to mine' session, and for some reason me and Brandon were sitting in my bath. It was empty and we were fully clothed, by the way, and we were putting the world to rights. It was at a time when house clubs had started to get a lot more pretentious, where dress codes were now in place and me and Brandon were arguing that it shouldn't be about what's on your back, and Brandon uttered the immortal words "Up Yer Ronson Lighter".

DJ Magazine reported at the time that *"at the after-party of an early Hannan promotion, a drunken Brandon kept saying "Up Yer….this", and "Up Yer…that"….before, while sparking up a fag, waving his lighter in the air and shouting the immortal words "Up Yer Ronson".*

What I was saying was Up Yer Ronson Lighter, which is modern-day cockney rhyming slang for Up Yer Shiter. Which, at the time, was my little way of saying "fuck it"…there's too many people too far up their own arse.

So the name of Tony and Adam Wood's legendary promotion Up Yer Ronson was born and I was quickly installed as resident, with the London to Leeds roadtrip soon a regular one.

I was up and down the M1 to Leeds all the time, with cohorts like Lisa Wharton, Baggy (always!), Simon Bentley (from Skunk Records), Tom Yates and Ruth Parrish.

With Up Yer Ronson on a Friday running alongside Basics on a Saturday (big up Dave Beer, RIP Ali Cooke), Leeds rapidly became the place to be. It was at Up Yer Ronson that I had the massive fortune of working alongside some of the great Americans DJs, including David Morales, Frankie Knuckles, Tony Humphries and the legend that is Erick Morillo. My fellow residents included Ian Ossia (later of Renaissance fame), Buckley, Paul Murray, Marshall, DJ Ease (Nightmares On Wax) and Neil Metzner. Great times or, as we used to say in Leeds, 'bang de breadbin'… a private joke, but if you were there you'll get it.

And as vibrant as London and the rest of the UK was at that time, there was a certain Balearic clubbing island that was much too much fun for me to ignore. And if I thought Sundays at Haven Stables, which were now over, were a good laugh, then it was nothing compared to what would unfold at a certain club in Playa D'en Bossa, with a fellow DJ I hadn't seen for some time.

Ibiza would also become a familiar stomping ground for Hannan, Wood and the Up Yer Ronson crew. The hit and miss Flying situation, along with his 'exclusion' from the Short Film About Chilling trip, only seemed to spur Brandon on where Ibiza was concerned and he was determined to make his mark there in the summer of '91. As usual, there was no shortage of drama.

With faithful friend Baggy Baxter in tow (Brandon's very own Bez!), the pair arrived on the Balearic clubbing island with the next two or three months their oyster.

We didn't know how long we would be there, but we knew we wanted to stay as long as possible. We had a bag of clothes each, £500 in cash and we turned up with five boxes of my records and headed straight for San Antonio.

We found an apartment nearby and took our bags up to the room. I immediately got chatting to this geezer across the balcony, and he said to me "you're Brandon Block, you know my mate Alex P". This guy, Matt Jahal, went on to explain that Alex had heard I was on the island and wanted to see me. That night we met up with a few friends we knew, Nicky Holloway and Del and Kate, who were running Nicky's San An branch of The Milk Bar, and, as you do in Ibiza on your first night, ended up getting smashed out of our brains.

The next afternoon, as me and Baggy were nursing our first of many Ibiza hangovers, suddenly there was this loud banging on the door of our apartment. Someone was screaming "open the door you wankers, open the fucking door". Standing there was Alex...paralytic, shouting things at me like "I've shagged your mum, I've shagged your mum's mate, your mum's mate stinks", making absolutely no sense at all, and then he left. It was both hilarious and bizarre.

We later found out that Alex had come out of Pacha that morning and had 'borrowed' a bus. However, this was no ordinary bus, it was a commuter bus, full of passengers, and Alex had then proceeded to drive it from Pacha to San Antonio, which is a good 20 minutes in anyone's book.

The bus driver had stopped for a sly toilet break outside Pacha and Alex in need of transport to San Antonio decided to see if his PSV licence was Euro-friendly. You can picture the scene as the people of Ibiza going about their normal business on the bus were suddenly whisked off by someone resembling a Greek God, missing every stop and finally coming to an abrupt halt in a bus garage in San An.

We saw Alex the next day down at Cafe Del Mar and he was black and blue, after being nicked by La Guardia and slapped around a bit. That was it, though, with nobody injured, apart from Alex, amazingly they had let him go.

So nothing like a nice calming influence to ease Brandon into his new Ibiza adventure…and Alex P was nothing like a nice calming influence! But what he did have was the keys to the soon-to-be legendary Space terrace, and that first meeting with Brandon and the commotion he had witnessed at Haven Stables was still fresh in Alex's mind.

Alex explained how he had built and opened the terrace at Space at the end of the season before, with his pal Jimmy 'The Switch' Mitchell, and wanted me to come down that Sunday and play with him. The actual main inside bit of the club opened at 6am and the terrace opened at 10am.

Before Alex built the bar outside, the terrace was used as a cloakroom and people would chill out there from the huge main room. The year before, Alex had approached the owners with his idea for DJs to play on the terrace. They agreed, but there was no DJ booth as such, the decks were behind the new bar they had built there. Me and Baggy got there that Sunday, with my five record boxes, and it was packed. And that was it, the gates to heaven and hell opened at the same time! I played my set and Alex said "great, I want you to do it every week", and I did, pretty much, for the next five summers, and for several of those seasons, three or four times a week. It was literally the best place in the world to DJ.

It became THE place for all the Brits to go, long before there were UK promoters at any of the other clubs, and eight years before DC10. It was the place the DJs went to unwind, where they went on their day off.

Musically, Brandon and Alex became known for dropping tunes that you just would not expect to hear during a standard house set, in true Balearic spirit, and just like Alfredo had been doing during the late '80s at Amnesia, when he wowed Messrs Oakenfold, Holloway, Rampling, Fung and Walker.

I remember Brandon playing Phil Collins' In The Air Tonight one Sunday afternoon to dramatic effect…cue everybody air-drumming to the famous middle section. The trick, though, was not playing too many tracks like that back in Blighty, because few of them worked as well on a winter's night in the West End.

They were brilliant times. We used to play all sorts - Depeche Mode's Just Can't Get Enough (live mix), Chris Rea's Josephine, Dire Straits' Money For Nothing, New Order's Blue Monday, Tears For Fears' Shout, Magnificent Seven by The Clash and Rolling Stones' Sympathy For The Devil.

At that time Liverpool DJ Steve Proctor used to play some really way out there records, and was a bit of a pioneer where the Balearic influence was concerned.

Obviously, the beginning of the Balearic thing has been attributed to Alfredo and quite rightly so, but a few people had the balls to play non-house records at clubs in the UK after that. I remember Proctor playing Lucy In The Sky With Diamonds by the Beatles at the Destination Moon rave in the morning when everyone was tripping off their nuts, for instance, and seeing people being brave and doing that when house or acid house was fully expected now, was a big influence and something that I took with me when I started on Space terrace. And ideal for me as I've always liked all types of music.

It's strange because before acid house came along, if you went to a decent nightclub or a so-called discotheque you expected to hear disco and funk and a fair amount of pop music, but now house had taken over, and the fact that you could drop Jesus On The Payroll by The Thrashing Doves or some of the Belgium stuff like Code 61's surreal Drop The Deal track, opened up so many things again. Those tracks wouldn't be out of place now and all came under the acid house umbrella, as such.

I remember one time, towards the end of my set on the Space terrace, getting so carried away, because it was going off in there so much that, one by one, I started throwing my records into the crowd. At the end everyone was shouting "one more, one more" but I didn't have any records left. It wasn't until a couple of people gave some back to me, that I was able to put another tune on.

Financially at Space, there was a unique arrangement in place for the first couple of years. Initially the deal was that Alex and Jimmy would keep the bar money, that they would stock it themselves and they'd pay the staff and me and keep the rest, a common practice in Ibiza, if you were hosting a bar or an area of a club for the season. But because the three of us were giving so many drinks away and getting so battered it just became financially unviable to do.

So Space bought the bar back off Alex and Jimmy and they paid me and Alex wages. Fair wages at that for the time, roughly £1,000 a month. And from then on we used to get as many drinks as we wanted at cost price. The plan was that we'd get paid monthly, and then our drinks bill would be deducted from our wages.

Me and Alex later discovered when we were sitting in the office one afternoon that we had both been signing our drinks dockets in each other's name. Crafty buggers. Then one month, I went to get my wages and was told that I owed Space £1,500! And remember, that was with all drinks I'd either drunk or given away to mates at cost price, but also due to the fact Alex hadn't signed anything for himself all season.

Somehow Brandon and Alex managed to foot their Space drinks bill. Meanwhile, Baggy had a unique way of trying to be the life and 'sole' of the party, out in the thick of the action.

It was mental inside the main room at Space in those days, really dark, and you'd be bumping off the walls as you walked through to the toilets. All the fun was outside on the terrace, though. I had been doing a bit of DJing with Brandon, so we were getting known as Brandon and Baggy, but when Brandon hooked up with Alex they just gelled straight away. I didn't want to be in the DJ booth anyway, I wanted to be out there having fun with everybody else. My thing at Space was snorting gear off people's shoes in the middle of the dancefloor.

As the summer progressed, and with so many fellow DJs and promoters from the UK and beyond flocking to Space on a Sunday, offers to play at other clubs in Ibiza and in the UK and all over the world during the non-summer months started to come Brandon's way.

But before all that, Brandon had a date back home, just outside of London at historic Hatfield House. The occasion was the 21st birthday of one of the party girls in his crowd, and the then other half of Matty D's, Lisa Wharton. A plan had been hatched to hold a themed event and the invite read:-

Good Queen Elisabess 1st invites you to celebrate in the grounds of her country estate, in the company of King Donegan "give us an VIII" Henry, Merry Mandy Queen Of Scotts & Sir Francis "The Pillaging King" Drake. Music will be provided by John & Mickey, Baron Block The Jovial Jester, Dashing Duke Dorrell, Earl Ashley Of Bubonic Black Plague Market Records, Friar Farley & Sir Babington Breeze. Feasting at 7pm, anyone arriving after 10pm will be beheaded.

Off their heads, rather than off with their heads, and while Elizabethan dress had been positively encouraged, there had been no mention of rollerskates. But that wasn't going to deter Brandon and Baggy, and in particularly Brandon, who the next day, because Donegan and Wharton had not surfaced from their room, somehow managed, after no sleep, to scale the drainpipes and guttering of the adjoining hotel, a full two floors and wearing those rollerskates, to bang on their window. A startled Matty D opened the curtains and could hardly believe his eyes.

THE LIFE & LINES OF BRANDON BLOCK

It was an achievement in itself, let alone on rollerskates. He'd been tearing around on those things all night, armed with a plastic sword. It was a great party, and everyone was sitting on the lawns waiting for Queen's to start and Brandon had decided he'd hurry me and Lisa along. It was classic Brandon.

Late summer/early autumn '91 bookings included a new Wednesday-nighter at The Gardening Club called Niche alongside Darren Emerson and John Edis. Brandon was also back at Venus in September for another Flying Bash, and he would also play at Wild & Peaceful in Birmingham alongside local DJs Jim 'Shaft' Ryan, Lee Fisher and Paul Moran.

And to cap a great 1991, in November, Brandon made it on to the line-up of Nicky Holloway's Kaos 5 Weekender (an event unconnected to Tony Hannan's party in Leeds of the same name) held twice a year at Pontins in Camber Sands since October 1989, based on the successful Caister Soul Weekender format.

The Kaos Weekender brought the leading house jocks and live PAs of the moment together under one roof, also serving as a great promotional tool for The Milk Bar, and vice versa.

For this weekender Brandon, fresh on the back of his summer success at Space, was given the 8pm – 9pm opening slots in the main room on both Friday and Saturday night, plus the 2pm – 3pm slot on the Sunday afternoon before Alfredo's finale set.

Headlining was Paul Oakenfold, Sacha (spelt wrong in the programme), Graeme Park and Carl Cox. Alex P had also made the line-up, playing in the downstairs room on both nights. Amusingly, a list of 'Things Not To Do At Kaos' on the inside cover of the program stated - No 5) Try to out drink Brandon Block.

I remember driving to Kaos in a friend's packed Escort van, the driver of which, who shall remain anonymous, had somehow managed to strap a huge lump of solid cannabis to the radiator

*(clockwise) * A FUBAR memmbership form*
* Kate and Sid at Milk Bar, Ibiza, 1990
* With Space terrace staff, circa 1993
* Lisa Wharton's 21st birthday invite
* Balcony action in Ibiza with Dizzi

THE MILK BAR

FUBAR Membership Application Form

Name:

ELIZABETH I

OOD QUEEN ELISABESS
VITES LADY Karon Dunn
CELEBRATE HER 21ST BIRTHDA
GROUNDS OF HER COUNTRY

HATFIELD HOUSE,
IN THE COMPANY OF

DONEGAN "GIVE US AN VIII" H
MERRY MANDY QUEEN OF SCOTS
RANCIS, "THE PILLAGING KING"

MUSIC PROVIDED BY:- JOHN & MICKEY
GOOD CLEAN MEN OF THE CLERGY.
CK THE JOVIAL JESTER & DASHING DU
EY OF BUBONIC BLACK PLAGUE MARKE
FRIAR FARLEY & SIR BABINGTON BREE

SATURDAY AUGUST 31ST
5PM – 2AM
FEASTING AT 7PM
ONE ARRIVING AFTER 10PM WILL BE BE

FLYING AT VEN
Stanford Street Nottin
Friday 27th September
DJ'S
DANNY RAMPLIN
DEAN THATCHE
PHIL PERRY
ROCKY & DIESE
SCOTT BRAITHWA
BRANDON BLOC

for what was an eventful trip down the coastal roads to Camber.

It was like something straight out of a Cheech and Chong film, and he completely forgot that solid puff combusts at a certain temperature. Not only was it shit gear, it stunk to high heaven, and we had more smoke coming from the bonnet of the van than if we'd broken a head gasket. Although we somehow managed to make it there undetected this guy did have his collar felt by the Kaos faithful, who were given more refunds than during an open day at TK Maxx.

1992 was another pivotal year for Brandon as he and the FUBAR gang launched their own night and he cemented his residency at Space in Ibiza with his first full season. He also played in Australia for the first time, and made his debut at BCM in Majorca - these glamorous international bookings all possible because of Space, with promoters and punters alike from around the world charmed by Brandon's infectious party-hard attitude.

With my birthday approaching in March, Nicky Holloway suggested we throw a party at The Milk Bar. We did it on a Sunday (March 10) to fit around our Friday and Saturday night bookings, and everyone came down after Full Circle.

They got me a stripper and it was hilarious. They put me on the stage there, but I'd got all my clothes off before she had. She took one look at me and ran out the club, and up the road in her bra and knickers, with me chasing after her in the nod. Priceless!

And it was an amazing party too, so much so that Nicky suggested we do something regularly. So on **Sunday March 31, 1992, FUBAR at The Milk Bar was born, and ran there every Sunday for two years.**

An old membership form reveals:-

Due to the popularity of FUBAR on Sunday nights it has now become necessary to make the night a members only night. This membership costs £1 and only gives you priority over non members, but does not allow you access when the club is full. We therefore suggest you arrive early, the club opens at 8pm but for Sunday August

30 we will be opening at 7.30pm. We do have an extension for music until 2am, but the sale of alcoholic drinks will cease at 11.30pm. There has also been a couple of incidents whereby FUBAR has had to pay for damages in the club. Due to this we will be vetting all applications for membership. We would like to take this opportunity in thanking you for your support over the past months and hope we can carry on having one of the most talked about club nights in London. THANKS, BRANDON, LISA, BAGGY & LISA

Myself and Lisa Loud were residents, and James Mac, Lisa's brother, and Danny Keith were alternate warm-up DJs, plus some other hand-picked guests like Dave Dorrell and Alex P played too. The other Lisa mentioned on that form was yet another Lisa….Lisa Wharton, who did the door and was another integral member of the FUBAR team, and also myself and Baggy's driver on many of our outings. Loads of people were inspired by the FUBAR name. There was even a nightclub in Stirling in Scotland named FUBAR, and a DJ pal of mine from Blackpool, Jason Barr, who produces as Ibiza Knights, actually took on the name DJ Fubar.

Lisa Loud picks up the story.

FUBAR was all Brandon's idea, a brilliant idea and the best name in the world for a club. Fantastic. Amazingly, among our little group we had basically decided that over the last few years, after being out on a Monday at Spectrum, Tuesday at Loud Noise, Wednesday at Future, warehouse parties on a Friday, Raw or wherever on a Saturday, and Sunday daytime at Full Circle, that we still needed to do a Sunday evening party. Bonkers.

I was working for a major record company, and you couldn't really get more high profile than that back then. All the record executives and people from the media would be trying to get in, journalists from ID, MixMag, DJ Mag, MixMag Update, the lot. There would be 500 people queuing down the road, unable to get in to a club that held 200, loads of people who wanted to go to The Astoria, also queuing for FUBAR by mistake because our queue was so big and, with everything going on, there was police everywhere. Total carnage.

Come the end of the week Baggy was constantly walking around looking like a window cleaner in a pair of dungarees, with one side of his face unshaven, one of his trouser legs rolled up, and looking like he needed his roots done. Baggy would be sitting outside The Milk Bar with all the tramps and then there was Blocko, the star of the show, who would eventually turn up and often fall asleep under the decks. All the promo we'd done all week and he'd be asleep under the bloody decks. After the club it was always 'all back to mine' and Brandon had had his kip so he was ready to go again.

Looking back, I always thought then, and still do now, that FUBAR was the best club in London at that time, but then I am biased.

Wherever I had played out that weekend I'd make sure I'd get back to London by Sunday night for FUBAR...it ended at midnight, but that was just the start for us, and I'd keep partying until at least Tuesday and sometimes Wednesday, by which time the weekend was almost about to start again.

We used to play some wicked records down at FUBAR, though, some great funk tunes like Tina Marie's I Need Your Loving... loads of stuff that we couldn't play in the house clubs at the weekend and, of course, our sing-along anthem, the 14-minute mix of Rapper's Delight, which, from under the decks, was often like an alarm call to me - you know - "a hip hop, a hippie, a hippie, to the hip-hop, you don't stop", etc, etc.

Sometimes when FUBAR had finished we'd go to Fish on Oxford Street, with our records, and try and see if they'd let us play some more. I'd be saying "c'mon, let's get round to Fish and play Rapper's Delight again, do it from the start, the whole way through". Silly arse!

We'd end up in all parts of London, south, north, west, east...all over, lapping up what our wonderful capital had to offer clubland at this very early stage in the proceedings. Our mates Pat, Paul and Bill had a flat in Harrow, which we nicknamed The Happy Hotel.

Popular Happy Hotel pastimes included pillow fighting on the roof of Lisa Horan's Fiat Panda, that old convertible model with the rag top, which for this pastime was fully open, the loser being the person who fell into the car, and all at some unearthly hour on a Monday morning.

Lisa Loud points out:-

The Happy Hotel was about as happy as a Happy Meal, and had a gammy old carpet and a minging old sofa with burn holes all over it. My flat, 105 Elgin Avenue, W9... now that was a completely different story.

Lisa Horan chuckles as she reflects on the chaos, and how the last thing that a DJ wants to injure before a gig is one of his arms.

All week and weekend it seemed that we were endlessly trying to get Brandon somewhere for a gig or, if it was a Sunday, get everyone to Full Circle.

Me and Lisa always managed to get some sleep, and would be up trying to organise things, but Brandon would always still be up.

One time he needed to get down to Torquay to play at Claire's, and while Lisa was ironing his shirt, he came careering down the corridor, and put his arm straight through her kitchen door. With blood everywhere and his arm half hanging off, we had to get him to St Mary's Hospital in Paddington for stitches before his driver could get him down to Torquay.

It's little wonder that the two Lisas were taking control where logistics were concerned. Despite the obvious fact that Brandon could not be trusted as far as you could throw him through a glass-paneled door, the duo both had jobs, albeit within the music business, but daily and weekly commitments all the same.

Horan had set up her own management company, representing A Man Called Adam, who were signed to Big Life Records, and also the all-conquering Leftfield, and would later manage D.O.P and Steve Dub, the Chemical Brothers' studio engineer. Loud, meanwhile, had set up Loud and Clear, an independent club and radio promotions company looking after Guerilla Records, Flying, Boys Own and working closely with Warner Brothers too.

Meanwhile, a certain Mr Block, still living at home, and when not being pampered by his mum clearly being mothered by the two Lisas, was finding it hard enough to keep fit for the dozens of DJ bookings that were coming his way each month. But he was also having the time of his life.

For me and some of the lads it had become the norm to carry on through to Monday and beyond, long after the Lisas and all the normal people had left and gone to work

I was already developing a reckless addiction where recreational drugs were concerned. However, I was settling into this irresponsible, yet fun-packed lifestyle, with consummate ease.

Today Nicky Holloway is proud of the part FUBAR played in the now legendary Milk Bar schedule. On his website, he explains:-

The club's residents list read like a who's who of 20th Century dance music. Darren Emerson and Paul Harris held court on Mondays at Recession Session. Danny Rampling's 'Pure Sexy' took over Wednesdays, Paul Oakenfold and myself ruled Friday's, Pete Tong and Dave Dorrell looked after Saturdays with the weekend rounded off by Lisa and Brandon's FUBAR on Sunday nights.

I guess I was in good company at The Milk Bar, and I could be found hanging out of the DJ booth there singing Rapper's Delight at full drunken pelt every Sunday night and then hanging out at various after parties until the middle of the week, all made easier by the money already earned at the weekend, the drugs that cash could buy, and with another handful of gigs only a few days away when that week's party was finally over.

FUBAR was our baby and our spiritual home in the West End, where we could call the shots. The Space terrace would become my Ibiza version every summer, and all on the back of the Haven Stables stint, it would seem that my most notorious work was done on the Lord's day! Lord help us, more like!

And the more drugs he could afford, the more he would take and the longer he would stay up. Nobody was vetting Brandon, least of all himself or any of the FUBAR faithful.

THE LIFE & LINES OF BRANDON BLOCK

WATCH THIS SPACE

With Ibiza looming, I was approached by a London clubber I knew to play at the opening of a restaurant in Sydney called Zoom. But, like much of my life then, preparations for my first trip down under were not exactly professional - a textbook three-day bender after FUBAR meaning, as usual, I hadn't slept for days.

Within the space of two years, I had gone from a jobbing London DJ who liked a drink to regular bookings throughout the UK, securing a residency at one of the superclubs in Ibiza and now a gig in Australia.

However, I'd done so much in such a short space of time that I think I quickly took it for granted. A lot of the other guys were out there DJing in the same places too.

There was already talk of us getting flown out to Majorca from Ibiza in the forthcoming summer, and I knew I'd start flying back to London every now and then for gigs too, because the demand would be there. Then shortly after that some of the Greek islands - Corfu, Cyprus and Rhodes - got on board as well, so going to Australia outside of the Ibiza season just seemed like one of those things.

Apart from trips to Majorca with Mum and Dad as a kid, the five or six weeks in Ibiza the year before had been the longest and furthest I'd been away from home. Don't get me wrong, though, I was excited about Australia. I loved the idea of going to different places, but mainly because it meant I could get off my head somewhere else and somewhere much warmer. Unfortunately, the first time I was booked to go to Sydney, was their winter. Not that I saw much of the weather!

I staggered on to an empty 747 in May, and set about getting nicely sozzled on the first leg of my journey.

For the first seven hours to Bahrain, I had four seats to myself, had a nice little booze and still had a bit of wallop left, so tucked into that too. My eventful first trip to Oz was underway in true Block fashion.

The guys organising the opening of the bar, also later went on to promote the massive Vibes On A Summer Day event, so they were well connected down under.

Years later I would completely freak out Norman Jay, by hiding under the decks while he played at a Vibes festival, in front of 50,000 people. Every time he turned round to look for a record I popped up and messed with the EQs or the pitch before hiding again...but that's another story.

For this first Australia trip, a guy called Joe picked me up from the airport and took me straight to the restaurant. When I got there another mate of mine, Nigel, was behind the bar, and Joe's brother Shaun was the chef. They had Bloody Marys with celery ready for me, the works. It was quite surreal, and about to get even weirder. I could hear banging upstairs and they explained that's where the finishing touches were being put to the club, and before I got a chance to have a look, there's "clonk, clonk, clonk", down the stairs and another old mate of mine Chris appeared with a big grin on his face and a big bag of wallop in his hand. And it wasn't easy to get that stuff out there then!

Turns out Chris was working out there plastering and had been brought in to work on the club. So I got absolutely bang on it there and then. The opening party was three days away, but everyone downed tools...booze, gear, more booze, more gear, and I was there with my jogging bottoms still on and my bags by the bar.

Later that afternoon we were still at it, and the supposed new club manager turned up, a large lady to say the least! I was coked up and feeling, shall we say, amorous, and was my usual chatty self. She was loving my accent and then around 6pm I persuaded her to show me the upstairs club. She'd had a bit of gear and a few drinks herself, and the next thing you know we were in the DJ booth, getting at it, with our heads wedged in the corner. I woke up the next morning at about six with her nowhere to be seen, covered in bits of MDF and wood shavings. Everybody had fucked off, the bar was shut and the cleaners were downstairs. I was bumping off the walls on my descent, but managed to help myself to a booze from behind the bar to get myself half straight, and as I couldn't get more than the odd "g'day" out of the cleaners I staggered outside. I was out on Sydney's Oxford Street, and kept thinking "well, at least I've had some sleep", as if I'd actually made some progress. It was about 7am, but in my sights was a Victoria Bitter pub, with a 24 hour licence. My luck was in, so I sat in there with some locals and got really pissed very quickly, drinking pints and pints of their strong VB beer. I didn't realise the time and suddenly it was about three in the afternoon and I was back out on the street, absolutely steaming.

Somehow I ended up in a record shop, with someone telling me they'd been told to look out for me. They put me in a cab, with the address on a bit of paper in my hand and the driver paid up front. When I got to this house, and knocked on the door, they were all in there..., and we all got bang on it again. Another day passed, and the next night it was the opening of the club, so another session after that and straight back to the airport.

My amazing five days down under had involved few sights, apart from loads of pubs and the odd Sheila, so still buzzing from such a 'rewarding' trip I felt it would be rude not to continue the party on the journey home. After boarding the plane I soon found an Aussie drinking buddy, who was on his travels to England for the first time. As our language and behaviour got increasingly more colourful, an irritated aircrew and the surrounding passengers had had enough. The captain was called to chastise us, which he did by handcuffing us to our seats. I offered little resistance and promptly passed out. His threat of being met at the other end by the boys in blue was enough to settle me for the rest of the journey.

But Brandon wouldn't settle very easily in London. FUBAR was in full swing, but he had other Sunday business to attend at Space in Ibiza, an opportunity that he just couldn't pass up.

I got back home, and I was so jet-lagged that after three days I just couldn't take it any more. I was due to go to Ibiza for the whole of the '92 summer in a few weeks time, but, rearranged some gigs, and said to Baggy, "mate, pack your bags, we're going now", and we headed straight to the airport.

As various promoters from all over the world started arriving without the massive budgets of later years, the obvious option was to employ myself and Alex, already plotted for the season, and available every night of the week. With Space always rammed on a

Sunday, our reputation was ever growing. Space was our place, just like Cafe Del Mar in San Antonio was Jose Padilla's place. However, we'd also drink at the Cafe Del Mar all the time during the week, and this was long before Cafe Mambo popped up next door in 1994, which we were also instrumental in the launch of.

For ages there weren't any British promoters doing anything regularly on the island. Later Clockwork Orange came in '94, and Up Yer Ronson did a couple of big parties the same year, and me and Alex started working for both those promotions, and many of the later influx of other UK promoters too.

In those days it was hard to fill all the big five Ibiza clubs - Space, Amnesia, Pacha, Ku and Es Paradis - one day of the week, let alone every day of the week. That would all come in the next few years, as thousands more clubbers descended on the island each summer. In the meantime, step forward myself, Alex and Baggy – "here to entertain you".

One Sunday I forgot exactly who I was entertaining on the Space terrace. I'd taken something that was particularly trippy, from a new batch on the island, and I was in the middle of my set, when suddenly a stranger than normal feeling came over me. Space was full, the usual palaver back then, when the decks were in the corner behind the bar and, if you were playing, your back was to the crowd. However, suddenly I had been transported back to Del & Kate's house in New Cavendish Street, London, W1, and we were having a nice little after-party for five or six of us. So I was looking through my records, and I used to have all sorts of stuff locked away in boxes under the bar at Space. I was wondering what my mates wanted to hear, and I picked out George Benson's Love Ballad, thinking it was going to be a winner, and everybody was going to go "woahhhhhh". I dropped the track, turned round, and there were thousands of people looking at me, mid-ecstasy high, thinking "what are you doing, what happened to the house music?"

The Space website states: "In 1990, Space brought to Ibiza the new sound that was being championed at that time in London, and with that sound came DJs such as Alex P and Brandon Block, who started the legendary Sundays at Space. The phenomenon had begun…Space Ibiza!"

So the approving nods and mutual backslapping were flowing nicely between Ibiza and London. It seemed that Brandon had quickly earned his stripes at Space, despite his boisterous take on the whole proceedings.

In 1997, when reviewing the Ibiza closing week for M8 Magazine, I had the pleasure of interviewing Space owner Pepe Rosello during his club's closing party. Already in his sixties, but hugely knowledgeable about the house scene that had revitalised his huge venue, I asked him to name his favourite Space DJs and he impressively rattled off the following ten names, and their respective 'best' years, there and then.

1 Sven Vath – 1994-97
2 Roger Sanchez – 1995
3 Darren Emerson – 1995-96
4 Brandon Block – 1992-97
5 Sasha – 1994-97
6 David Holmes – 1994
7 DJ Reche – 1991-97
8 Danny Rampling – 1993 + 95
9 David Morales – 1994-96
10 Carl Cox – 1994

Pepe told me in 1997:-

In 1988 I was studying the Ibiza licensing laws and noticed that you had to shut your club at 3am, but for some reason you could reopen at 6am. Nobody did, of course, and although it was strange, I decided to do just that. Ever since, Space has opened only during the day. We don't open the terrace until 10am, because by then most of the tourists in the hotels opposite are up and have had their breakfast.

When we caught up with Pepe in Ibiza in summer 2011 over a mid-morning glass of wine it was with a huge sense of pride that he reminisced about the glory days of the Space terrace.

The terrace was an amazing experience. It was the first time, since the party really began in the '60s, that we had the authentic spirit of Ibiza back...the free lifestyle.

I remember when Brandon was playing behind the bar, the energy was amazing.

But Brandon and Alex did create a lot of jealousy on the island, about the success of the terrace...the island has always been about hospitality, and parties, though, and it has been that way since the American hippies came in the '50s.

Before Space I had the Playboy club in San Antonio since 1963, so now I am 48 years old in this job. We opened Space in 1989 and from the start there was a big queue, the crowd waiting to come in at 6am...and I discovered that lots of my friends, their teenagers were suddenly telling them that on Sunday they needed to get up very early to go fishing...but they weren't at the sea, they were fishing inside Space. Lots of friends used to come to keep an eye on their sons and daughters.

You met everybody at Space, from nowhere, from everywhere. The energy, through the body, through the music, you felt yourself, that you could be yourself. Nobody cared how anybody dressed. There were lots of celebrities and it was like a big theatre show. I was very proud, because the terrace at Space, it was the most beautiful men and women in the world, per square metre. And it is the crowd that always push us to make the club what it is today.

Space has been voted the best club in the world eight times since 2001, a fact Pepe is immensely proud of. After being in the business for half a century, that the grandmaster of Ibiza clubbing still craves the plaudits is surely why his club has remained on top for so long.

I think for Brandon and Alex, the terrace was the facility for them to get near to the crowd. They always felt very near to the crowd. The crowd related very well with them and they always had a very nice proximity with the crowd. There was something high around them, and you don't know what, but it was authentic.

Space opened with just the inside in 1989...one year later, 1990, we opened the terrace, and, of course it was Alex's idea and with James he made the terrace. At first we were selling hamburgers and sandwiches on the terrace, and then that didn't go with the smoking or whatever, so we took the hamburgers away and we put Brandon and Alex on there cooking music instead. Things went better and we didn't have to throw the hamburgers away anymore.

It was also during the season of 1992 that Brandon and co first travelled to play at BCM in Majorca, another massive European nightclub, who were putting on huge club nights, featuring leading UK jocks, long before leading British club nights became brands in their own right and replaced the DJs as the headliners.

Majorca was just a half hour flight away, and the first time I got booked at BCM over there Baggy came with me. We were met by a leather-clad British Hell's Angel, the right hand man of an infamous BCM promoter, who had always had a keen interest in making sure his DJs were well looked after. Later that night, as we arrived at the club, the introductions were short and sweet, with one question on all our minds, ie, "donde esta el wallopo?".

A well-known acid house legend was able to escape our grasp so he could go and play his set, and later after mine, I legged it back to my hotel room with a generous doggy bag. As with many like-minded club owners and promoters I worked for, another long-standing business and personal relationship had begun and the BCM set-up remains one of my favourites to this day.

On-going, over the next few summers, myself and Alex would be booked as a duo, with 'Space, Ibiza', after our name in brackets, itself an increasing feature. We would play alongside other London jocks like Darren Emerson. And when Darren was playing at BCM the management's strategy was to put me and Alex on first, and then they'd put Darren on last, around six or seven in the morning, to play his hardest techno, and clear out the club so we could carry on the party on our own.

One of these such evenings Graham Gold was also booked. A friendly rivalry has always existed among DJs so to be told you'd been relegated to the lower floor of BCM where house music was taboo must have been soul-destroying, but this was unfortunately Graham's fate for the evening. You can only imagine the banter between myself, Alex and Darren that night.

One trip over to BCM from Ibiza had followed one of my and Alex's infamous play-fights on the terrace at Space. This particular scrap had seen my right arm swell to gargantuan proportions. From one side I looked like Arnold Schwarzenegger, and the other a skinny Mr Bean.

On arrival at Palma airport we were met by the fantastic Paulino, who took me to the local pharmacy to collect some painkillers. While stood at the kiosk window of this late-night chemist, I decided to stock up on some other bits too. And of course, in those days, you had no need for prescriptions when abroad so I asked for the strongest sleeping tablets available on the market.

It was also around this time that BCM had a staff villa for DJs, dancers, cabaret acts and general guests. It slept about ten people and there was always room at the inn for us. As there was also room for season-long residents, Roberto and Carlos, two Columbians who made an annual pilgrimage to Magaluf with plenty of excess baggage.

At our disposal were green and yellow Renault Twingo hire cars. One night we took to the road in our "Magaluf Minis" in an attempt to reenact one of my favourite films, The Italian Job. My journey came to an abrupt end when we returned to base and I inadvertently decided that parking on the driveway wasn't challenging enough, somehow ploughing through the entrance of the villa and literally parking in the hallway. I wasn't supposed to blow the bloody front doors off!

I got out of the car, made it as far as the toilet, where I sat down for a well-earned rest and treated myself to a sleeping tablet before I retired for the morning. And boy did it work. I quickly passed out on the toilet and because I was so skinny through my now extensive use of cocaine, when I was found, I had slipped inside the actual toilet with my arse touching the water, and with a big red mark around my back and under my thighs where I'd been wedged in the actual pan (for most of the day…). Despite alarming incidents like this - which, were also hilarious at the time - in my mind, I was enjoying life so much that I saw no reason to slow down.

Jon Jules, with his photographic memory, remembers those Twingos well and one BCM visit by Alex and Brandon in 1995.

I was over there for the summer, as resident at BCM, and my heavily pregnant girlfriend Katy, now my wife, was with me. And she was proper pregnant, like seven months gone.

BCM had two staff villas at the time, a smaller one, which we were sharing with the club's podium dancers, which wasn't particularly ideal for a pregnant woman, and another larger, much plusher one that the guest DJs would stay in, which came complete with the two Twingos, which the DJs could pick up from the airport on arrival.

I was always hassling BCM owner Tony Palma, asking if we could move into the bigger villa, but he was having none of it. It was six or seven weeks into the season and Katy was already fed up with the 'Brits abroad' who were around all the time. So with all this in mind, for a few days I had been trying to find the right moment to tell her that a couple of guys I knew were coming over, DJs who would be in the bigger villa. But knowing how mad Brandon and Alex were, I just couldn't find the right time.

Then on July 4, I remember it vividly, because the boys were imminent, I mentioned it to Katy over lunch. We left the restaurant and were driving down the main strip in Magaluf, and suddenly this bright green Renault Twingo was driving toward us, the wrong way down the road. I was like, "what the fuck?". Then it hit a parked car, bounced off that, and the wing mirror on the driver's side snapped off, and ended up through the open window on his lap.

The Twingo pulled over and Brandon got out with the wing mirror in his hand, shouting the odds at everyone, thinking someone had thrown it through the car window at him, completely unaware what had happened. I looked at Katy and said "that's Brandon Block".

We actually hung out with him and Alex for the rest of the day. I was due to play football with Des Mitchell, another resident at BCM, and a load of other workers and Alex and Brandon, both famously mad about football, didn't even want to check in to the villa, they came and played a game with the rest of us.

The next day Brandon, who had worked out we were in the smaller villa, said we should move in with him and Alex for the rest of the week they were there. All of a sudden Katy decided we were OK where we were, thanks.

Meanwhile, another venture in Ibiza in 1992 saw Baggy somehow secure a FUBAR party at the 4,000-capacity Amnesia venue...not bad considering The Milk Bar held 200 people and the night had only been going for three months in London.

However, not all the Ibiza promotions Baggy was involved in were a success, or exactly built on solid foundations, and as Brandon and Alex became more in demand at Space terrace and at other clubs, their mascot seemed to be running his own renegade promotion.

I bowled into the Amnesia office asking if we could put on a FUBAR party one night, and the guy there looked at me as if I was mad. However, I had a copy of MixMag with me, which said FUBAR was THE best club in London. His ears pricked up when he saw Lisa Loud's name mentioned, and said he was a big fan of her. I managed to get her on the phone from his office line, and she spoke to him, and we got the gig. It was mad, Amnesia was the biggest club in the world in those days, bigger than Pacha. We had the whole club for one midweek night. Brandon, Lisa, Alex and A Man Called Adam, who we'd robbed off the Cafe Del Mar, all played, and I remember standing in that amazing DJ booth there, looking down on the crowds thinking, "how the fuck did I manage to blag this?".

We did FUBAR parties at Exstasis, Summons and Star Club, but I was up for doing any old fucking club, really, because I was having fun and some money of my own would have been useful.

I thought if we could catch that crowd that were in between things, after the Saturday night clubs shut and Space Terrace opened then we might even be able to rival Space at some stage. So I started an early hours FUBAR party in a gay club just outside of Ibiza Town, along from Pacha, but that fell flat on its face.

*(clockwise) * Blocko hits down under*
* With Space owner Pepe Rosello outside his Ibiza superclub, 2011
* At BCM, Majorca (l to r) Alex P, Tony Palmer, Darren Emerson and Graham Gold
* On the Space Terrace in usual fine form
* A rare early '90s Space Terrace poster

EVERY SUNDAY
AT THE TERRACE
ALEX P.
&
BRANDON BLOCK
CADA DOMINGO
EN LA TERRAZA
space
space
HOH

Meanwhile, The Star Club's adjoining Star Cafe, was another popular hang-out for Brandon and co, and hang out they did!

The Star Cafe in San Antonio was where me and Alex always ended up after we'd been DJing during the early seasons in the '90s. It was somewhere we went when nowhere else was open, and was most notable because of our 'office' at the back.

They had this head barman there - I can't remember which Juan it was, now - who used to give me the key and a big bag of wallop whenever we turned up because I always had so many people in tow, who wanted to carry on drinking. I knew he used to knock out some gear, but I didn't realise he was one of the biggest guys on the island. He got involved very deep and did 12 years bird in the end, which was a lot in those days.

The cafe had a big palm tree in it, and when you moved a load of its leaves away, it looked like a huge kebab shawarma rotating spit. Well, when you're off your head, it did. I'd be standing there on a pair of step ladders, pretending to slice it, shouting..."chilli sauce...chilli rocking horse".

Later at the Star Cafe it got to the stage where people weren't exactly queuing outside the office, so much as hanging around the peripheries, and every now and then I'd poke my head around the door and beckon someone in. That lucky person would be like "wooooo, I'm going in the office with Brandon". And this person would suddenly ditch their mates and rush in, usually with supplies. To their dismay, it wasn't so much an office. It had a bed and a table and it was boiling hot. It was like a prison cell, really, and we'd sit in there for hours, talking bollocks, having the crack.

At that time, we weren't to everybody's taste, certainly not where Ibiza was concerned, but back then you couldn't not know us, we were everywhere. And at that time the Star Cafe was certainly a place that you wouldn't go to if you were so-called trendy, but you could go in there and have a right laugh.

I slept at the Star loads, after being locked in, and had to climb out over the wall. It was open air, there was that big palm tree in the back, and about six or seven times I had to climb out of the roof of the office first and shimmy up the tree to get out of the place.

We took it to the limits of partying hard, days on end, and then I'd carry on, continually not sleeping. My speciality was hanging off/climbing up or down apartment blocks. Quite how I'm still alive to tell the tale, I'm not sure.

When Baggy and I returned to London after a punishing, but invigorating Ibiza season, our FUBAR homecoming party in September was large to say the least.

And after that second full season in Ibiza (and the surrounding Mediterranean 'counties'), just like I had cemented my reputation with Alex and the Space crew, Alex had also been well and truly blooded into the FUBAR clan.

As part of Alex's inauguration, as with any fledging FUBAR member, a night at Baggy's house in Sudbury was a must. During his first evening there an unsuspecting Mr P had foolishly fallen asleep. So in preparations for his awakening myself and Baggy tipped two bottles of amyl nitrate on to his pillow and let it diffuse. We also set Baggy's home strobelight on full 'nutter rave speed', and placed it carefully on the bed. Alex woke up shortly after screaming. Initiation ceremony complete!

As well as the regular Venus parties in Nottingham, 1992 also saw a weekly Flying residency at The Arena in Middlesbrough, with Brandon booked on rotation on a monthly basis alongside familiar faces from the Flying roster.

London's West End was thriving with packed house nights, and would be good to Brandon and his fellow DJs over the next decade.

As well as Flying, clubs like Naked Lunch at Studio Valbonne in Kingley Street, run by brothers Simon Hanson (Gat Decor) and Steve Hanson (Tag Records) with the Deja Vu boys (Barry Ashworth and co) and Sean McClusky's Love Ranch, at Maximus in Leicester Square, dominated 1992, with the Gat Decor anthem Passion typifying the chuggy, yet still uplifting progressive house sound that Brandon and his peers had adopted. These West End clubbing institutions provided an infectious, if not sweaty, backdrop to weekend proceedings.

Darren Emerson, Fabi Paras, John Edis and Laurence Nelson, the other man behind Gat Decor, were resident Naked Lunch DJs, while Lisa Loud, Paul Daley (who as one half of Leftfield possessed his own killer progressive house anthem Not Forgotten) and Andy Weatherall, by now a prolific remixer/producer, were all Love Ranch regulars, where anthems included Photon Inc's Generate Power, Joey Beltram's Energy Flash, Last Rhythm by Last Rhythm and the Hard Hands Mix of Not Forgotten and TC1992.

Labels of the moment like Guerilla were king, with acts like Supereal, Spooky and D.O.P, aka Brandon's mates Kevin Swain and the other Kevin, Hurry, all particularly prolific that year.

You could buy your new Supereal twelve inch at Flying or Tag Records on a Saturday afternoon, then hear it at Flying, 'the Lunch' or 'the Ranch' later that evening.

Brandon would guest at all these Saturday nighters, as ever, getting into various scrapes along the way.

'Borrowing' things had been a constant theme since joyriding as a teen, 'mugging' that shop dummy at Burtons and, of course, The Guv'nor.

On another occasion, at a house party in Brixton, myself and Swainy pinched the front room carpet from the flat in question, rolling it up, walking out of the place with it under our arms and then waiting on the Stockwell Road for several hours for a big enough mini cab to transport the 20 metre pile back to Lisa Loud's flat.

At least we were resourceful and used the carpet to make the wait for the cab more comfortable. It was hilarious, me and Swainy had rolled up this rug, telling the people who were dancing on it that we'd been asked to move it because it was getting damaged. We put it on our shoulders and walked straight out of the flat. At the cab office we had insisted on an estate car big enough for the carpet, but had to wait ages for a suitable one to come back to base. Lisa Loud wasn't best pleased, because it ended up back at her flat, rolled up in her garden.

Loud remembers:-

Brandon and Swainy had been to an after-party from my flat one Saturday night and then turned up back at my place later with this girl's carpet. And suddenly the girl was on my phone at my flat saying, "hi Lisa, erm, I'm really sorry, but I think some friends of yours have been here and have stolen my carpet out of my party".

I didn't know her at all, but she had managed to trace them to me, and was on my phone. It was so embarrassing, I was mortified, and I said, "you boys better get that fucking carpet back or I will never have you in my house again", although we did take it out in the communal gardens for a bit because it was a nice sunny weekend. I think she got it back on the Tuesday morning in the end.

MixMag gossip columnist Dan Prince noted at the time:-

Poor Paula noticed that her new Persian was missing. Looking up she noticed Block and Swain making a hasty exit with it over their shoulders. Will the carpet turn up at FUBAR or even on the grass at Full Circle?

Meanwhile, paintings and carpets were small fry to Brandon and co. Pinching an actual bar from a pub, or 'kid'-napping a goat was much more of a challenge, even if it was always going to hard living in the shadow of Alex P's bus heist!

Alex will always be difficult to beat with the bus blag in Ibiza, but the piece de resistance for me and Swainy came when we actually nicked the bar from a pub. It was The George in Soho. One end was loose, so we unscrewed the other end and legged it down D'arblay Street. That ended up in Lisa Loud's garden as well!

Another FUBAR phase was climbing, and trees were far too obvious for our lot. After famously throwing condoms full of water from the roof of The Wag Club, while I was meant to be DJing at The Brain Friday-nighter, me, Baggy and Swainy followed that up by staging our own 'Strangeways sit-in' on the roof of The Firs Hotel in Slough, where Phil Perry and Chester would throw Full Circle after-parties.

Meanwhile, Dizzi managing to get halfway home with that goat from a Labrynth rave in Hackney is also well up there in terms of FUBAR folklore, and he explains:-

Myself and a couple of friends, Ally and his girlfriend Sam, came out of a Labrynth do in Hackney, and there was this baby goat in the middle of the road. Considering what we'd been taking that night we weren't sure if we were seeing things at first, but we quickly realised it was real. We bought it some crisps and a Mars bar and named it Finbarrrrr...after a promoter we knew. We were saying "c'mon on Finbar...c'mon Finbar" as we walked to Hackney Wick station. It followed us all the way to the platform and it actually got on the train with us too, as all the other people going about their normal Sunday morning business looked on in amazement. We didn't have any train tickets so when we reached Liverpool Street we told the inspector that the goat had eaten our tickets and we'd brought the goat with us because we didn't think anyone would believe us otherwise. Genius. The driver was in stitches when he got off and saw what had been on his train. Ally and Sam wanted to take the goat home, but the station manager waved us through and made us leave Finbar with him, which was just as well, I guess.

Despite the fun and games there was some work, in the loosest sense of the word, taking place. Brandon was clocking up DJ guest spots and picking up regular re-bookings.

As 1992 drew to a close, I had a weekly Friday residency at Leeds mad house Up Yer Ronson, then held at the Music Factory, and my association with the Up Yer Ronson crew remains strong today. Not surprising, considering I came up with the name in the first place.

At the start of 1993 FUBAR began to spread its wings too, with Lisa Loud and me booked as a duo on tour nights across the country.

FUBAR's home, London's West End, was still heaving, clubbing-wise and I was more often to be found at Club For Life at The Gardening Club on a Saturday, a hugely popular basement venue in the main Covent Garden plaza, which was twinned with the adjoining Rock Garden, often used as an overflow.

But you were just as likely to find me travelling up the M1 to the ever-expanding repertoire of house nights, in various towns and cities north of Watford.

With an apparent open invitation to play at Up Yer Ronson on Fridays, Brandon also made his Wobble debut in Birmingham for Phil Gifford and Si Long, while gigs in London in the first quarter of '93 included Best Of British at Ministry Of Sound alongside Justin Robertson and Colin Hudd, Shakavara at a "central London venue" and A Tennis Ball at the David Lloyd Centre in Middlesex, where he was billed as Brandon "Boris" Block and played against Paul "Navratilova" Daley and Nicky "Nastasie" Holloway.

Sundays were still all about FUBAR, and a messy end/start to the week, with more and more cocaine and pockets full of pills keeping Brandon partying longer and longer.

Among all the madness a pattern was emerging…each year another Ibiza season would be upon Brandon, and each time, as far as his health was concerned, it was the last place in the world he needed to be.

THE LIFE & LINES OF BRANDON BLOCK

PASS THE DUTCH 'E'

Another Ibiza season was looming, which, after the last couple of summers, I was extremely excited about. But a few weeks before that, Nicky Holloway, who was planning an ambitious event at the new EuroDisney complex in Paris, asked me and Steve Lee if we fancied going on a recce/ticket drop-off trip with him and we said "why not?"

The three of us got the ferry to Antwerp in Belgium, and Nicky drove down to Amsterdam, did the rounds there dropping tickets off to various outlets including trendy clothes and record shops and, needless to say, the odd 'cafe'. That evening we were off to The Roxy to see DJ Dimitri, a legend at that time, and also an Ibiza veteran. Suffice to say, on arrival at the venue we were greeted with open arms and given the keys to one of THE drug capitals of the world.

After The Roxy we were invited to someone's house, and it turned out this gaff was actually the local school, which had been closed for refurbishment. A local practice in those days in Holland was to employ a permanent resident to keep squatters out, and one such guy was our after-party host for the night.

So picture the scene, there we were, three absolutely Eeed-out-of-our-heads London loons, in a closed school with access to absolutely every single department. We undertook our new self-appointed roles with an unbounded vigor. First stop was the gym for our basketball workout with PE Master Mr Brandon Block (BA/PHD/MDMA), followed by a quick tour of all the other departments, in particular the chemistry lab, where we helped with the refurbishment in our own inimitable style.

The next day we were on our way back to the port and with a few hours left got smashed up in a bar in Antwerp. There was this fit mature barmaid behind the bar, a real MILF, long before the term MILF had actually been invented, and more like a BILF, I guess. I was trying to crack on to her, but she was having none of it, so myself and Steve decided to do some local 'window shopping'.

Nicky was playing teacher still, though, and saying "c'mon on guys, we haven't got long before the ferry leaves", but me and Steve were already out the door. We had no money left, so our shopping trip was ambitious to say the least. We had about 30 guilders between us, so roughly a tenner, and were getting chased out of these bars as I was trying to blag us both a cheap nosh. We made our way back to base, but Nicky had left and the MILF was smirking, saying "he's gone, for sure".

Nicky had got our passports so we couldn't go anywhere. It was off to the police station to sort out some paperwork to get us home. We called a friend who managed to pay for some new ferry tickets for us over the phone on his credit card, and then once we got to the other side jibbed all the way home from Dover to Bermondsey where Steve lived.

It turned out Nicky had felt sorry for us and went back, missing the ferry himself and arriving back in London a day after us! How's your Donald Duck?

Brandon would be on his Ibiza travels again shortly, and chomping at the bit to get back to his Balearic bolt hole for the 1993 season.

We were now entering into 'way of life territory', as it was rapidly becoming. As people began to realise and start living the Ibiza dream, coupled with what was going on in the UK, the modern-day dance music scene had not only been born, but nurtured and was growing very quickly at a very healthy/ unhealthy pace.

Throughout these early years of the legendary Space terrace and Ibiza outings, the people we met and partied with were pioneers in hedonism, irresponsible behaviour and a general love of all things Balearic, and were becoming a very big global family very quickly.

At the time, some of the influences and colourful characters who I remember fondly, and who opened my eyes to the Ibiza phenomenon starting to take root, were people like Czech, Sirikeet and Yella from Amsterdam and Yella is now the owner of Blue Marlin; representing the German and French contingent, George and Jessica, who both went on to open KM5; and never forgetting the wonderful Italians, 'The Spaghetti Brothers', Roberto and Ernesto of Tahiti and Zenith fame, and also the Italian Tribe, Saro, Simone, Eduardo, Adriano and Stefano, responsible for Aqualandia and various quarry parties back in the day, before MTV had even stepped on the island. And not forgetting my good friend Carlos Diaz, an amazing DJ and a true gentleman. Apologies if any of these names are spelt wrong, but it's been hard enough remembering them in the first place!

Carlos Diaz was born in Uruguay, grew up in Argentina, and moved to Ibiza in 1986. His DJ career on the island began in Brandon's beloved San Antonio, at the Nightlife venue on the corner of what later became 'the strip'.

In 1986 after Amnesia closed you would be in your bed by 7am. Then the next year in 1987 a club called Glory's was the first to do later after-hours on the island.

We would come out of Nightlife at 6am, but you could never be sure Glory's would be open. If it was, once you were inside, the sensation of pleasure that you still had another four hours to go, until around 11am, was amazing. But the after-hours at Glory's was for one year only.

In 1988 there was a club called Manhattans doing after-hours for a few weeks, and then in 1989 Space opened, when the after-hours there lasted until around midday, but only inside then.

Alex P created the terrace in 1990, and then Brandon played there in 1991, and I started to see that the habits of the people changed. They weren't going out on a Saturday night anymore. they were waking up on Sunday at midday, eating something, going to Space, staying until 4pm or 5pm when it closed, and then going to KM5 after that for the rest of the night. Now Sunday was the day.

I feel that Brandon and Alex, through what they made happen on the Space terrace for the next five or six years, were the main DJs who made a real contribution to the the early days of Ibiza. In the late '80s and early '90s there were two DJs from Ibiza going to the UK, Alfredo and Jose Padilla, but a hundred coming the other way.

Out of everybody that came to Ibiza, Brandon and Alex did something Balearic, something real. They created something that wasn't there, they created the terrace. Before that everyone was inside at Space and it was dark techno. Brandon and Alex created the alternative, and that's when the timetable started to extend.

Diaz also guested at Space in the pre-Home/We Love era and went on to become a resident at Zenith, the promotion Italian duo Roberto and Ernesto launched after their pioneering Tahiti beach session, playing numerous full seasons at the likes of Pacha and Amnesia from 1995 onwards.

In the mid-noughties Diaz further enhanced his reputation on the island as founding resident of Blue Marlin on Cala Jondal beach, where he can still be found, as well as at modern-day all-singing, all-dancing Playa D'en Bossa beach club hotel Ushuaia.

I first met Brandon in 1991 at an Aqualandia party in Majorca. I was playing at this party with him and Alex, and Brandon was dropping five Es to start the night. I met these crazy people and for me, they were two DJs that made a difference.

There is always the argument within Ibiza that the English came here and they fucked things up, but Brandon and Alex did bring something different. And they were both lovely guys, and that's how they achieved so many friendships with so many different people.

And it's funny, because in the early Ibiza days I also made friends with people like Nicky Holloway, and used to stay at Nicky's flat in Maida Vale in London, but he never booked me to play at The Milk Bar. Brandon, did, though, for FUBAR...in fact, he was the first person to give me a booking in London, even though I was staying with the guy who owned the club.

In the summer of 1993 Brandon was in so much demand back in London and the UK - frequent flights back home from Ibiza were needed to keep up with the booking enquiries flooding through.

With his big residency at Space on a Sunday firmly in place, it meant every other weekend he could fly back for Friday and Saturday gigs, all over the country, and then catch the early Sunday morning flight back to Ibiza, in time for another afternoon of madness at Space.

Not bad work if you can get it, but also, when you're now used to cocaine fuelling this enjoyable, yet punishing schedule, both an expensive and unhealthy vocation too!

It was quite common at the end of another epic day at Space, that I'd lay on the bar as the bar shutter came down, wedged between the bar and the shutter, protesting at not being allowed to play another record, and often the security would relent and allow us to play another three or four records, behind closed shutters, so to speak.

Space was very different then to how it is now, and even how it was at the end of the '90s. There were no teams of security guards in uniforms walking around the place. It was basically Cheeko and Tony managing the venue, and Ariel running the door. Although their English wasn't fluent we seldom had to use anything more than sign language to communicate.

I think the reason they tolerated our tomfoolery was because we not only brought good business to the club, but also a sense of fun. Many of those guys are still involved in the management of Space, and we're still treated like royalty when we go there.

A few years later, it was also down to our shenanigans behind and in front of the decks which saw the club put CCTV in the most awkward of places. But it didn't take us long, particularly after various reconnaissance missions to the office, to find out the all-important blind spots, which just happened to be where we got up to most mischief.

Me and Alex were on such good terms with the staff and the security that we were able to have people both admitted and ejected at will, from the very meek to the very influential. A few of the 'ejectees' included the now world-famous Flying frontman Charlie Chester (EJECTED!!!), pop luminary and renowned Simply Red frontman Mick Hucknell (EJECTED!!!). While 'admittees' included all close friends, soap stars and any up-and-coming A-listers. Over the years we partied with loads of celebs, including footballers, musicians and actors, as literally people

from all walks of life descended on the island, and especially Space.

Lisa Loud does her best to create those glory days on the Space terrace.

I don't care about any of the big names who have played on the Space terrace since, when Alex and Brandon were on there it was always amazing.

I'd been going to Ibiza since 1985 and experienced the whole Amnesia thing in 1987, and my mate James Mitchell, who had been there since the early days too, created that terrace at Space and tirelessly promoted it, and when the Blocko and Peasy injection came, it was absolutely absolutely absolutely magic, and you just didn't want to leave there.

If you go right back to Amnesia in the '80s, Alfredo, and the famous mirrored Pyramid there, that early magic evolved into Space terrace. Complete nutty-ness, pure acid house, all the people who started that scene, then all the other enigmatic people and influences from everywhere else who came in, travelling from different scenes from all over the world. Everyone out in the sunshine, the DJs loved it, playing out in the open air.

There didn't appear to be any rules, maybe because there was no roof you naturally felt like you were breaking all the rules.

Then the planes going over and the noise they made resonating through the whole place. All this would excite anybody, no matter how old or who you were.

Everything the boys did was an extension of the crowd, and at the end of the day, they weren't doing it for the money, they always owed more money than they were paid because of the drinks they drank and gave out. Fortunately there was always someone prepared to write it off for them.

Baggy recollects...well, sort of...

One time I went to Ibiza with Brandon for a week, but lost him on the first day. The next time I saw him was on the last day. I'd met some Italians and a week later I woke up somewhere with one shoe on, wearing only a pair of cutdown jeans. The Italians took me to this beach, where Brandon was wrestling in the sea with Tommy Mac. I joined in and asked Brandon what we were doing that night, and he told me we were leaving for the airport any minute. I thought we'd only been there a couple of days. We went straight to FUBAR after we landed, and when we got there my shorts were still wet. And I couldn't remember a thing about the whole week.

London gigs for Brandon in July and August included usual monthly commitments with Club For Life in Covent Garden, alongside the likes of Healy and Dave Dorrell; a one-off Art & Slippery When Wet party at a film studios on the same bill as Weatherall, Emerson, Rampling, Perry, Farley and Steve Savva: an Up Yer Ronson tour night at the Hacienda with Steve Lee, and a special Ronson night in Leeds, billed on the advert and flyer as "THE RETURN OF BRANDON BLOCK FROM IBIZA", again with Steve Lee.

There was also an appearance at the recently-opened Club UK in Wandsworth, which was launched a month before by the Georgallides brothers, Chris and Marios, who had transformed cheesy Romford disco Hollywood, the home of Sharon and Tracey, into a decent place to hear house music on a Friday, through its Culture Shock night, launched earlier in 1992.

Brandon and all the leading house jocks at that time would make decent money from the Georgallides' First Continental empire, and when they opened the 2,000-capacity Club UK in 1993, the good times were set to roll some more, particularly as there were also Hollywood venues in Southend and Ipswich, and a Midlands UK in Wolverhampton on its way too.

At the start of August, Brandon would headline Club UK, with Pete Heller, his good pal Dominic Moir, Rocky & Diesel, Aussie Andy Morris and the 'Balearic milkman' Phil Mison also on the bill. Three years later, Brandon would be one of the headliners at Club UK's 3rd Birthday bash, alongside Boy George - the Culture Club frontman now a fully-fledged house DJ on the circuit - and Danny Rampling, with Fabi Paras, Phil Perry and resident Steve Harvey also playing.

More and more it was the same DJs' names appearing on flyers and magazine adverts, and the line-ups at these clubs seemed to be self-perpetuating. This was before the internet was in full swing and most promoters didn't have websites up and running yet.

Before the '93 Ibiza season was over, Brandon was back on the island to wrap up another summer, and one particular beach bar and its daytime after-parties was the talk of the town.

The Tahiti Bar in 1993 just happened, and took off really quickly. And it meant the fun continued each time after Space... brilliant, magical afternoons and nights! The most amazing after-hours on the beach. The Italian duo who ran Tahiti down on the beach at Playa D'en Bossa, Roberto and his brother/partner Ernesto, invited me and Alex to play there, because they'd seen what we were doing at Space, and how could we turn that down? Great guys and great days. Roberto and Ernesto's parties were and are always amazing.

I remember one fateful day at the Tahiti. I had been seeing this beautiful Brazilian heiress, whose multi-millionaire parents just happened to own a huge cattle farm, just outside of Sao Paulo. We'd been partying for days and I was on my last legs.

I'd put the five record boxes that I'd used at Space in the back of Up Yer Ronson duo Tony and Adam's hire car, and made my way from Tahiti to Las Salinas beach with my south American friend Anna, and carried on partying.

To my surprise about half an hour later I saw a forlorn Tony and Adam pacing up the beach. With heavy hearts they explained they'd dropped the key to the hire car on the beach near Tahiti, and it had obviously been found because the car had been stolen, with every record I had in Ibiza for the summer in the boot.

Unable to contain my angst, so drug-riddled and partied out, I literally broke down in tears in front of them, which hardly made them feel any better about the situation and only added to their guilt. I was so distraught I was shouting my head off and calling everyone everything under the sun... under the sun.

*(clockwise) * 'Hanging around' with Alex P and Baggy before leaving for the Ibiza 1993 season*
* At the Dance Europe party with 'Sasha & Digweed', 1993
* Letting it all blow with Dave Beer at Dance Europe
* DJ Magazine piece on Velvet Underground opening, 1993
* With Ernesto from Tahiti and DJ Magazine piece, 1993

James

...hiti beach parties in Ibiza
...weird, wonderful and just
...tainly had them reaching
...ly D'en bosa, the **Tahiti**
...ally closed. Nearby early-
...colourful people including
...the beach when it closed
...hange and most were still
...c supplied by the likes of
...remy. Tahiti boss Roberto
...(around £25) working his
...m a seemingly mild-man-

..., London
...Matthew James

...n we caught up with him during build-
...ated Milk Bar. And good old Brandon
...unday night Fubar is restored shortly.
...ough away from its similarly-sized prede-
...y has London buzzing with anticipation.
...aurant, the club is set to provide a wel-
...'s nightlife. And a return to the "alright
...al Bar before it closed in April. Nicky points
...this club. Somewhere they know they can
...e of old regulars, the same raised dancing
...te-night licence means every night can end
...eans you can stock in at the off
...and just pay for

I stormed off, leaving Anna, Tony and Adam at the beach. My punishment (and everybody else's) was that I would walk from Las Salinas, which is in the middle of nowhere, back to our base in San Antonio. But not by road, 20-odd miles itself...no, I was going cross-country.

After walking for about two hours, still fully-charged and off my maracas, I stopped in the middle of a pine tree forest and realised that I had no idea where I was. I looked behind and Las Salinas was but a dot in the distance.

I woke up three hours later with pine needles up my arse, with no money, no records and not a 'Danny La Rue' where the hell I was, and all in complete darkness. I got up and headed for the nearest light, which turned out to be a remote village, like the land time forgot, with not a single phone available. Somehow, I managed to thumb a lift back to civilisation.

The next day I was awoken by Tony and Adam and a hastily (and pastily) arranged search party for my records. Each year in Ibiza a certain model and colour of hire car is the most used – this year was no exception, namely a dark green Renault something. Every single street around Ibiza was filled with Renaults, all the same colour and all the same model – the phrase 'needle in a haystack' comes to mind.

We visited various police stations in search of my tunes, but to no avail. Eventually after hours of searching we decided to call it a day, but not before one more look down a road in Ibiza Town we'd already been down twice that morning. Would you believe it? Second from last, at the end of that street was the hire car, with my records still in the boot. Two Italian lads we knew, Davide and Angelo, had found the keys on the beach, seen the registration number on the key ring, found the car and decided they could save a fiver's taxi fare back to Ibiza Town and drove off.

Once back at their apartment, and after checking in the boot, they'd recognised my record boxes and quickly parked up, and planned to let me know later the next day. All's well that ends well, but, as usual at that time where I was concerned, not without a bucket full of gear and dollops of drama involved.

Tahiti promoter Ernesto explains:-

We spent a lot of time at Pacha after Tahiti, making the Zenith name, then we also did big weekly parties at Amnesia in 2001 and 2002. We were also working a lot in Miami at Nikki Beach, for many years in Majorca too and Roberto was helping to manage the DJ Luciano as well.

For sure we don't forget the big influence of Brandon, in the early days, and particularly at Tahiti where we first made our name. We have a big new promotion launching at one of the big clubs in 2012 and we will be fusing the new DJs with some of our favourite old DJs and for sure Brandon will be playing for us again.

Meanwhile, another year and another driving escapade for Brandon, and this trip, this time from San Antonio heading towards Space, was not so successful.

Towards the end of the '93 season, we'd finished a FUBAR party at Star/Kaos one Saturday night/Sunday morning, and were on our way to Space. Jeremy Norris was driving his own car, because he was actually living in Ibiza at the time. Jeremy pulled out of the back road, behind Star Cafe, skidded on the road, and a truck came from nowhere and took the whole front end of the car off...literally leaving our shins and knees exposed, in the same position, but slightly nearer the ground, due to the nose of our car lurching forward. I decided the best plan of action was for us to jump in the nearest cab, leaving the remaining half of Jeremy's car at the side of the road. Unfortunately, an hour later La Guardia nicked Jeremy from behind the bar at Space while he was DJing. God knows how they found him. Maybe after tracing the car back to Jeremy, they noticed his name on one of the many Space posters up around the island?

At the end of summer '93 Brandon would return to another autumn in the UK, with the prospect of The Milk Bar closing, and with FUBAR relocating at the turn of 1994 to Velvet Underground, Holloway's new club, literally five minutes away on Charing Cross

Road. Brandon and his already long-suffering mother had a new lodger too, as Baggy explains:-

Brandon dropped me off just down the road from my mum and dad's place, after the '93 season in Ibiza. I turned the corner and the house was all boarded up. I hadn't been in touch with my parents all summer and we didn't have mobiles in those days, so we couldn't text each other, or anything like that. Turned out, they'd moved up north.

I walked round to Brandon's house, knocked on the door and asked if I could stay for a few nights, and ended up staying about six months. His mum wasn't too happy about it, particularly one day when I came out of the bathroom naked, swigging a bottle of vodka, and said "now Viv, we've been living together for some time, don't you think it's time we took this further?"

Another ground-breaking occasional MixMag feature My Local focused on Brandon in the November '93 issue. Pictured alongside a 'local', the piece read:-

Brandon's local is The Mitre in Sudbury. It's here that he has a skin full with his mates – Baggy, Ted The Barman, Five 'Es' Matlock, Larry Outback, Rocket Rogers, Bowlsy, Big Jack and Nugget. Brandon's been a regular for eight years in which time he's run the successful Under The Pool Table Club and regularly sneaked in through the toilet window for a beer while the landlord slept unawares. From the jukebox he chooses the Black Crowes' Hard To Handle, his favourite drink is a pint of snakebite with a large vodka, a Pernod float and Dubonet top, with two bags of pork scratchings.

Also, in that November issue of MixMag, there's a hilarious picture of a gurning Brandon playing a trumpet with Dave Beer, and an accompanying review of Dance Europe singled out Brandon as "Best DJ" stating "everyone was magic but Brandon Block slowing it down on Friday night was top".

Brandon's inclusion in the actual line-up for Dance Europe in September showed that he had now cemented his place in the upper echelons of the house scene.

Either side of Ibiza, I was travelling the UK, and internationally building my reputation too, albeit becoming as known for my partying as much as my music. The disappointment over my treatment at Flying was now a distant memory.

At EuroDisney, Sasha had top billing, with US superjock Tony Humphries, Paul Oakenfold, Andrew Weatherall, Graeme Park, Pete Tong, Justin Robertson, Slam duo Stuart McMillan and Orde Meikle and Holloway himself in the middle order, with the last two names on the bill, other than European jocks like Laurent Garnier and Sven Vath, mine and Miss Moneypenny's head honcho Jim Ryan.

As soon as we got to France, I sorted out my Plat De Jour for the next three days... and proceeded to hold court in my room with Paul Avery and, at one point, a certain Sasha and Digweed. Dance Europe was a small line-up, but I had been doing a weekly party at Nicky's venue, and I was going with him to his new place, Velvet Underground. I was honoured to be on the bill of one of Europe's first dance music festivals.

Bookings that wrapped up 1993 included a slot alongside Pete Tong at The Arena in Middlesbrough; more regular Up Yer Ronson parties, including one with Sasha and MC Kinky in November; an Ibiza tour from mid-November to the start of December, with Alfredo, Holloway and John Kelly, taking in Birmingham, Liverpool, Stoke, Manchester, Sheffield, Brighton and Nottingham; he played with Digweed, Carl Cox (playing a hardcore set!) and Colin Dale at Destiny: The Cream in Clacton on Boxing Day, and at a special Up Yer Basics collaboration the day after, again with Sasha, and also Phil Perry and Ralph Lawson. Then it was back to London for New Year's Eve at the Ministry Of Sound with New Yorkers Kenny Carpenter, Tedd Patterson and Bert Bevans, and Holloway.

I had photographed both Holloway and Brandon at the building site that was Velvet Underground, complete with shovels, for an article that appeared in DJ Magazine at the end of 1993. In the piece I made necessary poor jokes like *"Brandon just cannot wait to get plastered when his beloved FUBAR is restored shortly"*, and he had added: *"I cannot wait to get FUBARRED again. A part of my life has been* missing since The Milk Bar closed. Everyone I have spoken to is bang up for it again."*

But Brandon was noticeably fidgety and didn't hang around long. FUBAR or no FUBAR, he was bang up for it anyway, and bang on it still.

I got asked to do loads of interviews like that, but around that time, in particular, I just wanted to get back to the pub or back to somewhere I could have a nose-up.

I had become addicted to cocaine very quickly. Any spare time I had, me and Baggy would spend in The Mitre. After FUBAR on a Sunday, and whatever we'd got up to following that, we'd settle into our weekly rota of boozing, and I can remember we were drinking more and more, and the gear and the booze was literally going hand in hand. It felt like I was electric, constantly plugged in, always with at least a quarter of gear in my pocket.

In my bedroom at home, my self-styled comfort shelf, just above my bed, which was meant for my alarm clock or my TV remote control, was now where I'd do my lines, and often as I got up and out of bed.

Meanwhile, as Brandon's fame and notoriety, as well as that of the scene itself, continued to increase at a frightening pace, Brandon was even able to send stand-ins along if he was too inebriated to attend certain gigs, particularly if abroad and the promoters had never met him. Dizzi remembers:-

For one trip to Tenerife, Brandon had convinced the promoter that me and our mate Connor were up-and-coming DJs from London and that when booking him for a gig at Bobby's Bar he should get us two out there as well while he could still get us cheap. I heard him on the phone talking about it one afternoon, and heard my name mentioned, and wondered what the hell was going on. Brandon had blagged us free flights and said "boys, we're off to Tenerife". However, we were so hammered on the night of the gig that Brandon couldn't stand up let alone DJ. He sent me along to Bobby's Bar, and I got into the booth, but didn't have a clue what I was doing. I pretended that I wasn't used to the mixer, but my first mix was total 'pots and pans'. It sounded awful, and I was escorted off, with the promoter saying "c'mon Brandon, you're too drunk to play mate, we'll have to leave it this time". That was the funny thing, that he actually thought I was Brandon, and that he seemed to accept the fact that he (or I) was too battered to play.

GOA, GOING, GONE

As 1993 drew to a close, and with New Year's Eve commitments out of the way, Tony Hannan felt that Brandon needed a break, and picks up the story.

I'd been spending more and more time with Brandon, and even then he was doing worrying amounts of gear. We all liked to party and get stuck in, but Brandon's intake was unbelievable. Despite the decent DJ fees he was getting he never seemed to have any money, because it was all going on drugs, and around this time he seemed down on his luck, so I said "c'mon mate, we're going to Goa for a couple of weeks and I'm paying".

So me, Brandon and my Up Yer Ronson partner Adam Wood and his girlfriend Sally went to northern Goa in India, a beach resort called Calangute. In those days we were all earning decent cash, our club nights were bringing in good money every week and spending £500 or £600 on a holiday for your mate was nothing to me then.

It was hilarious, me and Brandon managed to blag some massages off some birds we met on the plane, and settled in nicely for a relaxing few days away from clubs, partying and drugs. We were so relaxed when we got there that we fell asleep on the beach and a sacred cow nibbled on Brandon's sarong while he was out for the count.

We even bumped into TV presenter and comedian Clive Anderson on the beach one day, and had a crack with him. We managed four or five days of sunbathing, eating good food and resting, and then we started to get itchy feet.

I'd brought a load of cassettes with me, recordings of Sasha's set at the Up Yer Ronson NYE party at the Corn Exchange in Leeds a few weeks earlier, and one night we found this bar called Titos and gave the staff in there a couple of tapes. Before you knew it, we'd met this Iranian guy, fittingly called Mad, and an Indian guy called Vicky, and they were dishing out these green gelatin squares of MDMA to everyone. People were dancing on the bar and the place was going off. We were back in business! Those green Es were the maddest I'd ever tried and that night, somehow, me and Brandon drove home on our scooters through the dark country lanes, absolutely pissing ourselves.

Brandon was speeding along looking at me, laughing his head off, when he suddenly drove straight into a sandbank. He literally flew off the bike, in mid-air, like superman and landed in a bush!

India was great, but I think Tony is being a little over-ambitious with five days, it was more like five hours! One day without any drugs then would have seemed liked five days now, though.

None of us had been to India before and we'd all heard the great stories about Goa and the forest parties out there. It had been a hectic New Year for us all, but our first attempt at what we thought was a half-decent hotel failed miserably as there was no room at the inn. Goa was a busy place, even in its tender years!

After managing to find somewhere to put our stuff for one or two nights, we headed to Baga beach, which was the closest one, and with portable stereo cassette player in hand and the latest Block/Sasha/Dorrell Up Yer Ronson mixes, the four of us invaded the beach. We were promptly told to turn down our racket by a woman who had approached us from behind. In unison, we turned round and gave her our views on the matter, in no uncertain terms. Turns out it was Michelle, the promoter of Claire's in Torquay, and who I'd played for only three weeks earlier. Goa is for her and many other people, their escape and chill time, away from their everyday lives. The fact that hers was dance music and her relative solitude and R & R time had been disturbed by three of the loudest fuckers to grace the idyllic beach, was a shock, let alone quite disturbing, I'm sure.

Brandon would kick off in 1994 where he left off in '93, playing regularly for Shelly Boswell at Club For Life – with Shelly famously stripping for a flyer for a new Club For Life party at The Cross.

Ministry Of Sound booked Brandon again for Open All Hours at the end of February, and he also made his debut at Clockwork Orange, a promotion run by Romford-based likely lads Danny Gould and Andy Manston, and who that night were celebrating their first birthday at Paddocks in Holborn. Also on the bill was Hastings born-and-bred John Digweed, making his London debut.

In February DJ Magazine had revealed details of a new FUBAR track called Power Of Love, featuring vocals from KLF singer Maxine

Harvey. The piece describes Brandon as *"chief loon"* and tells of the *"frightening possibility of a FUBAR band on tour"*, adding *"God help us"*.

In March Brandon was back at The David Lloyd Centre in Middlesex for an Ibiza Reunion party, hosted by Black & White, alongside Judge Jules and Alex P, and part of an Up Yer Ronson tour with Fluke (live) and Alistair Whitehead.

He was also booked for Clockwork Orange at The Old Vic Theatre in London with Rocky & Diesel and popular transvestite DJ Jon (Pleased Wimmin), and when Paddocks rebranded as The Leisure Lounge, with Breeze (RIP).

In April 1994 Brandon returned a compliment by taking Hannan with him to Hong Kong on a club class, all-expenses trip, which had been set up by Shelly Boswell. And Hong Kong would be another jet-set destination which would go on to have great significance for Brandon and his health.

My residency at Club For Life was well under way, and Shelley had a hook up for me in Hong Kong under the Club For Life banner, and I invited Tony Hannan to come along. It was nice to return the favour. I had a booking there at a club called Neptunes 2 in Wan Chai, and another one in a hotel.

I remember we stayed in the New Territories with some ex-pats we'd met out there - Peggy, Jane and Nina. Thanks for your hospitality girls. One of the dogs roaming around out there was such a mad bastard that they named it after me...*Blandon Brock!*

Like Ibiza, I immediately fell in love with Hong Kong, and always enjoyed going back there. On that first trip I remember ringing up whoever was picking me up from the airport and ordering a bag of gear, so I must have been completely addicted by then.

Hannan remembers:-

When we got there, one of Brandon's dad's friends, who was living there, took us out for a really nice meal and showed us around a bit, so it was nice to have a friendly introduction to Hong Kong, but, as usual, it didn't stay very chilled for long.

At one of the first bars we went to the next night on Kowloon side, we bumped into this guy who I knew from Manchester. After some niceties, we got chatting and it turned out he had a kilo of MDMA back at his apartment... like you do. We were suddenly very popular with the locals and ex-pats.

I always remember me and Brandon returning to Heathrow, and walking through customs, and an official asking us "anything to declare boys?", and me and Brandon looked at each other, and back at the guy, and in tandem said "yeah, we were the bollocks". To his credit the customs guy laughed his head off and waved us through.

It didn't seem to matter where I went in the world - Australia, India or Hong Kong, let alone Ibiza and the rest of Europe - someone always had some gear. It was always on a plate for me, and I could tell that the use of drugs recreationally was quickly becoming a global epidemic.

Back home a MixMag cover mount cassette called Mad Hatters Tea Party, mixed by Brandon and Jeremy Healy, accompanied the May '94 issue.

Already an Ibiza legend, Brandon set up shop with Alex in the summer of 1994, renting an apartment directly above the Cafe Del Mar. And, as well as Space was going, ever the promoters, the duo decided they would try and put on a few of their own smaller events that year as well.

I had the dubious pleasure of interviewing the pair in said apartment, and an article I wrote for DJ magazine included: *"The poster for their new Exstasis Saturday-nighter Sac Le Nez (French for nosebag) depicts a horse with his head buried in a bag of oats and probably explains much".*

Those aforementioned 'likely lads' from Romford, Danny Gould and Andy Manston, were also in Ibiza at the start of the 1994 season, hoping to roll out their central London-based Clockwork Orange brand in Ibiza. Brandon was instrumental in finding them a base in Ibiza, and he and Alex were a perfect trophy signing for their project.

Clockwork Orange would be good for Brandon financially, with Gould and Manston becoming the longest-serving British promoters on the island come the turn of the Millennium, with a record seven consecutive seasons in Ibiza by 2001. Manston remembers:-

I first met Brandon at FUBAR one night… a group of us used to go up to The Milk Bar regularly on a Sunday night. We had started Clockwork at Paddocks in Holborn in January 1993, and Brandon played at our second party there in the February.

In 1994 we started making noises about wanting to do something in Ibiza and it was Brandon who suggested Es Paradis as the perfect place, hooking us up with Clara (aka Miss Bisto) who worked there. We went out to meet her at the start of the '94 season and agreed to do a run of Wednesdays to see how it went. In a way it was that easy in those days, no months of planning. I remember booking Judge Jules up within a month of that and for a few hundred quid. Me and Danny gave out flyers ourselves and Brandon and Alex were our residents. In fact, when we got there at the start of the season they were both already in our apartment because they'd got booted out of their one.

I had known Clara for a good few years. She was working at Es Paradis as a dancer, and became the resident DJ there, and became a dear friend of mine. Marisol, my ever faithful friend and daughter of Es Paradis owner Pepe, she came to Space all the time (besos...), and we'd also done a few FUBAR things at Es Paradis, so there were good links with the club.

Danny and Andy were doing some great parties in London, along with promoters like Shakavara, and I soon became more of a resident, than a guest, at Clockwork.

Clara had asked me to recommend an English promoter for Es Paradis, and with the venue being located in San Antonio, I didn't hesitate in recommending the boys. Clockwork was perfect for San Antonio. Danny and Andy were completely down to earth, just like Clockwork, in fact, and their weekly session was on a Wednesday, just when it started going bonkers throughout the week in Ibiza, not just at the weekends.

For Danny Gould, a larger than life clubland character himself who became one of the 'stars' of Sky One's cult Ibiza Uncovered TV series in the mid-to-late '90s, partying in Ibiza was his destiny.

THE LIFE & LINES OF BRANDON BLOCK

When we started in Ibiza, as far as I was concerned, Brandon was THE Ibiza geezer. He was earning top dollar, but like me, he didn't see a lot of the money. It all went on gear and 'larging' it.

It seems funny looking back now, but Brandon and Alex were people I aspired to emulate, in terms of caning it. In fact, they invented the so-called caner category, long before all the awards for that sort of stuff came about. When Ministry Magazine announced their Top Ten Caners Of The Nineties, Brandon and Alex were No 1 and I was No 3... and I was well happy with that. I felt like I'd achieved what I'd set out to do.

I don't know about Brandon, but I've got no regrets at all....I believe it was meant to be. It was pure drugs, sex and rock 'n' roll for me and I always saw Brandon as a complete part of that. We were in Ibiza, the best playground in the world, having the time of our lives and it was simply amazing.

One year I spent at least £30k on gear, another year our drinks bill at Es Paradis was £20,000 and that was with £15,000 knocked off for goodwill by the owner.

I was spending £1,000 a week on Dolce & Gabbana clobber, eating in the best restaurants, drinking the best champagne and pulling the best birds. Brilliant... simple as that. In 1996 we came back £2,000 down and a couple of years later returned £250,000 up. When we stopped doing Ibiza in 2001 I personally didn't have a lot to show for it, but I wouldn't swap those years for five million pounds now. If I had a time machine, I'd go back and do it all again, exactly the same way.

If you turned up and you were really scruffy and pissed, then you might not get into Clockwork, but if you wanted to have a good time you were all right by us. We were never up ourselves with our door policy. We gave the crowd what they wanted - mainstream stuff with a bit of old school and Brandon typified what we were all about, giving the crowd what they wanted.

One party we did at Es Paradis was Brandon and Alex vs Tall Paul

(clockwise) * With Alex at Aqualandia water park, 1994
* Andy Manston from Clockwork Orange DJing behind the bar at Space Terrace at a Clockwork 'Carry On'
* A poster for infamous Blocko promotion Sac Le Nez, 1994
* with TV presenter Clive Anderson and Up Yer Ronson duo Tony Hannan and Adam Wood in Goa, 1994
* With Cafe Mambo owner Javier Anadon, 2011

EXTASI
PRESENTS
SAC LE'NI

EVERY SAT

DJS
BRANDON BLOC
ALEX "P"
DANNY KEITH

WITH RESIDENTS STUART WINTER, ROBERTO Y AG
+MORE TOP LONDON DJS TO BE ANNOUNCED

and Seb. Brandon and Alex were on the balcony upstairs with one set of decks and the other pair were downstairs on another two, and they were going backwards and forwards between them, Brandon with his pants right up to his nipples, arsing around as usual.

When I went to Ibiza, as soon as I stepped off the plane, I used to take a deep breath and sniff it all in. You can really smell that place in the air.

Space on a Sunday was simply the best day out you could have. We'd always make sure we'd have a good sleep the night before, get up, have a cooked breakfast, a joint and a line, get ready, and head down to Space. I used to get these butterflies in my stomach because I knew we were going to have such a good crack. That was the old Space, long before they moved the DJ booth in the late '90s, and actually covered the terrace over in the noughties. This was the proper Space terrace, with the top bar at the back, up by the fences, and with the planes going over.

I remember one year Brandon and Alex were on, playing Erik B and Rakim's Paid In Full. I was on one of the podiums going for it and just as I'd had a massive go on some poppers, they dropped one of my all-time favourites, A Guy Called Gerald's Voodoo Ray. I was dropping shapes all over the shop and the whole place was going off big time. I looked over at Brandon and Alex and they were standing there with empty record boxes on their heads.

They were amazing days out! Loads of British clubbers mixing with local Spanish and Italian club kids, south American lap-dancers and gangsters and villains from all over the world. Unbelievable. Brandon and Alex's chemistry, particularly at Space, was amazing. They were born entertainers, and everybody wanted a part of that, everyone was trying to get into their circle of friends, their little crew.

These days Danny Gould and his partner and Andy Manston and his family go camping regularly. Gould adds: -

I've been clean and sober seven years, and the money I earn as a construction manager I really earn. I'm not going to waste that money on drugs or booze, because in my eyes I really have worked hard for this money.

Manston, who is also now in the building trade, concludes:-

We lived the dream for years and smashed it. Brandon was like a rock star at the time. We did go bonkers, particularly out in Ibiza, and I am surprised we're all alive to tell the tale. I was a bit more sensible than Danny and actually kept some of the money we made. I'm married now with two kids. In fact Brandon and Alex DJd at my wedding in 1999.

Danny Gould is spot on when it comes to Space, never a truer word spoken, in fact.

Those first few years of the terrace not only cemented myself and Alex's DJ career, but also Space the club's reputation. Without those first few years of Ibiza, I'm not sure dance music would have had the same impact as it has worldwide today.

Around 1994/95 the promoters coming to Ibiza realised that putting on weekly events was a big deal, and elaborate promotional tools, including parades through Ibiza Town, were vital. Manumission and Clockwork were the forerunners for the parades and Danny and Andy spent loads of money promoting their night. It obviously worked because Clockwork ran for so many years at Es Paradis.

There were many potential heirs to the 'Blocko' throne of caning, and Danny was right up there, and gave me a run for my money at times. When I 'retired' from cocaine in 1996, it was safe in the knowledge that the likes of Danny were coming through the ranks. And like any professional caner, it's good that Danny was able to stop eventually too.

Among all the weird and wonderful people Brandon has met in Ibiza over the years, various characters along the way reminded him of his own humble beginnings. Like Jason Bye, who quickly swapped driving a delivery truck in Walthamstow, in east London (just down the road from Clockwork duo Gould and Manston) for the life of a respected Ibiza DJ, soon hobnobbing with DJ heavyweights like "Healy, Coxy, Blocko and Peasy", on his way to holding down some of the most coveted DJ residencies in the world.

In 1993 Bye stumbled across a PR job at a bar in San Antonio, whose owner had an ambitious plan to take on the Cafe Del Mar just around the bay.

Bye had first come across Brandon at one of his favourite San Antonio haunts in 1993, but wouldn't get to know him or Alex 'properly' until his first full season at Mambo in '95.

The first time I saw Brandon was in The Star Club. He was DJing with Alex, who had the longest hair I'd ever seen and who was trying to mix in Frankie Knuckles' Your Love.

Your Love is obviously one of the, if not THE, greatest house tunes ever, but it's got a little bit of an off-beat at the start, and I never really realised until I started DJing why it was so hard to mix in. Alex had his hair down over his face, trying to mix the track in, and we could hear it coming in, and just as me and my mate Greenway were ready to start bustin' our moves, he'd start all over again. He got it in eventually, but it took a good 20 minutes.

Brandon was stumbling around with a set of curtains on his head, doing the lights, and everyone's chins were going ten to the dozen. In fact, you could have powered half of the UK with their chins that morning.

It wasn't real hands-in-the-air stuff, everybody was just marching around, stomping, in fact. It's just one of those things you never forget, the energy when those two were playing, everybody tuned in together.

But I didn't talk to Brandon or Alex that night, not actually until the year after at Mambo. They quickly became like brothers to me. I was 21, and nobody in London had ever given me the opportunity to play before. Mambo boss Javier Anadon and both Brandon and Alex always gave me a chance, and the boys in particular always respected me for my knowledge of music.

Brandon and Alex were the only DJs who would even talk to me at the start, the only ones who would even remember my name, even though they quickly called me Ha-son, instead of Jason, like Jesus in Ibiza is pronounced He-zeus.

That night Jason saw us at The Star Club, which the Star Cafe, our other favourite haunt, was adjoined to. It would have been one of our FUBAR nights, which, with the help of Baggy, we started promoting at a few venues so we had our own night in Ibiza.

We had various mates playing for us too, people from London that we knew on the island, like Spencer Broughton, Jeremy Norris, Von and the Star Club's resident Stuart B, who was a great DJ, particularly over three decks.

We had the best times at The Star Club. One night Von was DJing there, and, as he turned round to look at his records, we emptied a bottle of amyl nitrate on to each slipmatt. He turned round and attempted to do this mix and, you can imagine, he started to rush, and this rush lasted for the whole of this record, and his face was a picture, because he couldn't work out what was happening.

Another night myself and Alex went on after Stuart B and locked him in the cupboard behind the decks for the whole of our set. 'Ha-son' Bye would be at the receiving end of many of our pranks too, but it was all in good spirits. We got Spencer Broughton so drunk one night that he vomited all over the mixer in the middle of his set. I think he ended up in the cupboard too.

In 1992/93, records weren't being played at Cafe Del Mar in the afternoon, but Mambo did have that when it opened in 1994, so we'd often tip up, play whatever, and then come in line for the sunset.

I used to play at Cafe Del Mar occasionally around '92, because we were staying above and always causing havoc there anyway, but when Mambo opened it was perfect for us. Javier knew me and Alex wanted to buy the place before him, and open up something, so he said "you two come here, and drink and eat here for free whenever, bring your friends and play when you want" so that's what we did.

I guess looking back it's mad that our pulling power was such at the time that we were being asked to sit in bars and drink for free, so that others would come and join us...but they did, and in their droves.

We were still using the apartment above Cafe Del Mar in 1994 when Mambo opened so we'd come out the back of the Del Mar and head straight down to our new 'home', Mambo.

I have had some of the best days of my life at Mambo, and the family there will always have a special place in my heart. Pete Tong has broadcast from Mambo loads over the years, but me and Alex did many of our Kiss radio shows live from Mambo too.

Javier Anadon remembers the early days at Mambo fondly, and is quick to heap praise on Brandon and co for their help launching the bar.

I have very good memories of Brandon in those early days.

In the first year with Mambo, everybody was laughing at me opening Mambo, but soon the same people who were laughing, well, I was very popular with them. But Brandon always believed in Mambo.

I opened Mambo on June 27, 1994, and, of course, Cafe Del Mar was so big, and I needed help always with Mambo, and Brandon was often here...in fact, he was here sometimes more than he was at his apartment. But he helped me to make Mambo.

But where hanging around bars by the sea was concerned, Brandon was also keen to build on his good work at Playa D'en Bossa the season before.

After the amazing Tahiti closing party of 1993, when myself, Baggy, Alex, Roberto and Ernesto drank the bar dry, we were wondering just what weird and wonderful beach activities the boys would have in store for us in '94.

So at the beginning of the very next summer, and after another amazing Space opening party, we headed to Tahiti, all 465 yards, directly across the road, and slightly to the left, and expected to be greeted by a smiling Roberto and Ernesto. But no, to our dismay there would be no after-Space nuttiness care of our Italian friends this summer. But, hold on a minute...what was this we spied?...50 yards to our right, a Caribbean-esque beach shack with our names

written all over it...as well as the grainy, but magical two words 'Bora Bora'.

And this was a far cry from what Bora Bora would become. Once again, as luck would have it, and possibly due to our thirst for hedonistic discovery, we were at the forefront of something truly special in Ibiza, even if we were three years early.

From 1994 onwards Bora Bora, and more about the latter-day version later, would be somewhere we gravitated after Space, - myself Alex, Tommy Mac, Del and Kate and friends like Sue Bennison, and our host with the most was barman Max Latino, who I still chat with on Skype to this day.

1994 was a great year in Ibiza, and a hugely important one for the island. Manumission opened that year, and I remember seeing a bald-headed naked man doing cartwheels on Las Salinas. Being rather well-endowed, Mike Manumission was like a huge catherine wheel spinning down the beach. From that moment on I thought that man should be on the stage... little did I know that stage would be in the middle of 12,000 people at Ku, and where each week Mike and wife Claire would host the world-famous Manumission sex shows.

BAGGY'S TROUSERED

In 1994 I was hopping between Ibiza and the UK throughout that summer season, with regular work back home for Up Yer Ronson, Club For Life and Club UK, as well as new bookings at clubs like The Steering Wheel in Birmingham.

In Ibiza, I was now playing three or four times a week on the terrace at Space, doing one day on, one day off with Alex - catching up daily with him at Cafe Mambo, if we weren't flying off to Majorca - and also appearing at some of the island's other superclubs, like Es Paradis in San Antonio with Reel 2 Real and Erick Morillo.

In August of that year, MixMag were back with another ingenious feature, as they set about wringing as much copy as possible out of the year's leading DJs. We'd already had the hilarious Stars And Their Cars, which saw Diesel showing off his Fiat Panda, with Rocky strewn across the bonnet.

Now came MUMMY'S BOYS, a feature about leading jocks who still live with their mums.

Of course, Brandon was a prime candidate for this and the ensuing Q & A, which featured a picture of Brandon's mum throwing some records in a wheely bin, included the following:-

MixMag: What's Brandon's worst habit?

Vivienne Block: He does like a little bit of a drink, but I think it's something the job encourages. There are times when he has come home worse for wear, and I only mind from a health point of view.

MM: Do you worry about him?

VB: I have had a few sleepless nights over the last 14 years but I like to think he's sensible.

MM: Do you spoil him

VB: I have been known to indulge him.

MM: Do you go to his clubs?

VB: His Dad goes. Me and Brandon go to the cinema together sometimes.

MM: What's your arch pet hate about him?

VB: The chronic messages his friends leave on the answerphone with swearing. They forget it's my house and I once phoned one of them and told him never to leave a message like that again.

That was Baggy, always leaving rude messages. My mum had a running battle with him, poor thing. He was always promising to decorate her house, because that's what he did...sometimes...and during this time he'd been staying at our house, sleeping on her couch, for half of the year.

One night we came back pissed, and he managed to spill red wine all over the main wall of our lounge...yes the wall! And only days after she'd finally redecorated the whole house herself. We didn't help matters by, in our drunken state, touching the red blotches with completely the wrong colour paint. She never forgave him for that.

And a couch would have felt like a four poster bed, compared to Baggy's varied sleeping arrangement in Ibiza in the summer of 1994. He explains:-

I would either crash out in a tent made out of a washing line and some blankets on the balcony of Brandon and Alex's apartment above the Cafe Del Mar; a large cupboard in an apartment rented by some friends above The Croissant Show in Ibiza Town; or inside a large holdall at another pal's place just outside of San Antonio. It was great. Having three places to crash in different parts of the island was ideal for me.

Mrs Block, meanwhile, was being confronted more and more by Brandon's fans.

I was in Lanzarote on holiday one year, chatting to some young people by the pool, and when they found out Brandon was my son, they asked me for my autograph...I mean, hell-oooo? I'm always amazed how many people actually know who he is.

I was on a Virgin flight to America with Brandon once, and we got upgraded to first class. I walked down Oxford Street with him another time, and couldn't believe how many people were stopping him, saying "all right Brandon, hello Bran..all right Blocks". It was just relentless.

And then there is our family friend, Allan Clarke, who was lead singer of The Hollies. When Brandon was growing up we were always close with Allan and his wife, and I still am today. We would have family Christmases at their house in Hampstead and with He Ain't Heavy, He's My Brother and The Air That I Breathe, Allan made two of the most instantly recognisable records ever. Allan was very put out as the years went by that his granddaughter was much more interested in Brandon than his own career.

Brandon went back to Hong Kong in the autumn of '94. On the way, with his coke habit spiralling out of control and some gigs in Australia to follow, he was caught smoking in the toilet of the upper class cabin on a Virgin Atlantic flight.

Little wonder he needed a fag, the amount of coke he had taken at the airport and during the flight.

I was escorted from the plane, and the only punishment was the downgrading of my seat to economy class for the return journey. Much better than handcuffs, but still lenient to say the least.

However, to make matters worse, I was unable to take my flight to Oz to hook up with Alex, because of some unpaid tax on a previous visit. A minor detail for a pub-loving cokehead.

Undeterred and grateful I didn't have to spend another ten airborn hours unable to smoke, I headed straight to the nearest bar for a 72-hour bender, spending most of the three day trip there (and at other bars) snorting, drinking and puffing, and still wearing my Virgin Atlantic pyjamas throughout. I still had them on at the gig, which I somehow managed to squeeze in between.

Around the winter of 1994, Brandon could be found as much playing outside of London as he could inside it. And as 1995 began he was busier than ever, his loveable rogue-ish qualities appealing to promoters all over the UK, week-in, week-out.

Brandon had always been welcomed north of the border by the passionate Scottish crowds. Colours in Glasgow, Fruit Club in Edinburgh, Ice Factory in Perth, Ministry Of Sin in Aberdeen, Ayr Pavilion (for Colours) and Lush in Port Rush, Network Club in Belfast and Boom Boom Rooms in Bangor were all regular bookings for him.

Meanwhile, the likes of Birmingham, Wolverhampton, Sheffield, Derby and Leicester seemingly could not get enough of him either.

Wobble had been one of the first promoters in 'Brum' to book him, and he headlined again for them in March 1995; April saw Brandon alongside Boy George, and residents Pete & Russell, at Progress in Derby; and in the same month he made one of his first appearances at Gatecrasher in Sheffield, this time with Healy, Alex P and Allister Whitehead, later in September playing alongside Tony De Vit and Tall Paul, at another 'Crasher gig in Sheffield.

Then there were the Chuff Chuff parties.

Chuff Chuff were just the best parties, and the Moneypenny's boys, brothers Jim, Dermott and Micheal Ryan and old pal Lee Garrick, turned their little party from the mid to late '80s into a global brand as Miss Moneypenny's and fair play to them.

After we all moved back to nightclubs from the raves, Chuff Chuff were events that weren't in a normal nightclub again. And this was when promoters started adding more imaginative drapes and other visuals. The various themes also made the punters feel they were being offered something more. Chuff Chuff and Moneypenny's will always be remembered for all the gorgeous girls. The best, in fact.

I was getting further away from my Flying roots, but I was hardly in any fit state to think long and hard about career implications and after all, I was earning a right few quid.

(clockwise) With Adam, Alex and Baggy in San Antonio, Ibiza, 1993
With Boy George at Chuff Chuff

united kingdom

NIGHT CLUB LONDON

SATURDAY'S UNITED

Saturday 7th August
Brandon Block
Pete
Dominic Moir
Andy Morris
Rocky and D
lison (Café del Mar)
Mark French

y 14th August
Perry
Fabi Para

BCM PARTY ZONE
BCM Inter-dance SECTOR 1
DANCE 94
THE GUEST IN THE HOUSE
ACTV DANCE 94 presents
JUNE
DARREN EMERSON
+ P.A. DOI-OING
NDON RATPACK DEAN SAVONNE
DENTS: DES MITCHELL + DAMON JAY

ateCrashe

eremyHealy02AlexP.03BrandonBloc04Ali
itehead05LeeFisher(Decadence).Date.Su
April.Time11.pmtill6.am.Allnight.Smartdress.

Brandon's cocaine intake was out of control, his sense of perspective and reality as eroded as his frail nasal passages. Surely one explanation for what happened next.

Spring 1995 also saw Brandon back in Hong Kong. And back with a bang! He quickly hooked up with the 'east London connection', a hardcore group of clubbers who settled there in the early '90s and were flying the British flag out there.

Whenever Brandon travelled to Hong Kong he felt at home with this lot, and this lot knew how to party, operating around the Lan Kuai Fong square of bars, with venues like L'Jardin, Soho and Atmosphere their main stomping grounds.

It was May 1995 and on arrival I quickly hooked up with the gang, Gilly, Tina, Debbie, Dale, Jackie, Gemma and co. There was a load of us on the Star Ferry going to Lama Island, on our way to someone's house over there. As usual, I was off my nut, and somehow decided I was going to dive off the ferry.

I wish I knew what made me do it, but then I could say that about a lot of things. Fortunately I dived off to the side, and not straight forward. I missed the propeller by about five feet. If I had dived forward into the swell, I'd have been chopped up into bits like a salmon. All my mates were thinking "What the fuck? What's he done that for?, Where's he gone?", and then I popped up above the water. They couldn't tell anyone, because I'd have got in big trouble for jumping in, yet, there and then, they weren't sure how they were going to get me out. Somehow they formed a human chain, like a downward Keystone Kops turnout, and dragged me out of the water with a big hook. God knows where they found that. Then as we walked off the ferry, I walked past the officials, soaking wet and they looked at me, as if to say, "nah, there's no way he's been in the drink, and even if he has, how the hell did he get out?"

Now, this isn't like jumping off a boat in the lake at your local park, or a leaping from a pedalo in the Med. This is the Star 'bloody' Ferry, in Hong 'bleedin'' Kong, a constant service linking Hong Kong island and the Kowloon mainland side across various routes, in some of the dirtiest disease-ridden waters in the world. Hundreds of thousands of under-privileged Cantonese families manage to live on the intricate web of junk boats and tiny, cramped water houses in and around the docks on either side, but this is no place for an under-nourished ten-gram-a-day coke-addled, pampered DJ from London.

Back home and it wasn't long before Ibiza was looming again. This should have been the pinnacle of Brandon's career, or the start of several pinnacles. However, it's difficult at the best of times to appreciate a pinnacle in your career, let alone when you're out of your mind, day-in, day-out, 24-7.

NOT ALL GIRLS A LOUD

Brandon was still raking in the column inches in the club press and consecutive MixMags in May and June in 1995 revealed Brandon had been coming to blows…literally!

MAY - CLUBLAND'S TOP TEN PARTY ANIMALS: "*Block was sighted at Full Circle wearing a motorcycle crash helmet, running along bent over double, bashing through some double doors, careering across the dancefloor, before smashing into the bar and landing on his arse. "Double Jack Daniels and coke please", exclaimed Blocko to a bewildered barman.*

JUNE - CLUB COUNTRY: "*Charlie Chester says he met two sisters who claimed they gave a top flight DJ a sneaky blow job in the bar at Back To Basics, the plush velvet curtains behind the decks, they said, made it easy to hide while the DJ pretended to be looking for a record. The DJ in question? Well it rhymes with Frandon Flock".*

When this was witnessed by Karen Dunn, Brandon's agent could only look on in horror.

Brandon and Alex had girls throwing themselves at them, and the blow jobs behind the decks were quite regular. I was privy to this many times at gigs while they were DJing. Those girls were so bad, but then so were those two boys. I would hate to be one of those girls, and I guess they'll have to live with that now.

Lisa Loud also witnessed more than most.

Where the female fans were concerned, I have to say I have never known anything like it. I DJd with Brandon on so many occasions, and those silly little dolly birds would have their own agenda, they'd be awaiting the superstar that was the Blocko. The amount of girls that I saw throwing themselves at him when I was DJing with him was phenomenal. Then when it was Brandon and Alex together, it was just like "what the fuck?".

One particular groupie got a little bit more than she bargained for, when she stalked Brandon back to his hotel room after Up Yer Ronson in Leeds one night.

Dizzi was with me that night with a couple of other friends. I'd been playing in Stoke the night before with Graeme Park, but when we got to Leeds, Dizzi was waiting for us with a flask of mushroom tea. Now this stuff was mental, but we all necked a cup full before we went to the club and it sent us 'garrity', so much so that I could only manage the warm-up before heading back to the hotel. There were a load of people in our room, but I was tripping off my nut, and screamed at everyone to "Get out!!".

I'd just managed to get rid of everyone, when this bird knocks at the door. Now, she was blonde and lovely, she'd been on my case for a while, whenever I went up to Leeds, but she was also a bit out there, and, up until this point, I'd always managed to resist her charms.

On this occasion, though, my defences were down. She came in the room, and was getting pissed on bottles of Bud from the mini-bar, and then Dizzi and Long'un knocked on the door.

It was already weird, because the girl had come with this guy, but when I'd said she could come in, she'd told him to wait outside, and so he was standing outside the room when the boys arrived and I was now inside about to get down to business.

Dizzi and Long'un came in and the girl, who was in the middle of stripping off what few clothes she had on, looked at them, and one of them said "oh, don't mind us, we're gay".

Well, this girl was so crazy she just carried on, and she told the boys to sit on the edge of the bed.

She started doing a floor show and then showed us a party trick with some self-dissolving 'crumble mints', which was a sight to behold!

The boys were sitting there, and she was saying "so this stuff, doesn't turn you on, then?", and they'd put themselves in a right position now... but nothing compared to the position she was about to try... as she uttered the immortal words "I'm going to do the froggy on Brandon now".

With that, she pulled my trousers down and jumped on top of me... the position so-called because her legs apparently look like that of a frog. Shortly after Long'un explained that, "actually, this is really quite strange, this hasn't happened before, but I think I am actually getting a bit turned on".

So she beckoned him over and he unashamedly joined in. Moments later, there was a knock on the door and it was Pecker, one of my old mates from Ibiza, who had come up to Leeds for the weekend. He was stood there looking at the spectacle in front of him and said "I'm only young, this is too much for me"... before running out of the room.

I can't even remember this girl's name, but she's out there, hopping around somewhere, possibly 'doing the froggy' every and now and then still... ribbit... ribbit...

Lisa Loud argues that she had her fair share of stalkers, but is thankful that, where the leading female DJs were concerned, the rules appeared to be different.

I was desired in the same way, but I think I managed it better than the boys, and, of course, it was different because they were boys...and boys will be boys. Guys queuing up for the female DJs just didn't happen and it wasn't really appropriate for some reason.

I always had long-term boyfriends and I was never out there on the pull and that was very evident. I did get stalked, though, and had to get the police involved at one point.

And the subject of Lisa Loud's so-called long-term boyfriends will always be a sore one for Brandon, who maintains he only ever had eyes for one person.

Lisa Loud was very unattainable, but to me she was always the most desirable woman in the world. Guys couldn't get near Lisa and Lisa because you had to get past us, and if anyone did they had to get permission from me.

Lisa Loud seemed to go out with a lot of my mates, which I was always unhappy about. It probably seemed more than it was, and was actually only a couple of people. I did snog Lisa Loud once and I will remember that until the day I die. It seems like a second ago.

But Loud hits back-

I loved Brandon too much as a friend and I just couldn't see me and him any other way than that. And in any case, I ended up being friends with every single girl he went out with.

Meanwhile, if Brandon was finding it difficult to hide his feelings for his FUBAR partner, then Loud was not completely enamoured with the 'Blocko & Peasy' DJ partnership, which was beginning to dominate proceedings. She reveals:-

Me and Brandon were the original DJ pair, and then he met Alex P and dumped me. Some muscley Greek God came along, who could pull another couple of thousand birds on top of the hundreds Brandon was already pulling and all of a sudden it was much more fun gallivanting around with Alex, dressed in togas. 'Blocko & Peasy' were born. Suddenly Batman and Robin had burst on the scene!

A picture is emerging of Brandon being not only an opportunist with his fans, but also a hopeless romantic and as Swainy recalls, the emphasis was quite often on "hopeless".

I remember, we drove down to Devon for a gig, and there were these really strong pills about. Brandon was driving back the next day, and I was coming round and as I woke up, he said "mate, we need to have a chat". I looked round and there was this bird on the backseat. Brandon had managed to fall in love overnight and persuaded this girl to leave her boyfriend and move in with him. She packed her bags and everything, except an hour or so down the road after talking it through with me, he'd changed his mind again. We pulled over at the next services and he gave the poor thing £100 to get a cab back home.

Meanwhile, where better to gallivant to than Ibiza, as the 1995 season approached?

Another stint for me on the Space terrace alongside Alex was guaranteed, and for the summer of '95, I would be playing almost every day at Space, plus regular sets with Clockwork Orange and

Up Yer Ronson, who after successful debuts in 1994 were both planning to up their games even more that summer.

The Clockwork Orange work was coming thick and fast for us, with nights at BCM in Majorca as well as Es Paradis, and then out of season back in the UK. Also regular work for Danny and Andy at their Ibiza reunion nights at Camden Palais, alongside other DJs who played regularly for the boys, people like John Kelly, Loudy and Seb Fontaine, not forgetting Clockwork's long-running monthly residency at The Cross.

Brandon and many of his fellow DJs on the so-called 'superclub' circuit were now in some quarters regarded, dare we say it, as too cheesy, and this signified the delicate genre splits and the pigeon-holing of certain DJs across clubland. The huge May Bank Holiday Tribal Gathering event in Oxford in the summer of '95 saw the Chemical Brothers headlining a largely electronic and specialist house line-up. It also featured the likes of Darren Emerson, Phil Perry and Justin Robertson, but there was already little chance of Brandon being invited to play at the likes of Tribal Gathering.

In Ibiza that summer, meanwhile, it was a couple of other familiar faces that would again provide a playground for Brandon and Alex to avail themselves of, because fortunately for all concerned, Roberto and Ernesto were back with some more Balearic beach activity.

In 1995, Roberto and Ernesto relocated to the beach at d'Es Codolar for some more fun in the sun during the afternoon after Space. This place was in the middle of nowhere. It was a pebbly beach - think Brighton - and someone had given them this huge parachute, which they had used to erect a canopy, while they had an old ice cream cart to put the decks on. Reche and Carlos Diaz were residents and we played a bit down there, but this was 1995, there had been a year's gap between the Tahiti and this beach party, and there were a lot more DJs who had made their names on the island since then, what with 1994 being such a pivotal year. We didn't expect to play every time we went and, to be honest, we had so much on the go, to have an afternoon off and simply get smashed was most welcome.

And in any case, there was plenty of fun to be had back at Mambo.

'Ha-son' Bye was now firmly on the firm, and as the summer of 1995 played out, he was quickly playing straight man to the two-headed funny guy that was 'Blocko & Peasy', and remembers:-

I'd be there every day from 2pm through to 2am, with various people like Brandon and Alex jumping on and off throughout the day. After about six weeks, Manumission asked me to be their resident at the back room at Ku, then Amnesia asked me to be full-time resident there, and that lasted four years.

In those early days at Mambo, Brandon and Alex would turn up in sarongs, constantly on their brick phones, Brandon with peroxide blond hair at the time. They had a big bag of roman sandals under the decks, which they would rummage through, saying "right, what ones are we going to wear today?". DJs like John Kelly would also turn up wearing sarongs, and they would all hug each other. And it was the first time I'd seen geezers hug before. It was all new to me, I was just out of Walthamstow, Hackney, that short of area.

But Mambo was so different then, anyway. You could have been anywhere in the world, there was nothing there, you didn't have the promenade, the hotels, which these days people stumble out of, straight down the parade to Mambo. It was just rocks.

Brandon and Alex were always so good to me, apart from anything else, giving me all the chill-out stuff they'd been sent because as Brandon would say, "we don't play any of that shit".

There were the times when you just couldn't get the boys off the decks...they'd be playing acid house when they were meant to be doing chill-out or whatever, and I'd be saying "do you mind if I jump back on boys?" and they'd be saying "fuck off Ha-son, we made this gaff".

I'll always respect the Del Mar...but they wouldn't have really encouraged the likes of me to play there. Jose Padilla was always on, and it was strictly chill-out, unlike Mambo, where it was a case of "on you go, let's see what you can do".

And soon the hospitality afforded to all DJs, up-and-coming and established alike, was the talk of Ibiza, and sunset aside, a non-chill out approach was positively encouraged.

A quick look at the priceless picture galleries in the main bar today reveals that literally anybody that is anybody in the global DJ world has played at Mambo. We haven't got space to list them here, but it is literally everyone.

Jason Bye was certainly green under the gills when me and Alex first stumbled into Mambo. In fact, we must have seemed like a whirlwind to him when we first turned up. Immediately, however, he became an integral part of our lives. Anyone who knows him well, will tell you Jason is a lovely fella, and he has gone on to do very well for himself. He must have played with virtually every big-name DJ at Mambo over the years.

Bye continues:-

Suddenly it was like a who's who of DJs. People like designer John Galliano would be hanging out there, Sasha and Carl Cox were asking to play, and Pete Tong started doing his Radio 1 shows live from Mambo with 5,000 people on the beach.

At the end of most nights, Brandon would be plugging my headphones into the mixer, so he could use them as a mic and sing Rapper's Delight, and Alex would be shouting something like "we've had your money, now fuck off". I've used that line all over the world, and people say, "that's a great line", but I always credit Alex.

Brandon and Alex's other catchphrase was "hold tight you nutbags"...and I reckon if they had got T-shirts printed with that on one season they'd have made a fortune...everyone was saying it.

There was always loads of girls around, but it always seemed to be more about having a laugh than anything else.

"Hold tight you nutbags" was born the night that Frank Bruno took on Mike Tyson in 1995.

Myself and Alex brought the West End of San Antonio to a halt with our plans for the biggest fight of Frank's life, which was scheduled for 4am, thus meaning everyone could get suitably smashed before the action started. For this momentous bout we were based at Simples Bar, owned by our great friend Julian, and now called Soul City. With the fight about to begin, I called for quiet and shouted over the mic, the now immortal words, "hold tight you nutbags". The place erupted.

Nutbag had been a word I'd used for a few seasons, and it was soon all over the island. Brad Pitt even uttered the words "he's a nutbag" in the film Se7en, so good phrases obviously travel fast.

That happened a lot in those days. Me and Peezee often came up with war cries which seemed to be taken on by everyone. "Avin' It" was a little number of ours, later to be shouted over a few Radio 1 Ibiza weekend broadcasts, by the man himself Pete Tong when caught up in the moment, and also adopted by many.

Since his big break at Mambo, Bye has gone on to carve out an internationally-acclaimed DJ career and has also played at the Sunday We Love...session at Space since the late '90s, but all that's a far cry from his daily orders from Brandon at Mambo to play probably one of THE cheesiest records ever.

I always wanted to play at Space on Sundays, because Brandon and Alex did, so it's amazing that I've been able to do that all these years.

But I'll never forget one unlikely Mambo 'anthem' - the Holiday Rap by MC Miker G and Deejay Sven. It sampled Madonna's hit Holiday and had the chorus line "we're gonna ring-a-reng-a-dong for a holiday".

The track was at the end of one of my Streetsounds albums, and I got distracted talking to someone out the front one day, and Holiday Rap started to play. I ran back, but Brandon shouted "Leave it!". And then that was it, I had to play it every fucking day. The cry would go out... "Ha-son... ring-a-reng-a-dong". And we'd all be in the booth singing it. And the thing is, if I'd just played it on my own one day, everybody would have said "what's that idiot doing?", but because this lot were with me, it was suddenly funny, and everybody would get stuck in and actually singalong to it.

For the record, the video to Holiday Rap, which can readily be found on YouTube, is probably one of the funniest, most kitsch, things on there. And a must if you're having a bad day at work.

However, there was, it seems, never a bad day's work at Cafe Mambo...not for Brandon, not for Bye, and especially not for coolest kid in his school, one Christian Anadon-Wilson.

Aged just 13 years old when his dad opened Mambo, this was one teenager who needed no encouragement where getting involved in the family business was concerned.

My dad is Spanish and met my mum, who is Scottish, in Benidorm 37 years ago. I was born in Ibiza and I've lived here ever since hanging around with these crazy people.

When Mambo opened it was really exciting for me, and I used to hang around there as much as I could after school, washing the dishes, doing anything I could to help.

I remember the day I first met Brandon. It was in 1994, and he was dancing around the DJ booth with loads of pretty girls, and my Dad said, "go and ask that man 'what have you been taking?'"... so I said "Brandon, what have you been taking today?"... and he looked at me shocked and said "nothing, mate, honestly, nothing". Knowing what I know now it must have been hilarious.

Brandon has been coming to Mambo ever since, and he was always really nice to me. I always used to admire him because everybody wanted to talk to him and he just seemed to be having so much fun.

I remember walking from the family house one day, and this jeep came past, and Brandon was in it with loads of people, and he was standing up in it as the jeep pulled over. He said "jump in", and they took me down to Mambo. I was hanging out on the beach with him and his mates, they were all wearing sarongs, with their Calvin Klein boxer shorts underneath, drinking loads of jugs of sangria.

It was fantastic for me as a kid. I was off school for most of the summer anyway, and I'd be hanging with Brandon, the guys from Faithless, John Galliano and Shovel from M-People.

These days the 'Mambo Family', as the Anadon family have dubbed it on their various websites, boasts enough San Antonio nightlife for a West End strip of their own - including one Irish pub; a Scottish bar; sushi, tapas and Italian restaurants; a live music venue; that themed pirate bar Bucanero and another sunset bar Savannah, just down the promenade, and managed by Christian.

And it could have been so different if Brandon had taken up his interest in the site, or at least, had been in a fit state to even contemplate opening a bar just down the way from Cafe Del Mar, previously his spiritual home in San Antonio.

But by the end of the 1995 Ibiza season it was clear that despite the fun and frolics and sun-soaked shenanigans, the Balearic clubbing mecca and its reckless devil may care attitude was only helping to fuel Brandon's coke addiction further.

Taking ten grams a day in Ibiza was 'doable' (for want of a better word) because he was DJing every day and hopping from after-party to after-party in between, and all on an island where excess is positively encouraged.

On one occasion that summer, sitting on the terrace at the BCM club in Majorca enjoying the afternoon sun with a group of girls, a piece of the septum from my nose fell out as I was chatting. Several of those lady friends vomited, while I calmly put the mangled piece of flesh, gristle, blood and white powder on top of an empty bottle of beer. I thought if the sun dried it out, that I might able to get some coke out of it?

Despite such acts of debauchery and an apparent licence to shock, Brandon was still DJing the world over, the notoriety from his sets at Space helping him clock up thousands of hazy road and air miles every winter. His rapid descent into cocaine addiction, not exactly the cheapest of pastimes, was only possible because of the DJ fees, now well into four figures, Brandon was able to command.

Earlier that summer Brandon and Alex had cashed in on their Ibiza fame by fronting a Clockwork Orange compilation, 'mixed live at Es Paradis', which one reviewer on Amazon describes as "verging on hard house, without being cheesy".

Now, in the autumn of 1995, Brandon had the first volume of his Fantazia Club Classics compilation to promote, with the second and third volumes following quickly in 1996.

Brandon's track selection for the releases shows an insight to his favourite house records up to that point (or what he liked from the big list of the ones available for licence, more like) and are:-

Club Classics Volume 1
1 Take Me Away (Pinned Up Mix) – True Faith
2 Made In Two Minutes (Rave Mix) – Bug Khan & The Plastic Jam
3 The Last Rhythm – Last Rhythm
4 Not Forgotten (Hard Hands Mix) – Leftfield
5 Go – Moby
6 On Ya Way – Helicopter
7 The 10th Planet (Ashley Beedle Mix) – Strings Of Life
8 Choc The Beat (Piano Mix) – Electric Choc
9 Temperature Rising (Bigger and Better Mix) – PKA
10 Hunter – Herbal Infusion
11 Move Your Body – X-Pansions
12 What You Need (LuvDup's Sat At Home Mix) – Soft House Co
13 Shine On – Degrees Of Motion
14 Right Before My Eyes (House Vocal Mix) – Patti Day

Club Classics Volume 2
1 Anthem - Joi
2 Such A Good Feeling (Inspirational Delight Mix) - Brothers In Rhythm
3 Everybody All Over The World - FPI Project
4 Don't You Want To Be Mine – Denise Lopez
5 It's My Pleasure - My Friend Sam
6 My Love – Collapse
7 Show Some Love – Jaco
8 Song Of Life – Leftfield
9 Energy Flash – Joey Beltram
10 I Kill Love - TNT

11 Rhythm Is A Mystery – Klass
12 Push The Feeling On - Nightcrawlers
13 Rhythm On The Loose (Rhythm On The Loose Mix)
   - Break Of Dawn

Club Classics Volume 3
1 Think About – DJ H & Stefy
2 Let Your Body Be Free – Volcano
3 Where Love Lives – Alison Limerick
4 40 Miles – Congress
5 Perfect Motion (Boy's Own Mix) – Sunscreem
6 It's Gonna Be A Lovely Day – Soul System
7 Plastic Dreams – JayDee
8 Out There – Friends Of Matthew
9 Everybody's Free – Rozalla
10 Berry – TC 1991
11 Kenetic (Frank De Wulf Remix) – Golden Girls
12 Degrees Of Passion – Gat Decor
13 Belfast - Orbital

I got gold discs for all of the Club Classics releases. Given how many were sold of each release, it was a shame because I only got paid something like £1,000 for each, a flat fee, no points deal, but again, great profile though. They are still some of the best-selling dance CDs to this day, 100,000 plus each of them.

I remember when I was due to record Club Classics Volume 1 and Jimmy, from Fantazia, was due down from Gloucester to record it at my mum's on a DAT machine, back in the good old days when you had to use vinyls and record decks.

I'd mentioned to him that my speakers weren't up to much. And on the day he turned up with this pair of brand new speakers, which he'd been sold by an opportunist white van man.

You know, the kind that used to hang around petrol garages in the '90s, looking for victims. Jim thought he'd had a right touch, but they only cost a score and were worse than what I already had.

I did use them in the end, and recorded the mix, off my knackers, and in only two takes, which wasn't bad considering I was more wired than the national grid.

I also did the Dance Nation and Trance Nation comps for the Ministry Of Sound, with Tall Paul, which both went gold too. All the discs now have pride of place in my poker room.

Back home from another Ibiza summer, Brandon's DJ schedule was so relentless he could be playing out six times a week across three or four nights. His days off should, and would, have been a perfect time to wind down and vitally be cocaine-free. But not Brandon! Somehow he managed to bring that Ibiza snorting form back with him and also managed to fund it too.

Not every day, but some days ten grams, so most afternoons, into the evening and through the night. Every morning, a line when I surfaced to get me going. Hedonistic when you're in Ibiza and you've got up at four in the afternoon, worrying when it's a rainy November morning in Wembley.

The backdrop to all this was still my mum's house in Sudbury. That small box room, always filled with records and designer clothes, and more recently covered with flyers, was now full of bulging ashtrays and strewn with empty coke wraps.

I never really had any money. I'd earn it and spend it on gear. But the more I earned the more gear I seemed to get through. Soon there simply was no time for me to recover, even if I wanted.

That addiction was my life, I lived for the shit. I can't explain how much I was doing. If I had been sitting at home talking to someone for two or three hours I would have done a quarter of an ounce, or about seven grams, while they were there chatting.... all day...every day.

Karen Dunn had witnessed both Brandon's meteoric rise in the DJ world, and his rapid decline into cocaine dependency.

Brandon was earning serious money now... but his coke habit was consuming all of it. He was one of my bigger earners... two or three gigs in the week, two or three on a Friday and two or three on a Saturday...and that lasted for many years.

Everybody loved him... and because he was getting so many bookings, I think that's why he began to take so much gear, simply to keep him up all night and week. But he wasn't a DJ's DJ. Lots of DJs who, let's just say were very into themselves at the time, didn't like his success. They were jealous of him, I think, because of the amount of work he got. They slagged him off for not playing the cooler records. But the crowd loved him because he was so naughty. He was a real crowd pleaser, in fact, just good fun to have around. He'd stand on the decks, all sorts, really play up to the crowd.

Tony Hannan agrees.

Lots of DJs have their sets mapped out beforehand, know exactly what they're going to play, and in what order, but Brandon was always one to get in there, have a good look first and give the crowd exactly what they wanted.

Critics may argue he was too busy mapping out his drug intake to pre-plan a set. Karen Dunn adds:-

Brandon soon became a nightmare to deal with. He made up so many lies, constant excuses and I became a very good liar myself because of him. I once had to charter a helicopter to get him to a gig because a promoter was so furious at him potentially not turning up, after all the money he'd spent on everything in the lead-up to the event, and the large deposit he'd already laid out. But Brandon was off his head somewhere and unable to get to the other side of the street, let alone the country.

And those promoters were paying him a lot of money, and had done loads of promotion. It eventually came to a head and it started to affect his work and his reputation. There was always a party to go to for Brandon, and he started going out and staying up for days on end.

Amazingly, Brandon cannot remember the helicopter ride! Or which club! But he had worked out that a complex network of dealers

*(clockwise) * The Star Ferry, Hong Kong*
* The blonde peroxide hair look with
Cafe Mambo resident 'Has-on' Bye
* Christian Anadon-Wilson and Jason Bye
*at Cafe Mambo * Lisa Loud at work!*

sundessential (BIRMINGHAM)
PRESENT
THE ULTIMATE MORNING PA[RTY]
AT
space
ON THE TERRACE FOR THE FIRST AND ONLY TIME THIS [...]
DJ'S:
BRANDON BLOCK & ALEX P
(KINGS OF IBIZA)
JOHN KELLY, LISA LOUD,
TONY ONETO & ANDY MANSTON
INSIDE
DJ'S:

GOODTIME PROMOTIONS PRESENT
EDE[N]
THE CLOSING PAR[TY]

BRANDON BLOCK & ALEX P.
PAUL JACKSON - JASON BYE - J[...]
NORRIS WINDROSS
FRIDAY 8th SEPTEMB[ER]
amnesia

was vital to help provide enough coke to keep the UK's best loved party animal partying. And there were more than enough dealers happy to relieve him of his cash.

Disturbingly, there was less and less emphasis on the party aspect of it all. More and more now, the coke was a necessity, not a luxury.

I'd stopped doing lines for a while. It was half a teaspoon full of coke at a time now. I tried to cultivate three or four dealers per day at different times. This rota was alternated on every third or fourth day, so as not to give the impression I was taking too much. Little did I know, they were all talking to each other, and keeping up the pretence for me too. It was also at this time that I discovered that Rohypnol (which were nicknamed 'roeys') could help me sleep, long before it was linked to date-rape. A chemist friend of mine would supply these, plus any extra painkillers when my need exceeded what my local GP was prepared to prescribe.

But the roeys would, at best, only ever get me three hours sleep as my coke intake greatly outweighed even the largest doses of the sleeping tablets.

During the winter of 1995 I was caning the painkillers, in this case distalgesics given to me by the family doctor for the increasing aches and pains that were crippling my body.

As well as the drugs, I was drinking like a fish. Hanging around in pubs waiting for supplies certainly wasn't helping.

And my GP was losing his patience. They don't say they know you're on the gear, but they do, they're not stupid. I was getting those cocaine itches, where it feels like you've got insects under your skin, and the most terrible pains in my back. I was at the doctors every week with some excuse or other.

But what Brandon didn't know at that time, was that he had contracted the disease tuberculosis, almost certainly a result of that idiotic plunge from the Star Ferry in Hong Kong.

My GP was saying he was not giving me any more painkillers, but I was getting extra on the side from my pal and banging away at the gear relentlessly too, and then there was the booze - beer, vodka, anything really. As well as my back, my chest was hurting badly as well, so my doctor sent me to hospital for some X-rays and they discovered I had TB, and an unusual strain of it at that. I was rushed straight to an isolation ward.

But despite the obvious desperation of this situation (well to most, anyway) I was still craving the cocaine that I had simply relied on more and more. I was slowly going crazy in there and, when I could, I was on my mobile begging friends to bring some coke to me at the hospital. I drove some so mad that they did in fact bring it in. Mentioning no names, because I really did have to persuade those in question.

And remember I was literally in isolation, it's like being in a cage at the zoo. The only contact with visitors is through two rubber gloves which are attached through holes in the wall, so I ingeniously conjured up a plan of biting the tip of the index finger off one of the gloves, enabling one visitor under particular duress to, instead of 'delivering me from evil', delivering me some evil, when I shook hands with him.

Then, when the visitors had gone, I'd use anything I could find in and around my bed to snort the coke off. I was in there ten days and getting a delivery most days. It was freaking the nurses out because they were doing my tests and the 'obs' (observation results) were all over the place. I didn't care, I just needed the gear.

Upon my release, I headed back to my mum's. I had missed a couple of week's worth of gigs, but would be back on the road again shortly, as long as normal business was resumed with my dealers.

They sent me home, I had this health visitor and I was on a triple therapy treatment for the TB, which is basically three different pills throughout the day.

The pills kill the TB, so that gets cleared quite quickly, then the rest of it is prevention, which I wasn't helping with the coke I was tucking away daily. The staff at Northwick Park Hospital did regular tests on me and I was told the TB was still there, but that it wasn't contagious. I knew I couldn't stop sniffing so I thought "fuck it". I was almost at rock bottom and all the gear was at least helping to numb some of the pains I had. But more and more smoking meant my lungs were taking a huge battering as well. I was still bang on the gear and back on the piss too.

And *"pissing all over Craig from Malibu Stacey's shoes because he thought he was a urinal"* as well... according to Dan Prince in MixMag, at least.

And the TB did at least, inadvertently, spare Brandon a drink-driving ban, although it is clear that by now, given his daily cocaine consumption, being behind the wheel of a car was the last place he should be.

After the dubious honour of 'doing the froggy in Leeds', Brandon's mate Toady cut short a stretch of bird in Manchester after one midweek DJ gig/roadtrip to the Hacienda saw Brandon spending the night in Salford Police Station.

Despite having various drivers over the years, I was still keen to drive to some of my gigs, especially if I'd just managed to scrape together enough money for a new motor, and for this trip I wanted to give my new BMW a run out. We were heading to an after-party and as I pulled up outside this house on the outskirts of Manchester I could see and hear a flashing blue light in the distance. I was unaware that we'd been followed, so I told my car-full to get into the house, while I dealt with the police.

They breathalysed me and I was slightly over the limit, taken to the station and banged up in a cell while they tried to persuade me not to request a blood test. However, my stay at the station was short lived after Toady called up and told them I had TB. The cell door opened, and I was quickly ushered out and told to leave immediately. The last thing they wanted was a disease-ridden DJ spreading germs.

As 1995 wore on the promoters of my residencies were putting up with my increasingly erratic behaviour, and somehow I was still managing to deliver behind the decks.

I'm convinced I got the TB in Hong Kong. It wasn't like I was hanging around crack dens, although, in the depths of my addiction, I was now dabbling with a bit of crack too.

TB is a nasty business. The disease killed millions before the discovery of antibiotics and even today it needs careful long-term treatment to be beaten. An airborne disease that preys on immune systems too weak to fight it, the bacteria infects your chest and eats you from the inside. Whether it was strong enough to fully penetrate Brandon Block at that point is debatable.

November 1995 came and went in a fog of motorways, DJ booths, bags of white powder and sleepless nights, as did most of December too. It was a struggle to make it to gigs like the Full Monty in Windsor with Rocky & Diesel, Malibu Stacey in London's West End with Stuart Patterson, and motorway gigs at Pimp in Wolverhampton and Karanga in Bath.

Then there was a high profile Boxing Day gig in Sheffield for Gatecrasher alongside Alex, De Vit, Judge Jules and Fontaine, but Brandon didn't make it.

On Christmas Eve he and Alex were driving to a gig in Harrow, when Brandon heaved and urged Alex to pull over.

I got out of the car and said to Alex "watch this". I felt it, could taste it, and proceeded to vomit a whole pint of blood all over one of the white lines in the road. Literally covered it in claret, deep red it was, like someone had cut my throat. Alex looked at me and said, "right... hospital... now!".

I spent the night in nearby Northwick Park Hospital. It would be easy to say I woke up in the hospital on Christmas Day, but I couldn't get any sleep I was so wired, especially not as my trusty 'roeys' were at home. Alex stayed with me, and we both missed our gig that night. Friends, including Jenny Rampling, my DJ agent at the time, visited as news filtered through. Other pals waiting for me at the club headed to the hospital too.

I was put straight back on the isolation ward and various tests were done. Despite my addled-state, I sensed that the doctors were starting to wash their hands of me, because they thought I didn't care, which in some ways was true. I started to think I was going to die. The doctors were saying that the TB wasn't dead and although it wasn't communicable, I needed to stop doing drugs.

The health visitors started coming to my mum's house when I got out and amazingly my blood pressure and other results seemed OK, but I was bang on it and bang on the scene still. I was out there on my own in terms of drug taking, nobody I knew could touch me in terms of volume, and despite that it still took me six or seven months to get to the point of even wanting to give up.

I was prescribed another six months' worth of pills for the TB, but after three months was advised to stop because I was mixing these strong prescribed drugs with everything else, and risking even more complications.

Jenny Rampling, who ran her Selective Management agency with Fran Cutler from offices in Brewer Street, Soho, remembers Brandon's admission to hospital well.

He was in a bad way at that time, and he was in and out of hospital for a while, but I always stood by Brandon, and always will. He's such a lovely fella with such a big personality and I have always adored him. It's true I did insist on my DJs being reliable and consistent and Brandon often didn't reflect well on our agency, so I guess I made an exception with him.

But he was also on the road to loads more gigs too – in February alone, Republica in Birmingham (with Scott Bond), Decadence at UK Midlands in Wolverhampton (with De Vit), Lakota in Bristol and also much closer to home for Clockwork's Third Birthday (with Judge Jules) and Frisky at The Ministry with The Shamen and Josh Wink.

The recreational enjoyment had long gone. Looking back, when I came back from Ibiza in 1994 I felt like I was still in party mode. Sure I was doing stupid amounts of coke then, but I still felt like I was partying. However, at the end of 1995 it was now a need.

I was weighing about eight stone and slowly getting jaundice. More trips to hospital and more pain. I was on the road to death, but I didn't give a fuck now. I was putting a brave face on it in public, a classic case of tears of a clown, but this was beat myself up time, take as much gear as I could, and if I died, then it was easier than giving up.

CANER GET A WITNESS?

Brandon's DJ diary at the start of 1996 was bulging at the seams, but so was his notepad of which dealer was owed what.

With the summer season looming, he had gradually moved into his "ounce a day" era...

It got to the point where I couldn't get out of bed without doing a teaspoon full of coke first. Then I'd sprinkle some gear on my Coco Pops and get through an eighth (three and a half grams) by mid-morning. Then it was out to get another eighth and that was done before lunchtime. Then back for some more and another lot done during the afternoon and so on. I hadn't even reached early evening yet, but there were more eighths to collect and if I was playing somewhere that night then more coke would be done at the club. I was up all night whichever way I looked at it. I'd have to take three 'roeys' just to get one hour's sleep. Then wake up bolt upright and off I went again.

And remember this was proper gear, nothing like the shit people have today. I'd get the coke in different eighths from different dealers during any one day so it looked like I was only getting through an eighth a day, but they weren't fools and weren't fooled.

Going to get the next eighth gave me something to do and, perversely, my life had a structure. The structure was making sure that I stuck to the rota and visited everyone at the right time. I was clearly all over the place mentally and it's mad to think I was able to keep up with everything.

One morning I woke at 7.30am, probably on the back of 15 minutes' sleep or something stupid like that, and I quickly realised that the cupboard was bare.

Now I was also suffering from agoraphobia and severe paranoia and could no longer face the outside world unless under the influence.

Most of my dealers lived locally, but on this occasion not local enough, so I called on a 'friend' who was in staggering distance, and who I thought might be 'holding'. He agreed to help me out, but stressed on the phone "please be discreet". Mishearing him,

and in my batty state, I donned a handy clown's outfit, left over from a recent fancy dress party, and complete with big red wig and floppy shoes, stumbled round the corner and banged on his door. My pal leaned out of the window, looked down and said "I told you to be discreet", to which I replied "I thought you said come in disguise".

I was now mixing my own stuff to make it last longer, because I knew that I would be sharing it with other people I'd meet during the day, especially if I was sitting in the back of a record shop, in the pub or at a club later that night. I'd make sure I kept some of the original cleaner stuff back at home so I didn't leave myself short, because by this time there was no way I could be without it.

Brandon played The Gallery at Turnmills and Miss Moneypenny's and Republica in Birmingham in one April weekend in 1996 alone, all under the backdrop of a MixMag article boasting the headline "DEATH RUMOUR ENRAGES BLOCK" which reported:-

Brandon Block has reacted angrily to rumours that he has died of a cocaine overdose. The rumour surfaced on the internet, posted by a student from Reading University on the UK Dance Bulletin board using the name "Sorcerer's Apprentice".

The message suggested Block died on Wednesday February 21, and called his death "poetic justice".

"I don't know who did this," said Block. "But they must be sick. It's the poetic justice bit that gets to me, they've obviously got no respect whatsoever. I've got the CID looking into it, to try and find who did it."

Reading University Ents co-ordinator Maxine Duffett confirmed it was a student who posted the message, and that Block didn't turn up to a gig, even though he let the University Union know two weeks in advance. "It was a fucking stupid thing to do," she said.

So the reports were exaggerated, but not grossly!

In May of '96, Muzik Magazine, which had been launched a year earlier by magazine giant IPC, the owners of NME and Melody Maker, as a dance music rival to MixMag and co, held their inaugural Saints & Sinners Awards.

An extension of the mag's Saints & Sinners page, of which Brandon was not surprisingly a frequent participant, the gongs became known as The SAS Awards, and first took place at the International Convention Centre in Birmingham. Dance music's royalty turned out in force for what was the industry's first such high profile awards ceremony.

Brandon romped home in the Caner Of The Year category. Other awards went to The Prodigy (Best Live Act), Carl Cox (Best DJ), Derrick Carter (Best New DJ), Underworld's Second Toughest In The Infants (Best Album) and Cream (Club Of The Year and Worst Toilets).

The accompanying issue of Muzik in July included a picture of Brandon, strangely looking reasonably healthy, being interviewed by Simone Angel from MTV, and explained:-

The Caner Of The Year award was hotly contested, with Paul Broughton of Brookside and Eden fame and Back To Basics' Dave Beer both arriving mob-handed. However, rumours of an untimely death clinched it for the winner, Mr Brandon Block.

To tumultuous applause, Brandon approached the podium under a barrage of bread rolls. During his acceptance speech, he waved a wrap of what must have been castor sugar and snorted heavily, leaving white powder all over his face. A deserved winner.

But castor sugar this was not!

My mates Lewis and Roey were throwing the bread rolls. I said "can I thank all the promoters and bar and club owners that have made it possible for me to win this award. I've got a little speech here", and I opened up a wrap of gear, which looked like I was unfolding a piece of paper, and sniffed the whole lot up, adding "thank you very much".

It wasn't castor sugar at all, let me assure you of that. Channel 4, who were filming, had to cut my speech out of their highlights show.

I think it was our era that really made that Caner Of The Year award possible, and if ever an award was made for someone, I guess that was it.

While Brandon was putting so much thought into his drug taking, his DJ agent Jenny Rampling, who had managed to sign him exclusively from a worn-out Karen Dunn, was booking him up for the rest of 1996 and beyond. Brandon's no-shows were becoming more and more frequent, though. Jenny points out:-

It wasn't easy dealing with the promoters at the time. In some instances they had paid 50% up front, and on some occasions I had to repay those deposits. But Brandon has always been a dear friend of mine and I will always protect him to the hilt. In fact, I became shit-hot at covering for him.

At Easter, Brandon had played at a Club 4 Life and Wobble collaboration in Birmingham, while May saw him guest at an 'Ibiza Sendoff' at Love To Be in Sheffield (a month before he would land once more on The White Isle), at Frisky at The Ministry, plus usual spots at The Gallery, Clockwork Orange and at Leicester University, plus Naughty But Nice in Hereford.

Despite those hospital scares, Brandon had settled into this potentially fatal routine and another season at his beloved Balearic clubbing Mecca was only weeks away. Residencies at three of the island's biggest venues - a punishing enough schedule for a teetotal, let alone this walking, snorting wreck of a man – meant he had a job on his hands.

However, that's where the coke comes in, because throw 28 grams a day into the equation, add some sun on his back and sprinkle with fawning fans, in particular the female variety, and there was a slim chance he might just get through until the end of September.

However, Brandon's situation was now even beyond his powers of 'avin it'. 'Ave it' he could not, well not for the full season, anyway.

He flew back from Ibiza for gigs with Gatecrasher, Passion in Coalville, London residencies and a trip to Ireland for an Up Yer Ronson tour date at Lush in Portrush.

But as well as his Space residency on a Sunday, he now had Saturdays with Up Yer Ronson at Amnesia and most Wednesdays with Clockwork Orange at Es Paradis, as well as various one-offs for Summons and Sundance. If he could manage to dodge DJ cohort Alex

P, then he wasn't going to evade the likes of Tony Hannan and Danny Gould for long.

A hilarious Up Yer Ronson photoshoot showed Hannan and his resident and guest acts and DJs for the season lounging by (and in) a pool, and included Mike Pickering, Paul Heard and Shovel (all then M-People), plus Allister Whitehead, Sasha and Jeremy Healy. Brandon hadn't made the photoshoot, and was increasingly withdrawing from these kind of circles too.

Ahead of that summer he and Alex P had mixed one side of a triple CD compilation from Up Yer Ronson, called Summer Of Ninety Six, with Marshall and Jon Marsh from The Beloved mixing discs two and three. And as well as his superclub residencies, Brandon was always in demand for sunset spots at Mambo and Kanya in San Antonio, as well as other guest spots for the Ministry Of Sound at Pacha, the huge Sundance raves at the old zoo near San An and at a new night called Beautiful at El Divino.

It was a relentless schedule and unfortunately, in just six years, Brandon was Ibiza-d out!

Tony Hannan reports from the frontline.

I'm not sure why Brandon wasn't in the photo of us all by the pool in 1996, which was taken at Pikes, but around that time he was in a bad way and if he could get out of things he would.

That summer, when we had the Up Yer Ronson villa in Cala Conta, Brandon was one of our residents and rooming with me, and he was in big trouble. As much as he was addicted to the cocaine, he had a massive problem with Rohypnol too. I remember he had about 300 of them with him, and he was doing loads every day just to come off the coke.

I needed some as well, to be honest, but nowhere near as much as Brandon. And that's when I saw him smoking crack as well. At that point there seemed to be not much off the menu for Brandon. There were lots of crack spliffs going around and it was like the rock and roll part of it all had gone too rock and roll. This was serious shit now. Something had to give and it was clear that Brandon had a massive battle on his hands.

The combination of everything he was taking and the TB simply meant that the game was up. Fortunately for Brandon, his body was still able to tell him that enough was enough. It was no surprise when he had to leave Ibiza early that summer.

I remember coming back from that full season myself, and that it took me a good seven weeks to really sort my head out. The partying was just relentless, and when I got back home it hit me like a train.

Still hungry for gossip, MixMag ran another groundbreaking feature in their August issue - 101 THINGS YOU WISH YOU'D NEVER DONE IN YOUR CLUBBING LIFE, with No 22, declaring – "Agreeing to a lock-in with Dave Beer, Charlie Chester and Brandon Block".

And in the same issue Dan Prince joked about *"the amazing sight of a naked Brandon Block standing on the hard shoulder of the M1 at four in the morning, being rubbed with dock leaves by his mates after falling head first into a bed of stinging nettles. God only knows what's going to happen when his telly show with Alex P gets going. The mind boggles."*

Back in London again and Brandon at least felt at home.

It got towards the end of the '96 season and I was so twisted – mentally and physically - but I wasn't going quickly enough. I couldn't see how I could carry on and the few days that I did get some sleep I hoped I wouldn't wake up. I just wanted it to end.

I was getting more and more paranoid in Ibiza. Everybody wanted a piece of me. I missed the relative solitude of my mum's place. Everybody was coming out to Ibiza on their holidays, wanting to party hard with me, the so-called Ibiza legend, and it was harder and harder to hide my addiction. A lot of people coming out were still recreational users, but I was tucking it away like there was no tomorrow, and quite frankly I didn't care if there was a tomorrow.

When I returned to London I felt better sitting at home on my own, doing the gear, without having to leave the house, well, not unless I needed any more.

Vivienne Block was now fully aware that her son was in dire straits.

As time went on things obviously became a lot clearer. I used to sit with him, at all hours of the morning, to comfort him and to see if I could get him to sleep. He wouldn't do the coke in front of me, but I knew he was going off to do it in his room or wherever. By then he was too far gone, I guess, and I would just try and be there for him, trying to calm him down. It was the actual state he was in that was so alarming, he was suicidal. And I was going through my own personal relationship problems at the time, so it was a very emotional time for both of us. I found the whole thing totally overwhelming and my weight dropped to under six stone.

I also started smoking crack more, washing it up from coke myself, just to get another, different buzz, and also to relieve the overall boredom.

My body was dying, I had pains everywhere. My nose was crusty around the nostrils and there was this terrible cocaine smell, that industrial, freebase smell that comes with crack or coke, and which I was largely unaware of. The pain reverberated throughout my chest, lungs and liver. I was so wired up, I could feel every organ in my body creaking. I felt dirty from inside out. The cocaine itches felt like there were spiders crawling up and down inside my veins, like one of those ant farms, insects constantly going up and down. I was forever scratching and itching, it felt like my pulses were pulsating with poison. The pain was in waves, but there were also dull aches, which were constant, and then more and more piercing, interspersed with muscular spasms, and knowing you're really ill and thinking that you might keel over at any point, just adds to the anxiety. Your brain can't tell you you're in trouble, you're oblivious, out of your head, but the pain is always there to remind you.

I suffered terribly with my teeth too, and ended up getting barred from the dentist, because I booked so many appointments, but couldn't keep any. I'd turn up late, not at all, or out of my head. The dentist was having to use so much local anesthetic, which is Novacane based, to get past the cocaine I'd already taken, that one day he said enough was enough. He wouldn't treat me again.

THE LIFE & LINES OF BRANDON BLOCK

Now I was caning it like never before. Then one morning I was so riddled with illness I couldn't even get out of bed. The TB was still rife, it had stayed in my lung. Not actively contagious, but still there and until I stopped doing everything else the drugs for the TB would never work. I went to Northwick Park A & E and was just sitting there shaking. I hadn't been to sleep for three or four days. They told me to go and get some serious help. These days, I reckon they would section me or something, but back then they didn't seem to want to get that involved.

I was missing more and more gigs too. Jenny would be ringing up the promoters telling them I wasn't coming, but it only seemed to add to my notoriety. A lot of these promoters wanted to book me now more to party with them than for my music, so that they could party with 'the legend that is'.

But it wasn't as if Brandon could hibernate completely at home, there was the little matter of his autumn/winter schedule to fulfill, and thousands of pounds to be earned so he could pay for his monster habit.

Brandon was booked for dozens of nights up and down the UK around this time, and until the end of 1996. Too many to list here, and he cannot recall if he played at any of them anyway.

I would take so much gear at these gigs, all laid on by various people, and to be paid for at the end of the night, that I started to sniff more than I was getting paid. At a couple of clubs I had to pay an extra couple of hundred quid more just to get let out of the place! So I stopped going to some gigs, and stayed at home instead, doing smaller amounts that I had there.

MixMag, meanwhile, were still plugging away with their coverage of Brandon, including a profile of him, in their DJ CORNER section in November, 1996. It included the following:-

(clockwise) * Death rumours in MixMag
* An interview with Simone Angel for MTV
at the 1996 Muzik Magazine SAS Awards
* As Elvis with great buddy Jeremy Healy
* Brandon's very own Viz comic strip

Death Rumour Enrages Block

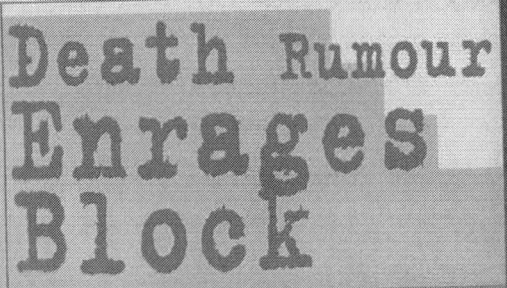

BRANDON Block has reacted angrily to rumours that he has died of a cocaine overdose. The rumour surfaced on the Internet, posted by a student from Reading University on the UK Dance bulletin board using the name 'Sorcerer's Apprentice'.

"...ted Block died on Wednesday ...etic justice."
..., "but they must ...ts to me, they've ...I've got the CID

Brandon Block

'avey 'avey 'avey
HE'S LIKE
BRANDON
BLOCK ON
CID...
CID!

Ronson
Ibiza

Brandon Block... on one again

mixmag

TIME: SUMMER 1996

thursdays at amnesia

SATURDAYS AT AMNESIA

AGENCY

FROM JUNE 27TH
FROM JUNE 29TH

DJS
JEREMY HEALY
JON PLEASED WIMMIN
JUDGE JULES
JUSTIN ROBERTSON
PAUL & RUSS (K-KLASS)
JOHN KELLY
DAVE SEAMAN
...VAN HELDEN
DOC MARTIN
DJ SNEAK
NORMAN JAY
TOM WAINWRIGHT
MARSHALL

CREAM RESIDENTS
PAUL BLEASDALE
ANDY CARROLL
PHIL COOPER

RONSON RESIDENTS
ALEX P
BRANDON BLOCK
PAUL MURRAY

BEST DJING EXPERIENCE: Probably Club 4 Life in Hong Kong in 1994

WORST DJ EXPERIENCE: I fell asleep under the mixer at FUBAR mid-mix...and I stayed there for the rest of the night

FAVOURITE FILM: Singing In The Rain

ADVICE TO ASPIRING DJS: Just enjoy your music and don't get disheartened if it doesn't happen immediately.

YOU'RE DEAD, YOU'VE GONE TO DJ HEAVEN, WHAT'S PLAYING IN THE ANGEL'S CHILL OUT ROOM:

Love Ballard – George Benson – "one of the greatest soul musicians with a song that is totally euphoric"

Glow Of Love – Change – "a very underplayed song, even today"

Back To The Beat – Todd Terry – "original house, tops"

Kaw Liga – The Residents – "top Balearic tune"

Play At Your Own Risk – Planet Patrol – "classic, innit?"

Friends were trying their best to warn Brandon about his extraordinary cocaine intake, but their concerns usually fell on deaf ears... and nostrils.

I drove down to a gig in Torquay one night and Paul Avery came with me. I had a quarter on me, in a bag between my legs and by the time I got there, with the help of a teaspoon, I'd done the lot. I was so wired I couldn't do the gig. Not until I'd sunk five pints, at least. Paul and a few other mates would tell me to take it easy, but I was just doing my own thing. However, their repeated warnings did eventually chip away at me, and I'm sure that helped.

Paul Avery had been chipping more than most, but wasn't convinced he was getting through.

You couldn't tell Brandon anything. He just wouldn't listen, but I'd like to think what his closest friends said to him did finally work. I didn't know anyone who could consume so much. That time on the way to Torquay, with that big bag of coke in his lap, he was literally eating it and didn't give a fuck. You sensed the music side of it had left him. I just couldn't see how he was going to play that night, but once I got a few pints down him and got him out there, he was off once more, and nobody could keep up with him again. He certainly had some constitution, probably unrivalled.

Matthew Donegan was as horrified as any of his old friends. Like many of Brandon's schoolmates, he had tried recreational drugs long before Brandon, but his old mucker had certainly made up for any lost time.

One day I was due to meet him at Wembley Park. We were meant to be going to have a bit of lunch, for a catch-up. He pulled up in his car at the station, with a big smile and loads of coke all over his face. He had a big bag of it in his lap, and he was shovelling it up his nose as he drove us to lunch. He ordered a big curry, and carried on snorting....it was only midday, but that was Brandon in his so-called prime.

It's terrible because I can't even remember those incidents with Paul and Matthew, and it's horrible hearing about them now. I can't imagine what some of my closest friends went through.

I'd also fallen out with Ali, around 1992, and I didn't speak to him properly for a good few years. One of the worst things about drugs is the paranoia, the simplest things being interpreted completely the wrong way. Me and Ali were sitting up somewhere, and it got out of hand and it was silly really.

After about four years, I broke the ice at Full Circle, and said "this is ridiculous". I was also fed up with having to try and sneak past him on the door at various places.

Ali was happy to be back on speaking terms with Brandon, if only so he could keep an eye on his old pal.

I think for me, because knowing him all that time and seeing how he was going, when we had that period, when we weren't talking, it was really hard for me, and I would find myself asking people around, how he was, and everyone just used to say "Brandon's Brandon", and it was so tough. I always tried my best to keep him out of trouble, but I wasn't around when he was really full-on, towards the end.

There was also a need to educate people around him, and make sure they were aware of what was going on, because his reputation really preceded him, and it got him in a lot of trouble because the more he could take, the more he would be offered.

Fortunately, somewhere, something inside told Brandon the game was up. Enough was enough, it was time to do something about this.

I was once again in the hospital emergency ward, clutching my sides, rocking backward and forward, completely wired after another night without sleep. The pain I was in was now debilitating, and no longer masked by the drugs, and I just couldn't tolerate this pain on a daily basis any more. It was then that I went to my dad and asked him if he knew anybody.

He knew the score and knew I needed help. A friend of his recommended Bill Shanahan, the Executive Medical Director and Lead Addiction Consultant Psychiatrist at Charter Nightingale Hospital in west London, who also practised in Harley Street.

Harvey Block explains:-

My partner at the time knew some people who knew some people at Charter Nightingale. And I was actually having dinner with her and her kids when Brandon phoned me and said he was dying, and didn't know if he could carry on. She put me in touch with a doctor there, who told me he would see Brandon. It was difficult for me because Brandon wanted me to take him down there, but I had been advised that, if he was in a physical condition to do so, he must travel there on his own, because that would show his willingness to try and get clean. So I said, "I'm sorry son, you have to go on your own, this is the address, they're expecting you, so get your arse down there". Thankfully, he did just that.

I can't actually remember going to see Bill, I was that fucked at the time, but I went on a Thursday and apparently sat there on this massive couch of his and literally paced up and down it, sitting down. He managed to pin me down at one point, though, looked

into my eyes and told me I'd be dead in two weeks and that if I came to his clinic he'd save my life. Something must have registered because I booked myself in for the following Monday.

Very sensible Mr Block, I hear some of you cry! But the eagle-eyed among you may have spotted that the initial appointment was a Thursday and Brandon hadn't agreed to check into the clinic until the Monday, so that left a whole three days to negotiate yet.

And he may have been "fucked" and he may not remember being there now, but that little detail certainly hadn't escaped Brandon's deranged mind either. A chance to go out with a bang, no less.

IT'S A WRAP

Brandon was facing the biggest battle of his short, yet so far charmed life, but how could he possibly be objective about the sheer scale of his problem?

I was certainly aware that I wanted a few days to get my head around it, not that I was able to get my head round much at that point. I had this gig at the Ministry Of Sound on the Sunday, but I was still focused on the appointment at the clinic on the Monday. I'd insisted I did the early set so I could be finished by about 1am, but I also had seven grams on me when I left my mum's house in Wembley, on top of a couple of eighths I'd done earlier that day.

I drove myself there and by the time I got to the club in Elephant & Castle 40 minutes later I'd done all seven grams, sniffing up a gram at a time at red traffic lights. The gear was not giving me a hit anymore, just keeping me going, giving me that wired horribleness I somehow craved.

Inside the Ministry a gaggle of my mates were waiting, some there because they had heard this could be my final hurrah, none believing it would be.

I sorted some more gear before I got in the club, gave a load out, did the rest myself and then headed home, shaking the hands of well-wishers as I left. Back in the car I wanted more coke. I headed to the flat of a dealer in Chalkhill, ordered up an eighth, did that with him and his mate, and got another one to take home.

Within an hour, I'd done that, and was on my way back to Chalkhill, doing another eighth with them, then back home with another eighth for me. That lasted even less time and so I was back at Chalkhill, at 4am, but the dealer had gone to bed. I was trying to climb up his drainpipe, so I could break in through his window. I'd done more than 30 grams now, but I still felt I needed more before I knocked it on the head. I think I was hoping for some kind of massive party, but I was on my own and desperate.

Back at my mum's I was tearing my hair out in my bedroom when I realised there must be some gear in my rug, eventually managing to scrape about three grams out of it! I washed it up myself and smoked it as crack, for what I hoped was one final time.

By now it was about 6am, I eventually managed to get about an hour's sleep, but it took at least seven 'roeys' to achieve that. I got up, tidied my room, had a shower and jumped on the train to Paddington, and checked into Dr Shanahan's Charter Nightingale clinic.

Admitting himself to the clinic in November, 1996, was no mean feat, but getting and keeping clean would be the difficult bit. And Brandon would have to do it all without his faithful 'roeys'.

I thought I was well prepared because I had a big jar of 'roeys' in my bag. But the staff at the clinic quickly searched that and confiscated the lot. They took me upstairs, did blood tests and took a gamma reading to check out my liver function. A good gamma reading is between 45 and 65, while a heavy drinker would register between 200 and 300. Mine was over 600!

Leading consultant psychiatrist Bill Shanahan had the unenviable task of trying to save Brandon Block's life and could hardly believe what he had found.

I have to say that then and, in fact, to this day I have never come across someone who was taking so much cocaine and was still able to stand up.

In 1992 we had been warned by the Americans to expect a huge cocaine epidemic, because of the amount that was getting through to the UK, but by 1996 we still hadn't seen the effects yet. Then Brandon walks in and he's doing around 28 grams a day. It was amazing.

The tests had revealed that Brandon had extremely abnormal liver ensigns, and years later an operation was needed to remove a piece of his lung.

Essentially, as well as the TB, Brandon had chemical hepatitis and on top of all this he was incredibly depressed. It was classic post-cocaine depression. He had been living for so many years with every day virtually like suicide Tuesday, because it's always the day after he had used. And because he was using drugs every day the depression was relentless. If you can't get rid of the cocaine, you'll never get rid of the depression.

But as he was slowly weaned off the cocaine, Brandon's resolve began to improve.

And he believes that sorting out his drug debt before his admission to the clinic was not only vital, but also showed that, sub-consciously, he was preparing to give up cocaine.

It's hard to remember or describe what state I was in. But at least I now knew I didn't want to die and I'd got my head around the fact that I didn't have to die. I'd had so much pain and mental torment by now that I just didn't want another day of that pain.

Despite the mess I was in I'd actually pretty much got myself straight financially, making sure all my debts with any dealers were paid up, so that when I did stop I didn't need to see anybody to pay up any tabs and in turn so I wouldn't be tempted to get any more gear. There was also a feeling somewhere inside me that if I didn't make it through for some reason, that at least I was paid up.

And this wasn't like sorting out a couple of credit card bills. I always had pages and pages of people to pay, people already paid and crossed off, etc. Most people have a 'to do' list, I always seemed to have a pad full of gear put on tic that I had to clear. But I always managed to muddle through. Just before I went to the clinic I made sure all debts were paid up, although that left me absolutely skint.

They were crazy times, and looking back I just don't know how I maintained that existence, let alone enforced it.

And a habit like this obviously doesn't come cheap. But like anything, bulk orders help reduce the cost. Fortunately, for Brandon, he cannot remember just how much was spent at that time, but hopefully, for his sake, as a valued customer, he was able to negotiate a considerable discount with all of his contacts.

Back at the Charter Nightingale Clinic, keeping Brandon away from any narcotics was obviously a prerequisite and right now a few days without even one line of the white stuff would be a start. Harvey Block continues:-

When Brandon was admitted we weren't able to talk to him for the first 72 hours. They had insisted on zero contact with him for the first three days. It was hard to get any details from them about how it was going at the start, but eventually I did get news, and they did let me in to see him, and he seemed on much better form than he had been.

I remember there was this nutty bird there, and her and Brandon were trying to get into each other's knickers, so there was sign of life, at least. There were also a couple of Yiddisher boys in there, whose families were quite well known in certain circles, who also needed some help.

When Emma Block was born her brother was 17, and the star of his own imaginary reality show...The Only Way Is north Wembley. She was oblivious to his continued rise to fame over the next decade or his massive drug addiction and admits:-

I first realised Brandon was a party person on Christmas Eve, 1994. I was 10 and my dad had the party at his flat in Belsize Park. There were loads of colourful and loud people there, and I forced Sasha and his girlfriend to watch The Little Mermaid with me.

I remember my dad taking me to see Brandon at the Charter Nightingale clinic and I remember not understanding what was going on. I didn't remember Brandon being unwell in the months previous and nobody would explain what had really happened. I was told he was sick, but I was confused because, apart from my grandad, I'd never seen anyone so ill.

I've never been to The Priory, but from speaking to people that have, as I understand it, the Charter Nightingale is similar but as opposed to The Priory, has got proper wards in there, with people on drips, doctors, nurses, consultants – in short, it's a real hospital.

Unlike The Priory, it's not so much about rehab. Bill said I didn't need rehabilitation, that, given the chance, my mind would recover mentally. He said I needed two good weeks in there clean,

to do the cold turkey the hard way and then build on it.

Bill Shanahan explains:-

We were unaware at that point about the link between the cocaine and alcohol, and that one was fuelling the other. When Brandon came in he was two years post-TB and terrified what might happen to him. As keen as he was to sort things out he really didn't like being with us and was extremely irritable. He was terribly negative in his outlook and a week into his treatment requested short-term leave to get some papers from his mum's house.

What Brandon didn't tell Bill was that he was in fact keeping an appointment to do an Essential Mix with Alex P for Pete Tong's Radio 1 show.

After a week in there I pleaded for them to let me out. The mix was obviously a big deal, but I didn't want to say leaving was about anything associated with clubbing. On my way home in the cab to get my records, like a force of habit, I got the driver to stop off at a dealer's house so I could get some gear. I just got one gram, which in itself felt weird. When I got home I went into the box room and it was really strange, like going into a morgue. It just felt really surreal. I quickly did the whole gram in that room and it sent me loopy. It was the cleanest I'd been for five years. I hadn't even been clean for one day in five years, let alone a week, and yet I was now really hammered.

I managed to get another cab to the Radio One studios in the West End where I hooked up with Alex, but I was wired, off my nut, and paranoid that everyone there knew I was. I did the mix, which actually came out very well, and got the hell out of there.

When I got back to the clinic they all took one look at me and knew what I'd done. I was placed in the suicide ward for the night and the next day I had to get up and speak to the group I was in and say I'd 'used', which was really embarrassing. Part of me thinks they let me out so I could slip up, so I'd take it more seriously, which I certainly did from that point on. I needed to feel sick about it and I did after that gram before the Radio 1 mix.

THE LIFE & LINES OF BRANDON BLOCK

Harvey Block had had his suspicions:-

After a week, they told me that he'd had to go home, that he said he needed his diary to readjust his bookings, and he had do to a mix or something, and it all sounded very dubious and I knew that he meant he was on the lookout. I was then told he had relapsed and was back on zero contact for 72 hours.

Another time, while I was in the clinic, Alex took me to Brent Cross Shopping Centre and reintroduced me to the not so wonderful world of hire purchase and I bought a Rolex watch for two and a half grand. I could have saved that money in a couple of weeks, especially now I wasn't spending it all on cocaine.

Looking back, it's amazing really, because on paper I can't have lost the plot too much to have been offered the Essential Mix, or at least have been playing that badly when I was out. That was a big thing at the time and we must have been pretty much on top of the game still to be asked in the first place. We were certainly still well up there in terms of DJ status, and we did a great mix too!

Bill Shanahan continues:-

When Brandon got back his raised blood pressure was causing him real anxiety, but he said to me "right, can we do this properly now?", and that's when his treatment really began.

Rather than the cocaine, repeated anxiety attacks were now part and parcel of Brandon's life, as his physical and mental battle to stay off coke intensified.

An intriguing insight into his mental outlook at that exact point can be found in David Davies' interview with Brandon for MixMag (December 1996, Vol 2, Issue No 67) as his fortnight at Charter Nightingale drew to an end. The photographs taken for that interview by Alexis Maryon, pictured opposite and on the cover of this book, are chilling.

* Main image by JaxEtta
* MixMag piece, 1996,
image by Alexis Maryon

HOW DJING ALMOST KILLED BRANDON BLOCK

ck is the good time
 guy guaranteed to
b and party you all
on afterwards. But
rtying too hard, too
he past year rumours
culating. He was

Amazingly, the magazine had seen it worthwhile to secure an interview with Brandon so soon into his rehabilitation, but then his clubland standing made this a fascinating exclusive, and it's even more intriguing now.

Brandon had been happy to oblige, the time spent with the MixMag crew at least giving him some kind of clubland fix. However, he seemed far from convinced he would stay clean.

Davies met Brandon at a cafe nearby Marylebone Station and the strapline HOW THE LIFE OF A TOP DJ AND FAR TOO MANY GOOD TIMES NEARLY KILLED BRANDON BLOCK accompanied the piece.

Brandon told Davies: *"Now is the time for me to calm down. I can't be fucking running around off my fucking head all the time. I've been somewhere. Detoxing. I haven't touched everything for two or three weeks, that's everything. I had to sort it out. There's still a few aches and pains, which is going to happen, but I'm not too late."*

Davies comments: *"But what Brandon Block is really doing is fighting his own fears. Ask him whether he thinks it will be the same completely clean and it's obviously something he's still wrestling with."*

Brandon adds: *"I'm still the same person. But no one says you can't do it again at a later stage. Just a gap, just a break, is always good, I mean, I'll party but sometimes you can just play your gig, have a good time, stay up all night and still get your head down."*

Brandon was now back home, back on 'civvy street' and, as ever, with a whole lot of time on his hands.

I came out after the two weeks and thought "brilliant, that's all sorted", but then it hits you. As well as getting the drugs out of your body, you need to get clean mentally for at least a month before you can start getting your head around it all. I remember when I did come out, it was horrible, the worst I've ever felt. I was still in cuckoo land. It was hellish and at the start it felt worse than when I was on the gear.

It's strange, because it takes you back to your youth, as if you haven't matured mentally yet. In the months directly after I came out I'd suffer these anxiety attacks, which would last days at a

time, like someone's pumping you with adrenalin, but negative adrenalin. I couldn't answer the phone, couldn't go out, couldn't do anything. But at least by now I was also too frightened to go back on the gear. I still have small attacks now, but I know they will pass, so they can never be as intense.

CARRY ON UP THE BYPASS

Bookings-wise, in the run up to his clinic admission, a whole host of gigs did not exactly come and go...more like, might never have been.

Brandon's inclusion on the line-ups of Up Yer Ronson in Leeds, Republica and Decadence in Birmingham, Musiquarium in Sheffield and Clockwork Orange, Club For Life, The Gallery, Malibu Stacey, all in London, were all advertised in September and October of 1996, but he has no recollection. If any of you do, then answers on a postcard... or Facebook...or Twitter...or whatever tickles your fancy these days.

November, 1996, had virtually been a wipe-out where work was concerned, but Brandon had a packed December diary looming with bookings at Ministry Of Sound and The Gallery, plus The Canal Club and Republica in the Midlands, Karanga in Bath, and on New Year's Eve both Menage A Trois on the south coast, and a massive World Dance event at the 5,000-capacity Wembley Exhibition Centre.

I know I missed loads of gigs just before I went to Charter Nightingale, let alone when I came out. Jenny (Rampling) was a like a law unto her own...and was very firm with the promoters. "No, he's not coming", she'd tell them. "He's not well, and that's that."

The first New Year's Eve without cocaine I was 100% clean, no drink, nothing. Karen Dunn had suggested that our mutual friend Brady started driving me to my gigs to keep an eye on me. And NYE that year was the first time Brady drove me, because I knew I really needed to do these gigs money-wise, as it was always double pay on New Year's Eve. I remember it was really nerve-wracking. We drove down to Portsmouth for a gig there first, and then back up to Wembley for World Dance, and a set in front of 5,000 people.

And 1997 would continue in the same vein, kicking off with a New Year's Day booking at Ministry Of Sound alongside CJ MacKintosh, Terry Hunter, Seb Fontaine, and boxer Nigel Benn (who for a few years joined the higher echelons of the DJ world as well). That year saw high-profile monthly or bi-monthly bookings at Frisky at The

Ministry Of Sound, The Gallery at Turnmills, Progress in Derby, Rise in Sheffield, Passion in Coalville, Essance in Nottingham and Slinky in Bournemouth. Brandon was now also a weekly resident at Club For Life in London and picking up a whole host of other regular bookings in the capital like Gatecrasher (The Cross) and Malibu Stacey (Hanover Grand), for whom he went on a UK tour.

All this ensured Brandon's name was plastered over the all-important dance press and that thousands of pounds continued to pour into the Blocko coffers. At the start of 1997 he had to literally roll up his sleeves (as opposed to any bank notes) and crack on with the job in hand, and all without drugs to depend on. But he did now have Brady.

When I sat down to talk to Brady about this new phase in Brandon's life at the bungalow in Ruislip in 2011, his former driver and minder was, later that day, going to hospital for triple bypass heart surgery.

I joined Brady for a delightful breakfast of bacon roll, jam donut and crisps, followed by doner kebab and chips for elevenses.

Brandon had popped out, and Brady's impromptu 'Through The Keyhole' Blocko special was hilarious. Who indeed would keep so many batteries, toilet rolls, cans of Perrier and tins of cat food in one house at the same time?

Brady reasoned that if his bed at the nearby specialist Harefield Heart Unit was not confirmed by the end of the day, he would be joining Brandon and the gang for their annual jaunt to the Cartier Polo knees-up in Windsor at the weekend.

I met him about 20-odd years ago at The Villa in Uxbridge. It was my gaff, because I knew everyone in there. I was usually 25-handed. Never any trouble because everyone knew us. Then one night Brandon came down, one of the young ones from Wembley. I half knew him, and he was pissed up, his usual self back then, you know, winding a few people up. And I saw this geezer, a mate of my brother's, take out this blade, and I said "oi, what you doing?", and he said "that lairy wanker, coming down from Wembley, I'll fucking give it to him".

Brandon was 19, 20. He was doing a little bit of DJing at the John Lyon and he came in that night wearing a pair of dungarees and a panama hat, off his fucking nut, and this wine bar was tiny, really. Everyone could see everyone in there. He got himself into trouble, and I got him out of it. We bonded after that.

Long before acid house, I was out on the New Romantic scene, doing my thing, going to places like Le Kilt and The Blitz. I'm in my late 40s now, and I was going to clubs when I was 15, knocking around with Spandau Ballet and all those boys. I knew Boy George double well when he did Le Beat Route. I introduced Charlie Chester and all Brandon's mob to proper clubs. They were little suburb kids, whereas my family was originally from Ladbroke Grove, so I was always up the West End.

I was very close mates with Chester over the years. We used to live together, but when I first met him, he'd never been up the West End. He was working as a cocktail barman in Regals in Uxbridge. At that time he was also a hairdresser, but he was a shit hairdresser. He's blind as a fucking bat, and he used to have to wear both contact lenses and glasses when cutting your hair. I used to call him Mr Magoo.

Now back in the big and bad world without cocaine, Bill Shanahan kept a close eye on Brandon's progress and he points out: -

Brandon appeared to quickly substitute the cocaine with alcohol, so part of my main task then was to get him to recognise that wasn't the answer, to reinforce that and to also make sure he attended CA (Cocaine Anonymous). He didn't like going to the meetings, kept them up for about three months and then asked if he could go it alone.

We gave Brandon a sponsor, someone who had been an addict, someone he could ring up if he needed a friendly ear, but I think he rarely called him. My main worry was that once we'd managed to get him off the drugs, and the drugs out of his system, that he would think he was cured.

The increased alcohol consumption was a constant concern and at one point his mother actually came into the reception at the hospital to voice her own worries. There were terrible side effects to Brandon coming off cocaine. He thought he was going to vomit the whole time, and at his most anxious was still convinced he was going to die.

Vivienne Block:-

When he came out of the clinic he would swear to me that he wasn't doing drugs, and if I asked him he would say "don't nag me, don't nag me", and then I'd worry that if I asked too much, he might go back on it, because I had stressed him out, silly things like that. It was very difficult to find the balance.

Only six months into his recovery, Bill asked Brandon to take part in a lecture at the hospital for a group of local students. Brandon had before, during and just after his treatment, broken the golden rule about relationships while in recovery.

It was great to be asked and when I walked in, a lot of the kids knew who I was and were shouting, "oi, oi Blocko". Maybe I should have done more of the counselling thing because I reckon I'd make a good sponsor myself. But at that time there were just too many things going on in my head.

At that time I remember flitting between two or three girlfriends within the space of two or three months. And this is why you should never start a relationship during recovery or treatment because I ruined probably some of the best relationships I could have had.

I won't mention the girls' names, but they had to go through the worst mood swings, and I can't describe what I put them through. They didn't know what to do. I'd like to say to all of them, and they know who they are, that I'm truly sorry if I hurt them at the time.

Meanwhile, as many old acquaintances as possible had to be put on hold for a while. It was horrendous.

Baggy Baxter knew enough was enough and is brutally honest as to why his cocaine intake fell dramatically.

When he came out of the clinic, I had to step away from him, because I just wasn't good for him. I loved him to bits, but it was best for both of us. I still kept in touch on the phone, but I'd got together with a new girl, and we were having a baby. When he came out of the clinic, I guess it was the end of the Brandon and Baggy partnership. And it was for our own good.

It was time, not to lose our friendship, but to have some distance. Otherwise, we would have killed each other. When Brandon came off the gear, his dad said to me "you've got to look after him", but I remember saying "who's going to look after me?"

Shortly after Brandon went to the clinic, I took myself off to hospital too. I'd been bang on it for a couple of days, and drinking double brandies. I tried to drink a pint of water, but it all came out of my nose. The doctor asked if I'd taken any drugs in the last 48 hours, and I had to tell him I'd had an ounce of coke, about 35 pills and 14 trips. They kept me on the intensive care unit for the next two weeks.

And as we had both ended up in intensive care by this point, I guess it was a case of "hang on a minute". Both of us knew enough was enough. I was that bit older than him too, and everything was taking its toll. I basically stopped murdering the coke, like we were before, because Brandon used to pay for it all. I did carry on in smaller amounts for a bit, but it caught up with me in the end.

I didn't do a day's work for most of the '90s, but I had an amazing time. Most Monday mornings we'd get a quarter in, and then kick on from there. Those years, 1988 - 96, were the best of my life, travelling around London and the UK with Brandon, and I wouldn't change a thing. Everything was paid for wherever we went. We were either in a club or a hotel or at an after-party, and usually everything was on the house. There were lots of perks, I had that lifestyle for at least five years, all week, every week.

For the first month I drank heavily, and I was substituting cocaine with alcohol on a regular basis, but I quickly realised that wasn't going to work. I had to change my whole life, for the time being at least, and keep going to the meetings, which for the first few months was literally every day, so I attended 90 meetings in 90 days, as advised. It's that intensive because you really don't know what to do with yourself on a daily basis. However, I found that being in meetings heightened my anxiety, not lessened it. I just felt too raw and vulnerable to be baring my soul so soon after cleaning up.

I was unable to share my experiences or listen to anyone else's. You're supposed to be able to do that, but I found myself too engrossed in my own turmoil. Someone would say they used to do two or three grams a week, and I'd think "shut up, I was at it all day, every day!". That's how self-centered I was at that stage.

There have been times where I have needed to open up, but I have generally used my support group of friends or Bill, my psychiatrist, who still to this day, I owe my life to.

And while I kept away from a lot of my friends, touch wood, I haven't had to lose any of them in the long run, including Baggy.

I talked to Bill and told him how I was feeling and he said "your recovery is your own, as long as you don't use cocaine, do it your way".

I got myself home, redecorated the old box room myself, so I managed to exorcise a lot of old demons then, and began trying to get my life back together. And as soon as I came out I had to try and create a new me, which wasn't going to be easy. Alex will tell you that he was getting tired of having to cover for me because I wasn't turning up, so we did more and more gigs on our own in the UK.

I came out of the clinic and had a year of being clean in the box room, which was hellish. I couldn't answer the phone, couldn't watch the TV, it was all giving me anxiety. I was missing a load of gigs. I spent so much time sitting, huddled up in the corner of the room, hugging my knees. I didn't want to leave the room or answer the phone let alone DJ to a club full of people.

When you're addicted for so many of your early adult years you don't mature mentally. So when you come off the gear it's like being born again, your brain has to take everything in again, has to process lots of experiences in normality for the first time. I reckon I was off my head for the whole of the 1993 – 1996 period. Never straight. The only gap I had was when I was sleeping... if I managed to get some sleep, that is. Now clean and trying to deal with being clean I'd clutch my arms and chest and sit there and shiver as the anxiety manifested.

The bookings I did make were few and far between. It would get to the afternoon of the gig and I would decide I was unwell and that I couldn't cope with it.

I did have one slip, a month after I came out of the clinic. And it was a stark reminder of what could have been. I was at a gig at the old Willesden cinema, with some mates, DJing before their band Single Mothers played live. These guys hadn't seen me since I'd come out of the clinic, and we were in the gallery when one of them got some coke out, and started racking up some lines. I hadn't really talked about the clinic to them because I was embarrassed about having to go in the first place and now it was almost as if I was too embarrassed to say no to the line when I was offered one. I took it and immediately thought "what the fuck are you doing?" I felt dirty and disgusting and that slip certainly did its job because I made up my mind I would never do one again.

It was during this time that Brady got more and more involved. He used to be known as the Lord Mayor Of Uxbridge... so-called because of his massive belcher chain, not because he was a local councillor or anything. And Brady really did keep people away from me, shielding me from anyone offering me gear, etc. He was essentially my minder for a couple of years and I couldn't have done it without him.

Fortunately, Brady had a plan.

The first six or so months were real dark days for Brandon. It was hard to even get him out of the house. I used to arrive at his mum's a couple of hours before we were meant to leave, to get his head right, maybe watch a bit of The Fast Show or something with him, or I'd take him out for a curry beforehand somewhere in Wembley, to settle him a bit, so we could go out and graft, because if I'm giving up my nights out, I want paying for it. I knew I could earn good money, if his head was right, and that the boy would be getting a lot more, earning some decent money for a change, not putting it all up his nose. Getting himself straight instead.

However, at the start, it felt like he couldn't leave the house without me. I felt I had to do it for him and, to be fair, it was a quite a strain on me. I've never said it to him, but it affected me as well, seeing someone go through all that. There was a time when he was a shadow of himself. He needed someone strong enough to deal with all the bollocks, and someone who also cared about him, who would steer him right, and I did feel a huge responsibility on my shoulders.

Often we'd be half way to a club and he'd say he wanted to turn back and go home, and I'd say "shut up, c'mon, I'm out now, you're out now, let's get it done". Half the time he didn't want to go to the gigs, but once you'd got him there he was the life and soul of the party.

I believe, even after he came out of the clinic, that he was close to death's door, not just physically, but in his head too. He was nigh on suicidal sometimes. Proper black times, and because I'm an outgoing bubbly person, I would try and take that away from him. Everyone's got a dark side, but when you're coming off something you felt you depended on, and it's been taken out of your life, having so much time on your hands, as a lot of successful DJs do, is hard. You know, those times during the day, when everyone else is working and there's nobody else around.

Harvey Block remembers:-

Brandon slowly managed to get through it, and he had his bad times, he let a few people down, when he got the collywobbles before a gig. People would never believe he'd given it up, so every time he walked into the club people would be offering him gear, "here y'are Bran...here y'are Bran", and it was difficult for him, because he'd turn it down and they'd insist, and he didn't want to tell them to "fuck off", because they'd paid money to come see him DJ, but he had to be forceful, and sometimes he just didn't fancy that battle all night. He did unfortunately develop a reputation for being unreliable.

Those couple of years before he went to the clinic, there were quite a few occasions when I took him to one side. But it always seemed to be a combination of the two - the gear and also the booze. I was obviously concerned for him, but it also became embarrassing, seeing him act like an idiot. That, for me, was the downside, I guess, of being at the clubs or at the parties. If it got too much, whether we were at a club in town, or at a hotel, or whatever, I would just say "right Bran, I'm going". There was no telling him at this point. He was on a mission and it would only get more frustrating for me. Once he was on a mission there was just no stopping him. I'd ring him the following day to check he was OK. I sat him down on three or four occasions and told him to take it easy.

You know, I've given up drinking recently, and often people would tell me I'd had enough, and I'd turn round and say "I know what I'm doing, leave me alone". And it was the same with Brandon.

If you're in the big league, well, it's the downfall of many in the music business, isn't it? You start to mix with some of the wrong crowd, a lot of hangers-on, who are all at the gear left, right and centre.

Brady became a very big part of my life. From around Christmas time onwards in 1996 he got me to nearly every gig, and having him around was good for me. He drove me around for the next seven or eight years. I was still at mum's when he started driving me, and the most important thing was that we had fun... and I mean belly laughs. Brady picked me up from the hospital after I'd had some extra surgery on my TB and I had stitches going down the side of my stomach. We were laughing so much at one point, that my sides were actually splitting. Blood was actually come out of the wound. And just starting to laugh again was the most amazing feeling.

Going from an ounce a day to nothing is like cutting off the blood supply to your body. It's a mental addiction and to stop it just like that is hardcore. They don't tell you it's going to be such hard work mentally and you wouldn't ever stop if you really knew how horrendous it would be.

When I got to the stage when I was over the edge I remember the moment vividly. People had been saying for ages "you're doing too much Bran" and then one day I knew I was gone, one million per cent in the shit!

I wasn't sure how I was going to handle club situations and still being around drugs. I was boozing quite a lot and there was the odd person who would set their minds on getting me to do coke by offering it to me all the time, but for the most part people were quite respectful about the whole thing.

Brady was doing a great job protecting me from people when I was DJing, keeping people who might offer me stuff out of the DJ booth, literally standing inside it by the door, keeping guard.

But I remember one club in Birmingham that I played at regularly had booked me a few months after I'd got clean, and they had this room which backed on to the DJ booth where the promoters, their friends and any DJs who were playing would hang out, drinking, smoking and doing lines. I was desperate for a pee during the middle of my set, so ran into the room mid-record and straight into the toilet there as I normally would. I was standing there having a piss and there staring at me was a big fat line of wallop that someone had left on the toilet cistern. I was locked in this little room and it was the weirdest feeling. I kept telling myself that the record was about to run out, and somehow got out of there in one piece. I know I was very close to taking it, though.

And that's what it was like for at least the first two or three years....a constant battle going on in my head. I won't lie, I have had my moments, when I've thought about having a line...that would only be human. But over the years I have tried to understand what causes the craving. It's obviously some kind of escape mechanism, which triggers the whole thing.

Brady continues:-

In the early days it was mainly going up to gigs and coming straight back. If I brought him home it meant he wouldn't get involved in any afters. There was always a hotel room booked for us, but I always thought if I brought him back it would be better for both of us. That way he wouldn't get involved in anything, and I'd still have some of my weekend left. I remember one time I called his bluff after a night at Bakers in Birmingham. He was getting tucked into some drinks after the club with a few boys, and I told him I wasn't going to sit there watching him get pissed, I'd had enough, it was time to go, but he didn't want to leave, so eventually I left him there, although you could tell he was torn as to what to do.

I turned my phone off, got a couple of junctions down the motorway and stopped off for some grub. When I got going again, suddenly this black cab pulled up alongside me and there's Brandon shouting out of the window - "Brades, Brades". He was eating a curry, which he stopped off to get at a local Balti house, before setting off after me.

The club environment really wasn't a healthy one for someone coming off drugs. I just wouldn't allow anybody to get close to him. Even all the silly little birds, I used to fuck them off out of the DJ

(clockwise) * As best man at Tony Hannan's wedding, 1997
* Water party action from the dancefloor at Es Paradis
* 'Blocko & Peasy' in the DJ booth at Es Paradis
* At Cartier Polo with (l - to r) Aves, Brady and Lee Stafford

	SI LONG	DANNY KEITH
	LAURENCE NELSON	BRANDON BLOCK
	STEVE LEE	LISA LOUD
	JON (PLEASED WIMMIN)	JON (PLEASED WIMMIN)
	TALL PAUL NEWMAN	LAURENCE NELSON
	PAUL WOODS	

6\8
PAUL KANE
JON DIGWEED
DARREN STOKES
CRAIG CAMPBELL
VIVIEN MARKEY
JAMES MAC

2\8
CRAIG CAMPBELL
SPENCER WILLIAMS
STACEY TOUGH
MATT FROST
PHIL PERRY

SIDENT DJ'S
REMY HEALY
RIS & JAMES

the Gardenin

booth. I wouldn't have none of it. Even now if I saw him do it, I'd smack him and smack the bloke who gave it to him.

Occasionally, Brady would take Brandon back to the Charter Nightingale in the middle of the night. Or just speaking to someone there before his DJ set started would be reassuring.

When we were playing clubs in central London like The Gardening Club in Covent Garden we were only 15 minutes away from the clinic. A couple of times I did take him back there after his set so he could see one of the shrinks on duty, at all times, middle of the night, early hours. Or he'd call them before he went on, say he wasn't coping, and just the knowledge that he had the option to go there was enough to get him through the night. Shelley at The Gardening Club was particularly good to him with bookings, regularly giving him the last set there on a Saturday, 4am - 6am, so we could play there on the way home.

Discounting his unique speech when receiving his Muzik Magazine Caner Of The Year Award, which itself had to be cut from the following broadcast, Brandon would have his first taste of prime-time national television when he was a guest an ITV debate show Thursday Night Live With Nicky Campbell, alongside Mandy Smith, the child bride famed for her marriage to Rolling Stone Bill Wyman. Brandon was talking honestly and openly about his drug addiction, and his mum Vivienne was horrified.

Brandon had come out of the clinic, he was back home with me and he was clean. I was watching the TV and there he was, saying that he spent thousands of pounds each year on cocaine. I remember getting my calculator out and wondering what sort of mansion we could have been living in, instead of a maisonette in Harrow Road. I was gobsmacked. I mean, like a lot of people, I'd smoked pot in the past, and quite enjoyed it, but all this money on that stuff. I was astounded.

In 1997 Tony Hannan asked Brandon to be best man at his wedding, but Brandon was still far from being best man material.

I know he was still in a bad way at my wedding in 1997, because he was hyperventilating and unable to do his best man's speech because he was having one of his anxiety attacks. In fact, he had to leave the wedding early, which was a shame.

But Brandon isn't the only one to have gone through the mill. A lot of leading people in the scene have had their down time. Brandon is not the only person to have suffered psychologically, but he is one who has come out the other side.

Brandon is so clever and bright, and because of his overactive mind, maybe, for him, the drugs just helped nullify that. There's obviously a long history of creative people destroying themselves over the years. He could have been a really good TV presenter if he hadn't focused on being a DJ, and there's no question that he could have been a comedian, he is a bloody comedian.

Brandon's infectious personality, raucous behaviour and unrivalled interaction with the crowd on the Space terrace had impressed radio station boss Gordon Mac in the summer of 1996, so much so that he offered Brandon a show.

Kiss FM was then still considered a worthwhile mouthpiece for London's clubland, and still fronted by the station's pirate founder Mac. He was keen for Brandon to team up with Alex P on air.

It was strange because by the time the show started I was clean, but Gordon came up to me in Space six months earlier when I was smashed out of my cake and talking to Norman Cook (aka Fatboy Slim). Norm had grabbed me on the terrace and told me he'd always wanted to meet me because I was such a nutter. Then Gordon asked if I'd like to do a show with Alex and I said "not arf!". It was surreal.

Norman Cook has fond memories of that messy Sunday Space session.

I do remember going up to Brandon at Space and introducing myself, and I remember being a bit apprehensive actually.

I played hip-hop and funk in the mid-'80s like everyone else, but then had been in the Housemartins, doing the whole pop thing, so I'd missed the start of the acid house scene. When I came back to Brighton after leaving the band I then carried on making records with rare groove samples in during the late '80s and early '90s, like Beats International, Dub Be Good To Me.

I didn't make a house record until Pizzaman in 1995, and I was always worried the original house lot would see me as someone who jumped on the bandwagon late. But I went up and introduced myself to Brandon that afternoon, said I liked what he did, and he returned the compliment. By the end of that afternoon, evening, morning, whatever, we were best of buddies. Space terrace was great, it was absolute lunacy back then.

The first Kiss pilot show was at the start of 1997. I remember it was on between 1am – 3am, in case we swore too much. It was an eye opener to me and Alex because neither of us had ever done radio before, apart from the odd show for local pirate stations.

Although I was off the gear now, I was still wired and taking antidepressants and anti-psychosis drugs. Ever since then I've tried to avoid taking any prescribed drugs. I stopped doing the antidepressants after three months because they were really fucking me up.

After a couple of successful pilot shows, and the installation of a ten second delay, we were given the 4pm – 7pm drive-time show, and it became very popular very quickly. As weekend presenters who were better known as clubbing DJs we only got paid about £30 each, which was pretty standard for Kiss and other mainstream stations at that time. In terms of profile it's great for work, though, and that's one of the main reasons you do it. Those that crossed over to Radio 1 didn't get paid much more than us, but you can command so much more money for your fees the bigger the listenership and reach you have, because you're obviously plugging your own gigs at every opportunity.

We were soon beating Pete Tong on Radio 1 in terms of listeners in London. Kiss had been known for using DJs like Danny Rampling, Judge Jules and Trevor Nelson, all well-respected in the scene musically and who over the years went to Radio 1 effortlessly, but we were the first party jocks on the legal version of Kiss, and our show was kind of like Steve Wright meets dance music, very comical, off the cuff and it came across as organised mayhem with less emphasis on the organisation part.

And we had some familiar faces helping out during the show. Paul Avery recorded some jingles for us, and Steve Long, Charlie Chester's partner in Cowboy Records, used to do some Jimmy Savile voice-overs.

There was no planning involved…we'd turn up with a couple of bags of records and off we went. We weren't playlisted at first, it was only when Emap got involved that it got more structured and unfortunately the show then lost its identity.

It's a shame because Emap started changing things around in 1998, re-branded the station from its original name of Kiss FM to Kiss 100 and moved our show to 10pm on a Friday because they wanted the same polished drive-time presenters throughout the whole week, no specialist club jocks on a Friday.

The later slot just didn't work because we had to pre-record so it wasn't as adhoc. I have it on good authority from insiders that Radio 1 were sniffing around and that they were weeks away from signing me and Alex up. As well as that Essential Mix we had been guests on various shows before, once when Danny Rampling was away and we sat in with Dave Pearce as cover.

Around that time I had also been booked to play at the Radio One Sound City event in Newcastle city centre alongside Pete Tong, Judge Jules and Seb Fontaine so the signs were good. However, this was just as we were getting totally disenchanted with Kiss and not turning up to some of our shows. Maybe someone at the Beeb thought we weren't worth the risk after all.

OUT OF HIS BOX

Shortly after securing a prime-time radio show, Brandon would also be the proud owner of his own house, as he finally plucked up the courage to leave the box room and his harrowing Harrow Road habit behind.

Even though I'd been earning loads for years I'd never had any spare money. It was only now that I started to see a few quid. So within that time I realised that I could get out of Mum's house, and that I badly needed some space to escape the memories of a bedroom that had been both my life and my prison.

For me buying a house at the age of 29 years old was a massive step, but once I'd made my mind up everything was completed within a matter of weeks. A lot of my friends had decided to buy their own place and the logical progression, from where we all grew up in the Sudbury area, was to move slightly further out to the leafier suburbs of Harrow, Pinner and Ruislip. For us, those were the natural areas to aspire to and at some point to settle down in.

One of my closest oldest friends, Rick Williamson, had moved there, so I decided to have a look around and I found a large bungalow. Brady had a look with me and I put the deposit down immediately. Paul Avery moved in initially and rented the front room, which I eventually converted to my poker room. I put a deposit down after managing to save that up from my DJ fees in a month.

Vivienne Block could hardly believe that Brandon was finally leaving home, and given the severity of his medical and emotional condition, it really was a case of 'if you love someone, let them go'.

When he thought he could move out and get his own place, I hoped in my heart of hearts that meant he was getting much stronger. And in that fact I took some solace, hoping that he had somehow managed to conquer this terrible thing if he felt he was able to cut this umbilical cord. Up until he had dried out, he was certainly in no condition to go it on his own. And then when he did I was left with all this time to myself.... and thousands of records.

I didn't know whether he would be able to maintain it and I didn't want my son to die. I didn't stop worrying, I was constantly concerned, and I would ring him all the time, every day, but he would get annoyed, so I stopped phoning him that much. As a mother, I did want to call every day, but I gradually felt more confident and eventually I began to trust him that he wouldn't go back on the drugs.

When he was doing it, I'm still not quite sure whether I didn't want to know about the drugs, or whether I really didn't know. I knew he drank too much, and maybe I should have been much more aware of the drugs, but I certainly wasn't aware of his increasing addiction to cocaine.

I just thank God he doesn't do it anymore. I also used to get annoyed when he'd go abroad without telling me. It's not a deliberate thing, it's just a thoughtless thing. I'd ring him and he'd often be in another country. God forbid anything happened to me, he is my next of kin, so I need to know what country he is in, at the very least.

In early 1997 I had a call from a friend, Jeremy Ansell, who was DJing out in Israel. He asked me to play at a club in Tel Aviv called Allenby 58, a venue in the town centre and Tel Aviv's most famous nightclub. Owned by an Israeli army officer, it also has a sister venue it uses in Old Tel Aviv Port called Octopus, where I would also later play.

I was in a right mess still, but the people were so friendly in Israel that I went back and played many times over the years, including shortly after my Brits experience. I took Mickey Finn out there with me one time, and I must give a special mention to the boys out in Eilat, down on the coast where I also played - Jackson, Gal and Jordon. They were all local radio DJs, as well as club jocks, but they were also qualified dive masters and they taught me how to dive, well as far as I was allowed, with my dodgy lungs and chest. I also played at Octopus one night with John Digweed. Fond memories indeed.

Back on the road, and also back DJing internationally, Brandon quickly began to enjoy splashing out on other things than drugs.

My new addiction was spending money on the house and on cars. And when I moved into my own place I was still buying all these cars on hire purchase as well.

Brady reasons:-

It wasn't just cars he was obsessed with. There were the trainers too. He'd wear them two or three times and then give them to a mate. And all the charity shops round this way were full of his clobber, the more stuff he bought. I got us a sponsorship with Tommy Hilfiger, and we'd get boxes of clothes delivered. On top of all the stuff he was buying, he just didn't have enough time to wear it all. And after he got hooked on eBay, well, the postman asked if he could build a sorting office in his back garden.

Although the Radio 1 deal hadn't come off, a more and more clean, if not always sober, Brandon was starting to enjoy his DJing again. The bookings continued to flood in, his fees were still increasing and more importantly there wasn't a Scarface desk full of cocaine to eat up his cash.

The offer of presenting a club tour show on MTV helped cushion the Radio 1 blow for Brandon and Alex, and the name Off Yer Med was apt, to say the least.

I guess myself and Alex were quite TV friendly. We'd done various cameo rolls on MTV before and had also appeared on a show called BPM, which my old mate Dave 'Doorbell' Dorrell presented on ITV.

Off Yer Med saw me and Alex act as roving reporters at clubs around the Mediterranean. MTV organised it all and it was good for gigs because we played at all the nights we were reporting on. We went to Crete, Rhodes, Ayia Napa, Majorca - where we played on the same bill as Dannii Minogue - and, of course, Ibiza. I know I shouldn't be negative about these times, because looking back it was great that people still wanted to employ me in some kind of capacity after all the carnage I'd caused, but I was still far from getting better, in terms of my recovery. I'd say it actually took me a good five years to get half sensible.

And there was the small matter of setting foot in Ibiza for the first time clean, and not being able to indulge in his favourite white powder on his favourite island.

I remember Ibiza 1997 was a nightmare, going back somewhere I'd specifically done so many drugs, and now clean. Everyone else was at it still, of course. I was staying at Pikes with Dad, but I ended up cooped up in the hotel all the time. One night Dad went out with Erick Morillo, Carl Cox and Jeremy Healy and the four of them came back three days later! Not exactly the best example Dad!

I felt that this was a new chapter, not only in my life, but also in my Ibiza career. That island is the maddest place in the world if you're sober anyway, and I was still drinking so it wasn't like I had to live like a nun out there. The island was awash with British promoters now, and as more and more of them got involved in Space around 1997 the club and the terrace were pretty much open every day.

For a while me and Alex would be used in some capacity at Space by all the new promoters, either at the start of the nights, or at the end. Space actually retained control of the famous Sunday session up until 1999, when Darren Hughes and the Home lot took it on, and turned it into a 24 hour event, and other residents like Biko, Jason Bye, Jonathan Ulysses and Steve Lawler were brought in. By then, me and Alex were playing regularly for the likes of Clockwork Orange at Es Paradis and for Up Yer Ronson at Amnesia. We went on to do Tonic weekly at Eden when that opened as a new venue in San Antonio in 1999, but we did still continue to play on the Space terrace at Clockwork Orange after parties on a Thursday morning and Manumission's Tuesday morning Carry On session, plus Tonic afters there too.

It was around this time that we were also asked to do the outdoor Sundance parties at The Zoo, which were mainly attended by the package holiday people and the Club 18-30 crowd. They were great fun, at a time when I felt Ibiza was taking itself far too seriously.

There were often three or four thousand people at those parties and I think me and Alex were asked because our music had become a lot more accessible in terms of your average man on the

street, compared to a lot of DJs who were trying to educate people at that time. We were the personality jocks that everyone knew, and the Kiss radio show helped that. Slipmatt was also used a lot, as well as Nicky Holloway and Roy The Roach, and we often had bookings there every week.

And if things were about to step up a gear on Sundays at Space, then so had activities at the unassuming beach shack just across the road.

In many ways the open expansive beach at Playa D'en Bossa was ripe for the beach party revolution that would take place at Bora Bora over the next six or seven years, after pioneering Italian duo Roberto and Ernesto had tested the water in 1993 next door at the Tahiti.

The man behind the Bora Bora success story, Gee Moore, is an interesting character, to say the least. With a history as a successful businessman around the London suburbs, owning various record and music equipment shops, he pitched up in Ibiza in the summer of 1997 intent on taking time out as a beach bum for a few years.

When he was approached to put in a sound system and be resident DJ at Bora Bora by the bar manager, a Belgian guy called Etienne, it was an offer he couldn't refuse.

When Etienne jumped ship with most of the bar staff weeks later to take up positions at the newly opened El Divino club, Gee and an Argentinian barman called Raj were left to run the place. And run the place they did, somehow managing to keep on the right side of the Jet Apartments complex which owned the bar, and the police.

Moore went on to hold residencies at all the major clubs on the island, including for Zenith at Pacha, creating a truly memorable legacy of beach-side clubbing in the process. And a certain Mr Block was never far away. Moore points out:-

Brandon is as much a part of Bora Bora as anyone else. He absolutely loved that place, and often, he'd lock himself in the toilet if he was meant to be DJing at Es Paradis or Amnesia or wherever else, with Alex P and co forever reminding him that he was late for his next gig.

I remember I was in the middle of my set one day, it was late afternoon, and there were a thousand or so people dancing by the bar and along the beach. Brandon popped up in the booth and dragged me off the decks, and through the crowds, on to the beach. It was impossible to get through all those people at the best of the times, but he had grabbed hold of me, and I was worried that the record was about to run out, and he was saying, "don't worry, don't worry" and dragging me towards the sea. We got down to the front and he bundled me in fully clothed, and when we both surfaced, he simply pointed back at Bora Bora and said "look at that, innit marvellous?"

Another time I was DJing, this hand covered in sand appeared over the side of the decks, and it was attached to Brandon, who was hammered, and could hardly see, let alone mix. But, without headphones, he proceeded to mix the next track in perfectly, before collapsing on the floor.

Other Blocko highlights included telling DJ Sneak to "fuck off" when he pitched up with his records asking to play. It was a typical cheeky Blocko - "what do want? nope, you can't play, fuck off" - as usual, unintentionally offensive, but poor Sneak didn't get the so-called British sense of humour, and off he went.

Today Bora Bora has been joined on Playa D'en Bossa by a host of upmarket and exclusive bars and beach clubs, the likes of Delano and Ushuaia filling the large barren spaces on the Space end of the beach, but nowhere as organic as the likes of Bora Bora or Tahiti, circa '93

With his Ibiza work done, Moore has taken his Bora Bora concept to Brazil and set up shop in paradise once more, via a sabbatical in L.A, where he blagged a walk-on part in the last episode of hit sit-com Friends.

By the way, if you're having a bad day, do NOT google www.boraborabrasil.com.

For the 1997 season, Brandon had importantly fully abandoned his tactic of plotting up in Ibiza for most of the summer. He had been flying in and out of the island on a regular basis for the past few seasons, but this time his 'management team' made sure he was never there for too long.

Brady believes the busier, more in demand, and in turn the more effective Brandon became, the greater his continued success was.

When he came out of the clinic and for the years after that, he never did a full season out there again, largely because he was too busy, flying back to the UK and all over the place. And he was lucky really, because if he had stayed there for longer than two or three days at a time he would have been in trouble, getting off his tits with all the other idiots. Keeping the Ibiza visits short kept him more focused in a way. He spent a lot of time listening to his records on the road, and started making records, of course. There was a sense that he wanted to be on top of his game.

Somehow, in the middle of another busy summer, Brandon jetted out to Hong Kong, also accepting a spin-off trip to Thailand straight after. A regular guest DJ in HK since '93, Brandon was booked once more by ex-pat Paul Honey to play at a massive "handover" party in July '97, and the generous promoter had thrown in a 10-day trip to Thailand to mark the historic occasion.

With the handover of Hong Kong back to the Chinese going through in 1997, lots of Brits out there were leaving and moving on, and there were some great parties because of that. Boy George was out there the same time as us, and I also played at a Club For Life party with Laurence Nelson that Shelley Boswell put on. The event 'Small' Paul Honey (as we had dubbed him) put on was amazing. He'd been putting on parties out there for years, and then straight after he very generously treated a few of us to the Koh Samui trip.

I'd heard all about Thailand, but hadn't been out there yet, and when I did get out there, I quickly fell in love with the place. Small Paul took us to the north coast of Koh Samui and I bumped into old pals like Simon Jonboy, who had been living out there on Bophut Beach.

Me and Laurence played at the Malibu Resort, a large Half Moon beach party, put on by Korn, Wudh, Sin and San, a great Thai family who at the time owned the Santa Fe nightclub in Chaweng, and now own Sound, Koh Samui's most popular nightclub. That beach party was a fantastic success and finished at 9am, opening a lot of doors for me.

And on that first trip, it didn't take me long to settle in, crashing my moped on the second day, and requiring daily

treatment on my various wounds at the local medical centre. You know, the typical Blocko stuff.

Thailand is beautiful and although then it was still pretty mental where parties were concerned, it had something much calmer and more relaxed about it than Ibiza.

However, on that first trip I still had lots of demons. It was only a year after I'd given up the coke, after all, and I also had tinnitus, which is the last thing you want when you've got lots of shit going on in your head. A lot of DJs get it, and it's like an annoying ringing in the ear that you can't control.

I can remember the exact moment when the tinnitus really took hold. It was a week before the Hong Kong/Thailand trip, after a flight back from Scotland. I was sitting with my good friend Alex (aka the lovely Bubbles) at Harrow Road and, as usual, after any flight/the night after a gig, my ears were ringing, but suddenly there was a different kind of ringing, and from that point on I knew it wouldn't ever really go away, and it hasn't to this day. I had already been diagnosed with loss of hearing at that point and as time goes on you just learn to deal with that, like the tinnitus.

The tinnitus had got really bad in Hong Kong '97, so much so that at one point I rang my dad and said I wanted to kill myself. I was still having some extremely low moments and Thailand had been just the tonic I needed, even though I spent a lot of it, like my time in Britain, dodging cocaine and people trying to give it to me.

After a busy summer jetting in and out of Ibiza, via Hong Kong and Thailand, Brandon returned home to settle into a hectic autumn schedule, which kicked off with a spot at Gatecrasher in September alongside Tony De Vit, who had become a legend in the hard house and trance circles during the '90s, and who sadly passed away in 1998.

It was extremely sad when Tony died. When I first heard we were driving home from a gig. We pulled over on the hard shoulder and I shed a few tears as the news filtered through. It made me realise how lucky I was to be alive. Tony was an ambassador for his genre of music and for dance music itself, a true gentleman. Everybody loved Tony.

Jenny Rampling ended her association with Selective Management when she split from DJ husband Danny in 1997, and went to live in Thailand.

I never sacked Brandon, despite all that went on. When you could get him to a gig he always gave 150% and no-one was more happy than me when he came through the other side. Apart from his massive personality (and it is huge!) he was and still is an enormous talent and a lot smarter than you might think. He's no-one's fool and he's a good person.

All the big DJs had different qualities and selling/pulling powers. Some DJs were very technical, some were great producers with records behind them and some were big in specific territories, but Brandon is a personality jock.

To use a modern day analogy, I'd say he was the Lady GaGa of the DJ World. It's not the most serious music you'll ever hear, but he puts on one hell of a show.

Jenny retired from clubland when she returned from Thailand, and after she met new partner Pat - and old friend of Brandon's - the couple had a baby girl. Now a junior school teacher, she jokes:-

Looking after a nine-year-old daughter or a classroom full of kids is a lot easier than looking after a roster full of DJs, and in particular Brandon Block.

The late '90s was a phase in his life where Brandon was slowly getting his head around never doing cocaine ever again. And he had still not conquered his drinking issues, not by a long way.

As I entered 1998 I again went through a big piss-up stage, going out on frequent two-day drinking sessions and telling myself that although it wasn't great, it was better than doing gear. I actually started to think that I was beginning to win the battle with the drugs now. It wasn't about going back to that, it was about starting a new chapter in my life.

And because I'd stopped doing gear, I went back for another course of triple therapy treatment to help shift the TB once and for all. However, although it was dormant, it was embedded in a

well in my lung, so a lobectomy operation was needed. And it's a serious op, they cut through my back and opened up my ribs and I was in hospital for about seven days. I remember in the days after the operation I ripped the morphine drip from my arm because I was feeling drugged-up and out of control. After being clean for two years that frightened me. It wasn't where I wanted to be, and I actually took that as a positive sign. I'd certainly come a long way from wanting cocaine brought to me in intensive care.

Meanwhile, another summer...another sunshine clubbing destination. Cypriot party resort Ayia Napa emerged in the late '90s as the latest "new Ibiza", and, although it naturally never quite managed to emulate its more glamorous 'colleague', Napa would go on to become a one-stop holiday shop for all things UK garage, with a sprinkling of house from the likes of Brandon.

Myself and Alex became residents at The Castle Club, Ayia Napa's biggest venue, in 1998. We started working with a promoter out there called Jimmy Buzzbar, who used to own a bar of the same name, and then we played at the massive promotions Jimmy put on at The Castle, which had a capacity of around 3,000 people. Ibiza was still hot property, and Ayia Napa was being hailed as the new Ibiza. Each year, as clubbing went worldwide, Napa, as well as some of the Greek islands, and basically any other holiday resort in the world where there was a party, would be branded the new Ibiza. You can't compare anywhere to Ibiza, but you cannot deny where Napa was concerned that there was a massive influx of British clubbers, with a whole host of British DJs, particularly from the UK garage scene.

And like I seem to do with most hot places that I spend a lot of time in, and grow to love, I invested in a bar out there. In 1999 my dad was out in the States with his third wife and was having one of his "I don't want to live in America" phases, and had talked about possibly opening a bar in Ibiza or Cyprus, so he came back, and with him, we put some money into a bar in Ayia Napa which had

(clockwise) * Limo promo for MixMag feature, 1999
* DJing on Space Terrace with Alex P and Tall Paul
* Enjoying a cuppa in Ibiza..how times change!

DANCE
NATION
SIX

TALL
PAUL
BRANDON
BLOCK

DNCD6

GODSKITCHEN®
BIRMINGHAM SANCTUARY, DIGBETH HIGH ST, BIRMINGHAM

grandopening.06.02.98

LAUNCH PARTY FRIDAY 6TH FEBRUARY
GEORGE, JEREMY B (MOS), JOHN 00 FLEMING
ANDY WARD, NICK RAFFERTY, A.J GIBSON

13.02.98 BRANDON BLOCK, ALEX P.
KIDDO, NICK RAFFERTY, A.J GIBSON

20.02.98 TALL PAUL, JON OF THE PLEASED.
ANDY WARD, NICK RAFFERTY, A.J GIBSON

TONY DE VIT, TALL PAUL, CRAIG CAMPBELL
KIDDO, NICK RAFFERTY, A.J GIBSON

already been built and was opening that season, called The Vibe Bar. Dad moved out there, as did Dizzi, who got involved too, and I was flying in and out from Ibiza or wherever, and it was great having Dad out there whenever I was in Cyprus.

Our interest in the bar only lasted a season, but I continued to DJ out there and in particular at The Castle Club, for many years, up until 2008, and often alongside other Brit house jocks like Danny Rampling, Graeme Park and Allister Whitehead. Paul Oakenfold went out there in the early days, and The Castle Club had a young Tiesto playing out there as well. Another great venue I played at loads was Mythology, for Bradley and Mick. Thanks for all the great nights boys.

British DJs who also increased their profiles out in Cyprus, and became good friends of mine along the way, include pioneers of the UK garage scene like Da Click, with MC Creed, The Dreem Teem (Spoony, Mikee B and Timmi Magic), Martin Larner, Mike 'Ruff Cut' Lloyd, DJ Luck & Neat, Pied Piper, Masters Of Ceremony, Unknown MC, who went to rap on a couple of my fledging hip-house anthems, under the guise of Phat Mustard, and not forgetting my old pals Norris 'Da Boss' Windross, Dominic Spreadlove and Danny Foster.

We would play at The Buzzbar for Jimmy, and then for him at his promotions at The Castle Club. always playing our usual brand of big room house, and it wasn't all about UK garage out there. Miss Moneypenny's were out there for many years, run by two great lads, Jit and Nibbo, and Hed Kandi had their own place at one point too. And I always remember the classic line in the Blues Brothers, when they ask the barmaid "what kind of music do you usually have here?", to which she replies "oh, we got both kinds - we got country and western". And that was the case in Napa, they had both kinds of music - house and garage.

And as Brandon has managed to transcend so many different genres and scenes in dance music, he has made and stayed friends with many DJs. One such DJ of similar stature on the house scene is Jeremy Healy.

I have a lot of warmth for Brandon. We've got into some scrapes over the years, like pushing hire cars into the sea outside Cafe Mambo, and then sitting there waiting for people to come back and say "what's my car doing in the sea"... really stupid stuff like that. I always look forward to spending time with Brandon.

As the '90s drew to a close, all the UK's leading promoters were still clamouring to employ Brandon. Monthly residencies in 1998 included The Gallery at Turnmills and Frisky at the Ministry Of Sound, in London; Godskitchen in Milton Keynes; Slinky in Bournemouth; Progress in Derby; Republica in Birmingham and northern heavyweights Gatecrasher in Sheffield and Golden in Stoke were also starting to book Brandon more and more, meaning that the style of house music that he needed to play at those clubs would naturally see him crossover into a more progressive house and trance style. This would not help endear him further to the house purists he had played with at the start of his career, but he was not the first to have sold out in that respect.

The trance stuff was something that I felt I needed to do at the time to keep up the level of bookings I was getting, but it never sat that well with me. My heart wasn't really in it and I was never really comfortable with it because it obviously wasn't my particular taste. But that said it was a time when big rooms were particularly massive, and playing in the main rooms at clubs like Gatecrasher and Godskitchen at that time was an amazing experience, to see it going off like that.

The Gatecrasher kids were funny...with their Kermit The Frog backpacks and Teletubby outfits. We used to giggle in the DJ booth when we were playing, but at the end of the day we recognised that they were enjoying the music and expressing themselves.

These days there's so many different DJs and producers making so many different types of dance music that you can get bogged down with it and it can be hard to identify your own sound. Tiesto is now filling stadiums around the world, Carl Cox is still as massive as he's ever been, but he's pretty much stuck to his guns with harder stuff and techno, and Sasha is still huge throughout the world, and in particular the States, having remained loyal to the progressive house sound he developed while at Renaissance.

Moving forward through the '90s, I was maybe one of the few DJs I started out with who got to play at most of the different

bigger clubs, because I never pigeon-holed myself. And where the trancier stuff was concerned I always only played the ones that I liked, and there was still a skill involved in dropping the right records at the right time, and a certain amount of pressure when thousands of people were in those big rooms.

I always thought Oakey was the first to really master that with his Cream residency, then Sasha and Digweed took it on, and, like Oakey, all over the world. Not always sticking to one particular genre of house might have been to my detriment at certain times of my career, but probably hasn't been to the detriment of its longevity.

When I used to play up in Leeds at Up Yer Ronson and Kaos and Soak in the early '90s, Sasha and Dave Dorrell often used to be playing up there and we'd meet up and have these little after-parties after the gigs, just a few of us, and play old hip-hop tracks, and that was the stuff we really loved, so I guess even then there was a sense that you had to play certain records because they were the big tracks or anthems of the time, although in the early '90s it was easier to identify big records because there was less of them.

Looking back I think late '80s hip-house was the favourite type of music that I have played during my career. Breakbeats in dance music had dated back to the roots of hip-hop in the late '70s, with DJ pioneers in New York like Kool Herc, and James Brown's Funky Drummer is one of the most sampled loops ever.

Then acid house took over and the Balearic influence from Ibiza filtered through, so being able to drop hip-house tracks like Young MC's Know How, Tyree Cooper's Turn Up The Bass and Toni Scott's That's How I'm Living was a real bonus for me. Dave Dorrell and CJ Mackintosh's mix of Young MC's I Come Off, in particular, was superb. I loved hip-house because it kept me linked with my past, a link between rap and dance.

Karen Dunn points out:-

Brandon did go more progressive when he was playing for clubs like Godskitchen, Progress, Golden and Gatecrasher... but while I never thought it really suited him as a person, it probably fitted in well with his 'arms in the air' party style of DJing.

Other regular work in 1998 came from Karanga in Bristol, Rise in Sheffield and Sundissential in Brighton. There was also that Radio 1 event in Newcastle and a spot on the line-up on the massive Gatecrasher and Ministry Of Sound collaboration at Lotherton Hall in Leeds, which was a 10,000-capacity sell-out. Ibiza residencies, meanwhile, included Clockwork Orange at Es Paradis and Decadence at El Divino. Brandon would also wrap up the year playing a New Year's Eve gig in London for Clockwork.

But as well as the inner demons Brandon was still fighting regarding drugs, there were other doubts creeping in and out of his fragile mind.

Around this time I was unable to perform sexually because my body was so ravaged, and even, for want of a better term, 'knocking one out' was tricky.

It took me about a year to contend with those concerns, as my body slowly recovered, and my emotions stabilised. It was then that I experienced one of my first loves after being clean and supposedly clear-headed.

I met Donna at a Slinky gig at The Opera House in Bournemouth just before my birthday in March 1998, and then invited her up to London for my actual birthday. I was with Donna for two years, but I reiterate, if you're coming off drugs, don't get in an emotional relationship with someone you like until you're fully recovered. It sounds like a cliche, but it's true that you need to like and love yourself again first before and even a year and a half after I wasn't ready. Donna moved into the house in Ruislip, and then out again about ten times. She'd pack her car, go back to Bournemouth and then she'd be back. Then when she'd had enough of moving in and out, she moved in with my mum, in Harrow Road (in the box room of all places!!), got a job in town and went on a bit of a mad one herself.

I'm still in contact with her today, and she's lovely, but I would also like to publicly apologise to her for what I put her through. I was a complete nightmare and I know in those years after getting clean that I messed up several people's heads because I couldn't cope with the mental and physical condition that my drug abuse had left me in.

Brandon broke down several times while talking about this time in his life with me. On one occasion, as he poured his heart out he asked himself **"what have I done to these people?,"** before adding **"fucking hell mate...I'm filling up here, I haven't had a little weep for ages, but it's good to get your emotions out every now and then, though."**

It's clear that those years after he cleaned up were particularly testing for Brandon, his conscience now continually wrestling with the great times he enjoyed living a rock 'n' roll lifestyle versus the shell of a man he became.

Bill Shanahan explains:-

I made sure that Brandon was invited back regularly for check-ups, and we tested him regularly throughout the first few years to see if there were any drugs in his system, and it always was and always has been, a negative result. He did come in one time extremely anxious, but we couldn't actually work out what he was anxious about. His career was going well and he was about to go on a lovely holiday to Barbados, so there seemed little to be actually anxious about. But when you're coming off hard drugs like that the slightest thing can trigger something.

Back in the comparative novelty world of Caner Of The Year awards, Brandon was not in a position to defend his 1996 crown in 1997. Then the 1998 awards saw the French dominate with Air winning Best Album and Daft Punk producer Thomas Bangalter collecting Best Single for Stardust's Music Sounds Better With You. A certain Derek Dahlarge won the Caner Of...gong by a country mile, following his own legendary exploits in Ibiza.

The editorial that year concluded: *"So to next year. Will the French be nominated for so many awards and will Brandon Block come out of retirement for the Caner award."*

So if it wasn't hard enough avoiding various accomplices and fans just outright offering him drugs, the dance music press were still anxious for more textbook Blocko shenanigans.

A year later in '99, fittingly, Brandon and Alex jointly scooped the SAS Caner prize, with alcohol Brandon's only poison. In true awards style, there was now an Outstanding Contribution To Dance Music

Award, won by Brandon's pal Sasha, and a Best Single award, voted by Sun readers, won by Phats & Small with Turn Around, the latter a far cry from The Sun ten years earlier causing panic across the nation about "evil acid house".

The SAS Awards editorial this time read, *"El Blocko protested: "But I haven't done any gear for three years." But this year's antics in Ibiza prove that when it comes to world class competitive caning, always being up for a right giggle is more important than chemical assistance."*

That Brandon was still the life and soul of the party, came as no surprise to Karen Dunn.

When he came off the drugs, it was very difficult for him to be upbeat all the time, and everyone was still trying to give him gear as well. But he slowly found himself and realised that he didn't need the drugs...and he really doesn't...he never needed them all those years ago at Atlas when we were at work or out drinking after work...he was always the best fun you could have.

Brandon's muse Lisa Loud is grateful that he somehow managed to sort himself out.

Thank God the drugs nearly killed him, because it stopped him dying from it, and it means we still have him in our lives today. It was the biggest of wake up calls, and for everyone else too, especially those who saw him in hospital each time.

To be honest, I always thought he was too clever for the drugs anyway. You may have been out partying with Brandon for three or four days, and you'd sneak off and get bits of sleep here and there and then get up, and there was Brandon, still up, with a bottle of vodka, talking away. He would remember stuff and he would amaze you, holding a conversation, remembering exactly who was at what the previous nights, what time the cab came, just telling you this whole detailed account of the last few days, which I think is rare when someone is so twisted.

Meanwhile, that later caner award was possible because Brandon could (and still can, if need be) drink and party for two days on end, without cocaine. And if he has had a few drinks, people will naturally assume he has taken coke. I was sitting with some friends one morning by the pool at Es Vive hotel in Ibiza in 2002 when a disheveled Brandon stumbled in and joined our group. Although there was no evidence that he had, I too was convinced he was 'under the influence', purely based on his account of the various places he had been partying for the last 36 hours.

Where boozing is concerned, these days it's once in a blue moon that I go out and have few drinks, and I get the worst hangovers in the world afterwards. However, I think my drug abuse was so huge that it has also increased my tolerance to drink, in terms of how long I can drink, and that's not a good thing.

No doubt there will be people who come forward and say "I've done cocaine with Brandon Block" over the last 15 years, but it was probably they that were off their heads at the time. I haven't taken any coke since 1996. Believe me, I don't want to go down that road again, and when you've gone as low as I have, and know just how far you could end up going again, you really wouldn't want to do any ever again. That's how I feel.

A QUICK DRIVE ROUND THE BLOCKSTER

After a brief foray into production with the FUBAR track in the mid-90s, Brandon embarked on a new chapter of his career in 1998 and a more concentrated stab at producing.

He hooked up with old pals Fran Sidoli and Ricky Morrison. Fran was Brandon's old mate from north Wembley and a jazz dancer he admired, while Ricky was Fran's mate, from Alperton, who had a sound system, simply titled The System.

Both had gone on to become respected producers in their own right and the trio were approached by Dancin' Danny D, a London-based producer/remixer of some repute, who had helped bring acid house to the masses in 1988 with his No 3 hit We Call It Acieed, under the guise D-Mob.

Danny D was looking after these guys called Baby Bumps and he asked Ricky and Fran, who were now recording as M & S and had done stuff with Michelle Weeks and Barbara Tucker, if they would do a remix of a track Baby Bumps were doing called Burnin', which had sampled The Tramps anthem Disco Inferno. So Fran and Ricky asked me if I would like to get involved, because we'd been talking about doing some stuff, and they suggested we go by the name of Blockster. My profile was very high at this time and I'd been clean for a couple of years so it made sense.

Budnik, a reviewer on online music bible Discogs, sums up the Baby Bumps release like this, commenting:-

It's not big, it's not clever, but boy did this do some damage in Ibiza, season 1998. This was absolutely everywhere. It's not the most creative piece ever, so if you're going to steal some Tramps strings and bass you have to execute it very very well, which Blockster has done here. Let's make no pretence, this was made as a pure party record, it does exactly what it says on the tin. I used to love this, and I still do, it's so chunky and so funky. It's those strings and that bassline that just make the drop on this so enjoyable and I really like those chunky hi hats that drive the track along so well.

And while many of Brandon's peers wouldn't have loved those "chunky hi-hats", they would have found the chunky cheques on their way hard to turn down.

Our mix of Burnin' got Baby Bumps into the Top 40 and so Danny D wanted us to do something ourselves and hooked us up with Ministry Of Sound, and we started working on our own release, a reworking of The Bee Gees classic You Should Be Dancing, which was an anthem from their seminal Saturday Night Fever soundtrack, and which famously included Barry Gibb's now trademark falsetto vocals for the first time. We had put out a white label promo using the original Bee Gees vocals, but then had to get them re-sung for the official Ministry Of Sound release.

We got a nice advance for the two singles, and an album. The record labels were still giving money away at the time, and dance music had been big business for them for the last decade or so. Ministry had set up lots of different labels to run alongside their successful club, and had realised that as well as putting out loads of compilations, they could save money in licensing if they owned a lot of the tracks that would go on those albums, as well as earning loads of money back by licensing those tracks to all the other big compilations other major labels were putting out.

We invested the majority of our advance in a state-of-the-art studio in the basement behind the old R & D record shop that we all used to spend so much time in, so hanging out in Rayners Lane appealed to us from a sentimental point of view. To get the highest quality sound, we built a room within a room, and paid for the best equipment out at the time.

Fortunately for the Ministry, their faith was repaid and upon release in January 1999, You Should Be Dancing went to No 3, and stayed in the national charts for 16 weeks. It meant that a spot on Top Of The Pops beckoned for Brandon, 26 years after, as a starry-eyed six-year-old, he first met the show's then producer, neighbour and family friend Brian Whitehouse.

The track was massive for us, and as well as being included on all of the Ministry comps, it went on all the other massive ones, like Now That's What I Call Music 42 and Now This And That... and it meant that my dream as a child of appearing on Top Of The Pops was actually going to happen. When the chart placing was announced on the Sunday evening I was at home on my own, because I'd been gigging all weekend. Fran and Ricky were listening together. We all screamed at each other down the phone and met up for a good old drink up.

When Blockster was released, Brandon's old pal Norman Cook, now in his Fatboy Slim guise, was No 1 with Praise You, a track accompanied by a hilarious and award-winning video directed by Spike Jonze. Cook had enjoyed No 1s in the past, first as the bass player of The Housemartins in 1986 with Caravan Of Love, then in 1990 with Lindy Layton in his Beats International guise and The Clash / SOS Band-sampling Dub Be Good To Me.

At the time I think I was one of the, if not THE, highest-placed modern day club DJs in the UK charts. Tall Paul had reached No 11 a couple of years earlier with Rock Da House, so to get to No 3 was fantastic, and it went straight in at No 3 too.

Norman had been involved in bands and doing his different things for quite a while now, but I wasn't a musician, let alone a pop star, so for me to get into the top three of the UK charts and to actually appear on Top Of The Pops, which had been such a British institution all my life, was superb. The Spice Girls had the Christmas No 1 a few weeks earlier with Goodbye and they were still selling quite a few records and obviously Praise You was massive too, so I was more than happy to get to No 3.

The Top Of The Pops experience was great. We were down at the Elstree Studios in Borehamwood, and it was a top day out. To be on TOTP was something I never ever envisaged, and it was an honour to be on the same stage as the various acts of the time, and a bonus to go out on prime-time BBC TV as well. I was on stage with Danny Love, our singer, a guy from Streatham, who had re-sung the Bee Gees original vocals (so no pressure there, then!). We had some cute dancers with us, but Fran and Ricky had stayed back stage so I was left to do the trademark DJ come producer wally bit behind the decks, which I was happy to do and which I'd always excelled at anyway. I was wearing this shirt with centres of records all over it and a big floppy hat, which a mate had given me. I tried not to take it too seriously because I was standing there behind the decks basically not doing a lot. I wanted to look silly, and I certainly did. It was great fun.

The kids in the studio were not exactly cheering for us, like the reception that Spice Girl Mel C got. She had done that track with Bryan Adams, Baby When You're Gone, which I really liked at the time, and so me Fran and Ricky met up with her, and Kate Thornton, who was presenting the show. It was great to be involved in Top Of The Pops, especially as it's no longer with us.

I did the usual rounds of interviews, including Mark Goodier for Radio One, and later that week I was on ITV's London Today show, with Mary Nightingale. That was weird, because it was like they were behind the times, asking about this dance music phenomenon of covering old records, but people had obviously been sampling other anthems for donkeys' years. Italian producer Daniel Davoli had sampled Loleatta Holloway's Love Sensation ten years earlier in 1989 for Ride On Time and got a UK No 1 with it, so we weren't exactly groundbreaking. I guess it was the Bee Gees angle that was creating such a fuss, because of their huge fan base, and them being the housewives' choice.

I remember Phats & Small reached No 2 with Turn Around, their cover of Toney Lee's Reach Up, a couple of weeks later, and we started to bump into each other on the DJ and PA circuit. We all did a big gig out in Dubai, soon after, in fact, and had a right old giggle. There was certainly always a friendly rivalry between the Blockster and the Phats & Small camps.

Appearances on The Pepsi Chart Show, recorded for ITV at the Sound nightclub in Leicester Square, with Dr Fox as presenter, also followed, but don't be surprised if you don't see broadcaster Mary Ann Hobbs interviewing Brandon anytime soon.

The Mary Ann Hobbs thing was so embarrassing. The BBC had set up this radio interview with me, Fran and Ricky at our Rayners Lane studio, and for some reason I'd gone out on the piss the night before, can't remember why, but maybe I was celebrating the chart success with some other friends. Anyway, I turned up for the interview the next day, half an hour late, and I was still drunk.

And I was immediately taken by surprise when the TV crew presented me with a cartoon drawing of me mocked up as Charlie in The Italian Job, Michael Caine's character. The Italian Job is one of my favourite films, but still to this day I can't work out why they had done this. In the picture I am standing by a vintage Mini Cooper, with loads of gold bars in it, and IBIZA on the number plate, with 'you were only meant to blow the bloody doors off' emblazoned across it. I don't know whose idea it was, but I've still got it up on the wall of my office now.

So, I had staggered in, rat-arsed, looked at the picture in amazement, swore at a few people, including Mary, collapsed on the sofa, and passed out. Mary Ann Hobbs said something like "I'm never speaking to that guy again," and stormed out. So that was another thing that Blocko fucked up.

But that wasn't the last we would hear of Blockster, albeit that the album would never actually materialise.

Our follow-up to You Should Be Dancing a few months later was a version of the Heatwave anthem Grooveline. I got Matt Darey, who was the man of the moment where trance remixes were concerned, to have a go at it, and it was his version that got to No 16 in the charts, so that meant two tracks, two Top 20 hits. It went on loads of comps again, and by the time they had finished with that, Ministry had recouped their money and much more.

After that, I think I kind of lost interest, and so the album never actually happened. We'd made another track at the end of 1998 called Something's Going On, under the guise Mystic 3, which Danny Love again sang vocals on, and that actually got signed to Erick Morillo's Subliminal label, which was really popular at the time, with that filtered disco sound, which the track was all about. That came out shortly after too, and sold a few thousand copies in the process. However, making an album as Blockster, of the sort of tracks that were now expected from me, and coupled with my DJ schedule at that time, would have been a tall order, I think.

The guys carried on at the studio for several more years, and had another Top 5 hit with M & S Presents The Girl Next Door and the track Salsoul Nugget, which sampled both Loleatta Holloway and Double Exposure. I was just too busy DJing to really get involved in any more production work at that time so I decided to knock it on the head.

These days you hardly need any equipment to make a record, though. All the plug-ins are available on Logic and the other various computer programs.

It's the same with actual DJing, kids don't buy record decks any more, they either go for CD mixers or straight for a laptop. You don't need decks any more, you just need to plug your laptop into the back of a mixer and you're off.

Increasingly, another fixture on Brandon's social scene was Tony Byrne, a radio plugger he met through Kiss FM, and who, like Brady, would go on to have a huge influence on Brandon's career.

I got to know Brandon first in the Kiss days because of my work as a radio plugger since the very first day the station launched legally. I was tight with Sarah HB, Dave Pearce and Steve Jackson, all those guys at Kiss, so I guess from the early days of Brandon and Alex's show, plus I was doing a lot of stuff with John Davis and Chris Brown in Ibiza, and we were all like part of a little gang going out clubbing, Stringfellows and various other places. Getting up to all sorts, really.

I'd already done some radio plugging work with Fran and Ricky, and I'd spoken to them about the Blockster track first, and then found out Brandon was involved, so it made sense for me to get on board.

I'd already had my own independent company, Single Minded Promotions. It was Matt Jagger from the Ministry who actually brought me in on the Blockster project so I got involved doing all the radio and TV promotions for the single. We did Top Of The Pops and The Pepsi Chart Show with Foxy.

I'd also been talking to BBC producers about doing an Ibiza special, because they still hadn't been out to the island. So in the summer of 1999 I'd put together an Ibiza special of the pop culture show The Ozone, with Jayne Middlemiss co-presenting alongside

Brandon. The BBC hadn't actually been to Ibiza before, and neither had Jayne.

The next summer I was also behind the Channel 4 Dog's Balearics show, which Jayne presented with a young Dermot O'Leary, and which also heavily featured Brandon and Alex. I was like a researcher/producer of the show, and also there to make sure Brandon turned up. At the time I was looking after big dance labels like Postivia Perfecto, etc, so I booked loads of big dance acts from their rosters to be interviewed and do live PAs on the show.

With a Top 3 hit and an appearance on prime-time BBC 1, Brandon's notoriety and fame was increasing by the week. New Year's Eve in 1998 had been topped off by an unusual mode of transport to his final gig at The Gardening Club. And while lots of clubbers get taken away from venues in a police car, it's not often a DJ gets delivered in one.

We were stuck in bad traffic in Covent Garden because of the festivities going on in nearby Trafalgar Square, and the necessary road closures. There were people everywhere, we were at a complete standstill, it was 'chocka'. I was already late for my set for Shelley Boswell so Brady told me to get out and walk the last half a mile or so with the smallest bag we had, and he'd park up when he could and bring in the other three.
So I got out of the car, and was getting one bag out of the boot when suddenly I was surrounded by Old Bill. I was shitting myself, but then suddenly one copper said "all right Brandon, where do you need to get to?". The next thing I was in the back of this police car, Brady had loaded the rest of my bags in the boot - which was apparently full of guns - the 'blues and twos' were turned on and I was taken straight to the door. I have to say, that was pretty special. Thank-you, Britain's finest.

Brandon's fame was still on the ascendancy and in 1999 he was asked to write a weekly dance column for national newspaper The Daily Star, as part of the tabloid's showbiz page Access All Areas. As well as charting Brandon's career over the next few years, 'Blockbeat' kept tabs on Brandon's naughty early noughties lap-dancing phase and his various celebrity romances, and running until 2001 the column was

THE LIFE & LINES OF BRANDON BLOCK

the perfect vehicle in which to talk about the various scrapes in which he found himself, in particular The Brits at the start of 2000.

Brandon played so many gigs in 1999, as the acid house generation club era reached its peak, the DJ fees earned each week, plus production royalties meant he could treat himself to a Ferrari...or two, among several other high performance sports cars!

At one time I had four cars, including a Ferrari, all imports and many first in the country editions - either parked on my drive or halfway up the road. Totally self- indulgent and totally unnecessary.

Then one day when me and Brady were driving through Ruislip we saw an old 2.8is Granada Ghia for sale. It was like an old Sweeney car. We said "we're having that", and we bought it there and then for £500. It would be our tool for DJ driving, so we were like The Professionals, and we'd use it for all my bookings. It was sumptuous, had electric everything and we put a decent stereo in and we were away. I'd always sleep in the back on the way to gigs and it went everywhere. We really drove it into the ground... Leeds... Newcastle... Blackpool, wherever. It was a much cheaper car than what we had on the driveway, but it was the nuts.

Brady points out:-

I gave a monkey for that, and that car lasted us for years. It was unbelievable, it was 1997 and it was a 14-years-old, gold, X-Pack Granada Ghia, loaded with everything. Then we bought a brand new BMW 7 Series, but the Granada was better than that. Brandon bought the 7 Series, and then I bought it off him. He gave 33 gibs for it, brand new, and I gave him 18 grand for it a couple of years later.

(clockwise) * Backstage at TOTP with Blockster colleagues Fran Sidoli and Ricky Morrison
* The red Blocko Ferrari F355 Spider
* The Mary-Ann Hobbs 'Italian Job' poster
* At TOTP with presenter Kate Thornton, 'Sporty Spice', Mel B and Bryan Adams
* Blockster promo shot with singer Danny Love

BIOKOS

THE ITALIAN JOB

TOP OF THE POPS

BLOCK

We had been using our own motors, and we were knocking the bollocks out of them. I said "we've both got nice cars, what are we doing here?" We were actually going to his mum's house, and there's this car dealer on the way, who had all these 'cheapies' lined up on the road. There it was, this gold Granada, and I thought, "this'll fucking do us".

Wherever we went, everybody loved the car. The first trip, we took it to Progress in Derby, and the car was so mint, that Russell, the promoter and the bouncers were all over it. It was originally owned by Lord Sainsbury, what a touch, the seats were massive and heated. It's the most comfortable car I've ever been in. We used to roar with laughter when we were in it.

Brandon suddenly had all this extra money, and he started wasting it all on cars. He'd buy and sell a car and think nothing about the money he just lost on it, as long as he was able to buy the next car he had his eye on.

He lost a few quid on one Ferrari in the space of six months, a F355 Spider. Before that he had a black 348GTS Ferrari, but that came and went as well. If a car was worth £10k, he'd be happy to get £8k back for it, because he was so desperate to get a new one.

One such high performance sports car didn't, however, stay on Brandon's drive for long, in another example of how it took him some time to put all signs of stupidity and recklessness behind him, despite cocaine no longer being in his life.

It was meant to be a quiet night in with a couple of mates of mine, and turned into what has become known as 'The Siege Of Block Manor'. It was March 1999 and I had taken delivery of the first Audi TT sports car in the UK - a beautiful, gun metal grey model with basketball stitching on the leather interior. I'd had my name down on the list ever since they'd announced they were making it a couple of years earlier.

I'd been out with the boys during the day, but later that night it was the old classic... we'd run out of fags. There's a petrol station two minutes from my house, so I said "c'mon let's jump in the TT", which I hadn't driven yet, apart from back from the showroom. We could have walked, but I was adamant we should

drive so we all piled in the TT, made it to the garage, got the ciggies, and headed back home.

Suddenly it got really foggy and I lost it on a bend, mounted the kerb, ploughed straight through a fence and crashed into the outside of our local pub, The Woodman. Literally through the side of it so my lovely brand new TT was half inside the pub itself, with guttering and drainpipes on top of it, totally mangled. And with my personalised number plate BIOXTA for all to see.

We all managed to scramble out of the car, thankfully without injury, and leg it back to my place. I was at Kiss at the time so this really was irresponsible of me, but I suddenly panicked about whether my insurance was valid on the new car.

We got back to the house, and an hour later there was a knock on the door and, surprise surprise, it was the police. The officer said to me "Mr Block, do you own an Audi TT?" I said "yes", and he said "do you know where it is?" Not so much telling a little white lie, as a dirty great big black one, I pointed to my mate and said, "it's round his place". The officer looked at me, dead-panned, and said: "It's not round there, Mr Block, it's in The Woodman!"

I said "you're joking, in that case, I'd like to report it stolen", and ushered them out of the door. I think all of us, including the police themselves, had a hunch they may be back.

Sure enough, an hour later… woo… woo… woo… woo… the whole of the cul-de-sac was under siege, with about ten police cars present, including two Volvos at the end of the road back to back, specifically so nobody could get out. There was a policeman trying to look through the letter box to see if we were in there.

One of my mates suddenly took all his clothes off and stood there naked right in front of the letter box so all they could see was his wedding tackle. The officer was saying "LET US IN… POLICE", and my mate was saying, "no, sorry, you can't come in, you haven't got a warrant, you've got no right", and all they could see was his bits and pieces. The police were saying that they'd got hold of CCTV from the petrol station, and my naked pal was saying, "I'm sorry, it's just not convenient right now…we're busy".

I didn't know whether to laugh or cry. Then somehow, my mate was on his phone and had managed to get through to Scotland

Yard. God knows how he knew or had the number, but he was speaking to this inspector, and quoting his name back to the police. By now there were police on the roof of the house, in the neighbour's garden, everywhere, and whoever this inspector was, he must have been high-ranking because suddenly they all went. It was quite amazing.

I got in a cab, and went to south London to hook up some mates out of the area, and I hung out with them all day, then came home and crashed out. When I woke up the next day, not for the first time, I thought, "oh no, what have I done?", and went down to Uxbridge police station to talk to them about it.

My insurance was all OK, and after being interviewed I was given a slap on the wrists. There was loads of damage to the car so I got that fixed and I also paid for all the damage to the pub.

WE WANNA PARTY LIKE IT'S £19.99

So with another tricky episode somehow successfully navigated, and amazingly, once again, without injury or loss of life, Brandon concentrated once more on his relentless DJ schedule.

As the months in 1999 ticked away, with the Millennium celebrations looming ever closer, he was playing for virtually all of the UK's top promotions as clubland partied like never before. And while clubland, as it had been known for the last decade, was almost spent, there were more than enough gigs to drive to – the sheer amount of bookings for Brandon in 1999, in fact, was phenomenal.

In the supposedly quiet month of January he played at The Gallery, Godskitchen and Golden. There was a crest of a wave to be ridden and Brandon and co were managing that with style. Club-wise, his monthly residencies at The Gallery, Frisky, Godskitchen and Progress continued, and Brandon also went monthly at Golden and Passion, with regular bookings at Mezzanine in Wolverhampton, run by his old sparring partner Charlie Chester, and Slinky also on rotation.

More unchartered territory was to be discovered in 1999 too, when Brandon was asked to play in Dubai.

In 1999 DJing in Dubai was still relatively unheard of, but a friend of mine, Paul Dwyer, was living out there. He'd started to do some parties and ask me to play.

I took my pal Gary 'The Phone', who I originally met a few times in the late '80s, but didn't get to know properly until the late '90s. Gary is so-called because he used to own a mobile phone shop and he is definitely someone who I associate with my clean years and who has also been a massive source of support to me. He's a bit of a boy to say the least, and I met him through my good pal and jazz dancer hero Rick Williamson on the forecourt of Rick's car showroom, negotiating the sale of a 735 BMW. At that point the buying and selling of cars was very much an addiction of mine. Me and Gary soon became inseparable.

For the Dubai trip me and 'The Phone' had two business class flights on Brunei Airways and it was all laid on. However, just as

we were about to land, it dawned on me that we were entering an Arab state, and that I had loads of stamps from Tel Aviv on my passport. I told the stewardess and was quickly whisked into the cockpit, where the captain wasn't that helpful, telling me that his mum had been to Israel, then had gone to Lebanon, and had been caught up in loads of red tape. Meanwhile, 'The Phone' was saying stuff like "fucking hell mate, you're in deep shit if they find out you're a 'four by two'. By the time I got to immigration I was a bag of nerves and was shaking so much I could just about fill in the landing card. It was after that I got an additional passport, which I could keep free of Israeli stamps, and vice versa.

On that first Dubai trip we were treated like kings. Paul had managed to get the gig sponsored by BMW and he was waiting for us at the airport with a BMW each for me and Gary to drive around in. We were staying at the Mina Seyahi Beach Resort hotel, which was amazing, and on the flight back, we were actually in first class. Champagne, silver service and lots of 'freemans' going on.

And there were more golf clubs than nightclubs out in Dubai at this point. There was one venue called Zinc, and then lots of bars inside hotels, and our gig was at a bar/club at The Atlantis, next door to the Hardrock Cafe.

There was a healthy scene of British ex-pats out there, and a few late-night watering holes, all of which were attached to hotels in some capacity, where they'd go to drink as late as they possibly could.

The second time I went out there, Paul booked me with Phats & Small because we both had big tracks out at the time, and we did a big party, me, Russell and Jason, at the Hilton Beach Club Resort, with 4,000 people down by the sea. It was amazing. The following night we were all taken out for a meal at an underwater restaurant at the seven-star Bari al Arab Hotel.

I must have DJd more than 20 times in Dubai over the years. At one point, around 2005, I was resident at a club called The Lodge, an open air place, and I went out there once a month for eight months consecutively. In those days I was like a celeb, I guess, and it was great fun, all expenses paid. We would get taken everywhere.

I played at loads of places in Dubai. Another one was Diamonds, but that got shut down after the promoter Danny Doubles, who I worked with loads as well, brought over Dezire Dubfire, the transvestite DJ. The powers that be didn't like that, and that night it was shut down immediately, never to return.

Brandon's star was still rising, and the Dubai experience was proof of that.

His Blockster success had seen him cross over effortlessly to the commercial arena, and for several years now the same DJs had been appearing at the same clubs, their names getting bigger on the full-page adverts that filled the likes of MixMag.

In May 1999, one advert for Passion at Coalville typified such repetition, advertising the Bank Holiday Sunday line-ups that month (May 2 and May 30) with exactly the same line-up – Brandon Block, Alex P, resident JFK and percussion by Mav. Hardly original, but Brandon and Alex and such leading DJs were putting bums on seats, and their stranglehold on clubland made it hugely difficult for new DJs to break through.

I could appreciate how difficult it was for up-and-coming DJs to get a chance. I'd always get people telling me about their son or their friend, that they were really good, etc, and get given all these mix tapes and CDs, and I'd tell them that I'd love to help, but explain that it wasn't for me to bring DJs along to play alongside me, or warm-up for me, and that the promoter in question booked all the DJs.

I'd try my best and mention a few names to the promoters, but they weren't interested. I was playing all over the country and they always had their local guys as the warm-up jocks, DJs who would bring a few people with them and had a decent local following. That was one of the main ways to get a foot on the ladder, getting a residency at the local club that was booking all the bigger DJs at the time, but obviously that would often be a closed shop within the general closed shop that we'd had for a quite a few years now.

But this is where production comes in, because every now and then a new producer would make a new record, or do a really good mix which was championed by Pete Tong on his Radio One show, and then they would start getting booked.

Pete Tong was very influential during the '90s, and that should never be underestimated. In particular, he helped bring through young DJs like Fergie and Eddie Halliwell. It was a shame for a lot of the up-and-coming house DJs, though. Later in the '90s it seemed that the kids coming through were listening to UK garage, drum and bass, trance and R & B more and more, and in those cases, it was easier for unknown DJs to break through into those scenes than the house scene, which was dominated by what I'd call the big-name old school DJs.

Also in May, Muzik Magazine ran an article in which old pal Nicky Holloway admitted he blew £50,000 on cocaine. Brandon was included in a fact file titled The Rich & Famous Who Had To Give It All Up, alongside supermodel Kate Moss and footballer Paul Gascoigne. His file read: *"The Blockster ended up on the dark side of the coke 'n' booze street. Currently wanted by the disco police for his Top 20 hit You Should Be Dancing"*.

Since then, Moss has managed to stay on the right side of cool, while Gazza took getting clean literally, and was allegedly caught by hotel staff getting friendly with a mop.

May 1999 also saw the first ever Homelands festival in Winchester, headlined by The Chemical Brothers and Fatboy Slim, with Danny Tenaglia given his own tent for a ten hour set and Brandon in the Slinky Arena. Creamfields also took place in August, with Pet Shop Boys topping the bill and Brandon in the Radio 1/Essential Mix Main Arena.

Brandon had been clean of cocaine for 18 months now, but he was still not averse to getting 'out of his tree'. In fact, he'd been branching out and Brady chuckles as he remembers one particular stunt.

Once he's had a drink, once he's got something in his head, he's doing it, whether it's climbing a tree, or kicking someone off the decks at Cartier Polo so he can play instead... he's going to do it. He went through this phase of climbing trees and one year when we were at Homelands Judge Jules was being filmed by MTV. Brandon climbed up a tree and jumped on top of him in the middle of the interview. Scared the life out of Jules, that did.

Ibiza '99 would be another busy three or four months for Brandon too...with a weekly residency on Tuesdays for Godskitchen at Amnesia, alongside the familiar names of Alex P, Seb Fontaine, Boy George and Jeremy Healy.

And with a steadier Ibiza season in 1998 following his erratic and often traumatic "clean comeback" season the year before in 1997, Brandon – despite his driving dramas – was in a better place for his latest Ibiza jolly.

Brandon and Alex were now completely out of the picture on the Space terrace on Sundays with Darren Hughes cementing his Home 24-hour residency and moving forward with his own resident team of Steve Lawler, Jason Bye and Jose Divina. But Brandon's Ibiza diary was as full as ever.

With Godskitchen in Ibiza going from strength to strength, in the summer of '99, Brandon also played fortnightly at Sundance Tuesday daytime sessions, regularly for Clockwork Orange at Es Paradis on a Wednesday night, had weekly spots at new San An superclub Eden and also had a new weekly Wednesday session at Summons. To cap it all off he and Alex also mixed a major release for The Dance Dept called Ibiza Anthems 2.

The summer of 1999 would also see MTV host an ambitious 18,000-capacity festival in a disused quarry a mile outside of San Antonio, featuring live headliners Faithless, Orbital and the Jungle Brothers, and a DJ line-up including leading Americans Frankie Knuckles, David Morales and Erick Morillo, plus Brandon, Alex, Paul Oakenfold, Seb Fontaine and Norman Jay.

I was writing for M8 Magazine and part of a delegation of journos sent out to cover the event, along with Bestival boss Rob Da Bank, then the Club Editor at Muzik Magazine, and all funded by sponsors Corona Extra and Smint, the handy new ecstasy tablet-shaped mints.

After regularly blowing at least £1,000 each week on the numerous occasions that I visited the island since the early '90s, the £50 in total I spent on that four day trip was a pleasant surprise indeed. And the sight of David Morales floating past on his Smint lilo at Pikes is a Balearic memory that will live with me forever. The exclusive live show

Moloko's Roisin Murphy put on for us at the notorious Manumission Motel, including a faultless rendition of that season's anthem Sing It Back, was also special, to say the least. But then so was the Manumission Motel!!!

A few days before the MTV party I played at a very important party - the second birthday of Zach P, Alex's son and my godson. From there we hotfooted it to an MTV Festival pre-party at Cafe Mambo, hosted by Erick Morillo, with Norm 'MBE' Jay, The Jungle Brothers, Knuckles and Morales all in attendance, and that set the scene for what was a great festival.

I didn't make it along to the Manumission Motel much, maybe once if at all, and that's probably a good thing. Who knows what we would have got up to in there in my heyday?

Over the years I also had the good fortune of playing at the flagship Manumission night itself a few times, in the main room, at Privilege, with the sex shows going on around me; Claire and Mike Manumission getting down to it in front of 11,000 people. Absolute madness, but that's what it was like in many of the main rooms out there, the same with Amnesia to a certain extent, where the DJ booth was up high, close to the ever increasingly erotic podium dancers. They filmed the Kevin & Perry film there, and it was exactly like that, with all the punters down below going absolutely berserk, and scantily clad birds and blokes dotted around the place.

Meanwhile, Daily Star readers were getting the weekly lowdown in Blockbeat. And Brandon must have been really keen on Donna. He even mentioned her tactically in his Daily Star column in July, 1999.

Played at London's Party In The Park, in front of 100,000 people - "such a buzz"...the girls were cool but I didn't sneak off with anyone because the only woman for me is my girlfriend Donna. Did you read that babe? This week I'm not going to recommend two tracks 'cos there's only one track worth buying - mine. Grooveline is a remake of Heatwave's Top 3 hit from 1977. It's out on Monday!

In the same month Brandon told readers:-

Rumours have been circulating that I had to put Happy Mondays legend Bez and drug-smuggler Howard Marks to bed. Nothing can be further from the truth. They're the last people who'd need Blocko to put them to bed. Admittedly, I did get very drunk with them at Space in Ibiza, but when I left they were still partying like never before.

Brandon's life has often lurched from one extreme to another, and it could be said he does extremes well...like an Ibiza stint in August 1999 when one night he was DJing to a Pacha crowd that included Madonna, and the next he was hanging out with Dean Gaffney and Sid Owen.

Meanwhile, the September '99 issue of MixMag was a bizarre one, even by their standards! The 200th issue of the magazine, it featured a two-page pull out from the front cover, which was a photo-shopped picture of a Royal Family wedding with DJs' faces superimposed over the happy couple and guests. Brandon was the king and Alex P the Queen. Other highlights include Judge Jules, Tom Chemical, Goldie and Karl Hyde from Underworld in dresses and Paul Hartnoll from Orbital as a bridesmaid.

Later in that issue Brandon was also named No 1 in MixMag's Nutters Of The Decade feature, and pictured with Bez (No 4), Derek Dahlarge (No 5) and Alex P (No 9). For the record, Danny Clockwork was No 8, finally beating one half of his heroes in the caner stakes, at least!

As the big countdown to the Millennium ticked ever closer, Brandon and Alex were installed as weekly Friday night residents at Area in Watford, a new 1,250 capacity venue just down the road from Brandon, opened by former Milk Bar owner Leon Lenik, Jeremy Healy and Club For Life promoter Shelley Boswell.

In November the DJ Magazine Awards were held at the Ministry Of Sound, and Brandon explained in Blockbeat:-

I missed out on the best DJ Prize, which went to Judge Jules, but the smile was wiped off his face when he was voted worst dressed man. I thought I might have scooped that, though, for some of the outrageous outfits I've worn.

Then as December of '99 started to play out, it quickly became apparent that clubbers across the UK were refusing to pay £100 for a ticket to a New Year's Eve club event, and most organized their own house parties instead.

The result for the promoters was calamitous. Many lost thousands of pounds, and in some cases the houses and nightclubs they had bought with previous proceeds, while hundreds of DJs had their gigs cancelled in the weeks leading up to December 31 as poor ticket sales left everyone with anything at stake in a blind panic.

I was initially booked to play at three events….Millennium Village at Three Mills Studios in Bow, east London, which was a complete disaster; Godskitchen in Birmingham which was reduced to just residents in the run-up and Golden at Manchester Academy, which I was pencilled in for, but that booking never happened either.

Brandon can reveal that at one point in 1999 he was offered an unbelievable £50,000 to play exclusively at the Godskitchen gig or £20,000 for a non-exclusive set.

I opted for the non-exclusive one, which meant I could do Millennium Village and Golden, and meant that I would earn more than the £50k in total. It also meant that I was spreading my options across three parties, so if there were any problems I stood a better chance of getting paid.

Once the big events were announced after the summer of that year, and it was confirmed that most of them would be charging

*(clockwise) * The esteemed MixMag Royal Family!*
* In Ibiza with Lee Garrick from Miss Moneypenny's
* with Dave Dorrell and Danny Rampling
Trace Edwards and Trevor Fung; Simon Dunmore;
and (centre) with revellers in Dubai, including
promoter Danny Doubles, kissing Blocko's head!

MIXMAG ROYAL FAMILY

KE TO THANK YOU ALL FOR MAKING THE LAST 200 ISSUES SUCH A LAUGH

Pissed Winnin 24 Karl Hyde 25
29 Brandon Block 30 Paul Orbital 3
34 Keith Flint 35 Goldie 36 Tom Ch

DAILY STAR, Saturday, November 4, 2000 17

LOCKBEAT WITH BRANDON BLOCK

s Vegas, party — full-on weekend
didn't get an up

£100, people had quickly started talking about whether the whole thing would be an anti-climax, so I tried to always consider that in mind when negotiating.

New Year's Eve had long been a rip-off where punters were concerned, with all parties keen to earn double what they usually do, starting with the bar staff, who somewhere along the line had began to earn so-called 'double-bubble' to cushion the blow of working while everybody else drunkenly saw in the New Year.

Bouncers had soon cottoned on to that fact too, as well as cab drivers, and when the clubs in turn started to charge promoters double the usual hire fee to cover their costs, the promoters decided to charge two times as much for a New Year's Eve ticket. It didn't take your average superjock or their agent long to work out that they could now charge double for their New Year's Eve fees.

Or at least, that's one theory, because there's definitely a bit of 'chicken and egg' about the whole 'double bubble' situation.

Whatever the case, for the Millennium it seemed that the promoters weren't content with going triple, they wanted to charge three times the usual double NYE ticket price. So whereas the punters were used to paying £30 on NYE instead of the £15 every Friday or Saturday throughout the year, now many of the promoters had decided to triple the NYE double to £90, and round it off to £100 for good measure. But don't get the violins out for Brandon just yet.

I accepted a cancellation fee worth a few grand from Godskitchen a couple of weeks before the event, as it was fast becoming clear that the whole thing was going tits up. Generally, the promoters thought they would have two or three thousand people paying £100 each, and so if that netted them two or three hundred thousand pounds they could afford to give four of us DJs £20,000 each, and still have loads left.

At the time I got offered the £50k I thought this was going to be the big one, the big pay day, and that I could clear my mortgage with that. But about a month before we knew it wasn't going to be as amazing as everyone thought because all the hype had been ruined by the ticket prices. I guess a number of things were responsible. Everyone involved was trying to earn a quick buck,

but I don't think most of the DJs ever expected to earn as much as we were being offered. We were on good money anyway, but when we were offered it, we were hardly going to say "no", and at least we had the cancellation fee clauses in our contracts. You couldn't blame the punters at all. I still had enough of a punter in me to appreciate what was going on wasn't right. They were saying "why should we pay £100 to listen to the same old DJs in the same old club when we usually pay fifteen or twenty?" And they were right.

Golden head honcho Jon Hill can shed some light on how he avoided paying Brandon thousands of pounds on Millennium Eve, and remembers those big DJ fees of the late '90s were a far cry from his dealings with Brandon's 'secretary' earlier in the decade.

I remember booking Brandon before he had an agent and ringing his home number and his mum Vivienne used to answer, and she was always lovely to me. Brandon wasn't the most reliable of DJs, but let's just say when he did turn up, he never let me down. I actually put on two parties on Millennium Eve, one at the Manchester Academy, which broke even, and one at The Void in our hometown of Stoke, which ended up just residents, and which I made five grand on. Both parties were basically just residents in the end.

I did bid for Brandon at one point, but like all the DJs for Millennium it was silly money, and I'm glad I got outbid. In fact, thank God I did get outbid. In the end we saw sense and basically charged what we did every other New Year's Eve. I think I was one of the few people who did make any money that year.

I always thought Brandon was unique in that he was probably the only DJ from the Balearic network in London who had a foot in both camps and then crossed over to the big-room trance bookings. I bet he made more money than all of the so-called cooler DJs who started out with him at Flying or wherever.

Despite the wave of ensuing Millennium NYE house parties, as well as Jon Hill's £5k, there were some other notable successes. Gatecrasher, in a bid to offer their faithful following something different, booked the Dom Valley Athletic Stadium in Sheffield, selling 25,000 tickets at £100 each in the process. Meanwhile, Carl Cox earned a reported £200,000 by playing the midnight Millennium set in first Fiji and then Australia, by literally flying back in time between the two in a private jet.

Karen Dunn, now back working with Charlie Chester for his Icon Ibiza holiday and VIP hospitality firm, remembers:-

The Millennium was a big disaster for a lot of people. Everyone got greedy and the bottom really fell out of the market. Where a lot of the top guys used to earn a couple of thousand pounds a gig, their fees now went down to a grand and under. Brandon was one of the DJs who stayed at the higher level for a while longer yet and is still working to this day, and three or four times a week as well, when many of the other DJs have thrown in the towel. That's because of Brandon's personality and notoriety and because he interacts with the crowd.

And Brandon had the perfect antidote to any Millennium blues – a trip on a Lear jet to Ibiza on the morning of New Year's Day for a Manumission party later that day on his beloved Space terrace with Alex P and Judge Jules.

Covered by MixMag, the editorial exclaimed: *"Outside the Kings Of The Terrace are warming up. There's no doubt that the Carl Coxes and Basement Jaxxes of this world rock the Space terrace, but no one does it with the spirit of Blocko and Peasey. Brandon's bought his "box of old chestnuts" and Alex goes one step further, putting on Wham's Club Tropicana."*

After the disaster that was…we had the perfect tonic with the New Year's Day trip to Space. We had to get to Luton Airport for 7am and although I was a bit drunk, I was clean and looking forward to the new Millennium. Space was packed and they didn't seem to have charged over the odds. It's expensive enough out there anyway, of course. It was brilliant to be back at our spiritual home and causing havoc on the terrace once more.

And, although he didn't realise it at the time, Brandon had a PR trump card in his hand, which would firmly banish the ghost of the Millennium, and give him more publicity than he could shake a publicist at!

BRITS & IN PIECES

On the face of it, going head to head with a Rolling Stones legend at The Brits was probably not the smartest thing Brandon has ever done, but like so many times before the devil inside him took over!

And once again he seemed to come out of the whole thing with all the extra controversy and attention adding to his worth.

The ceremony came at the start of an extraordinary fortnight, even by his own standards.

While this little episode in his life could not be blamed on cocaine - he'd been clean almost four years by now - alcohol did have a major part to play.

The dreaded champagne reception was at the route of the problem and we've all been there, peaking too early on an empty stomach at a wedding or corporate function…just haven't ended up on stage at Earls Court bickering with Ronnie Wood in front of a TV audience of ten million and counting.

This was Brandon creating the latest instalment of Brits-gate, which had previously seen Samantha Fox and Mick Fleetwood 'die' on stage, Jarvis Cocker moon at Michael Jackson and Chumbawumba drench MP John Prescott.

It was an interesting cast already, but now Brandon, Wood, Big Brother presenter Davina McCall and American Beauty movie star Thora Birch were entering stage left or, in Brandon's case, stage front.

No stranger to awards ceremonies after those various Caner Of The Year gongs from the likes of Muzik Magazine, Brandon's association with The Brits started in February 1997, and around that time each year the annual awards ceremony celebrates music released the previous year. His old pal Matthew Donegan had booked him and, for the two rollerskating teens, it had been some journey.

Donegan points out:-

When we hooked up again for The Brits, we did both look back and laugh, and say "fuck me, we've come a long way". We were a couple of boys from suburbia who didn't come from a privileged background, with no help up the ladder. Everything we'd achieved up until that point, we'd done off our own back. Every step we'd made, we made it for ourselves. We didn't have any relatives in the music industry, no lift up whatsoever. We'd achieved what we'd achieved through our merits, our hard work and our tenacity, so at the time he had the Blockster thing, and I was organising the after-party for the Brits, and we were like "yeah, we've done all right here".

The first year I booked Brandon for the after-party was 1997, and I was working for Cymon Eckles at his Riki-Tiks bar in Soho. Brandon had come out of the clinic in October '96, and by February '97 he was still a bit shaky and he came up to me after a few records and said he wasn't feeling quite right. I booked him again for the '98 and '99 parties, and then again in 2000, when he was nominated.

I was delighted to play all of the after-parties at The Brits. It was obviously a good gig, and I always thought I'd be able to blag a couple of tickets to the actual event and make a night of it. That all went well each year, and then a couple of weeks before the 2000 ceremony, I got a call from The Ministry Of Sound saying that the Blockster track had been drafted in as a late addition to the Best Dance Act category.

Wamdue Project, who had scored a massive No 1 national charts hit with King Of My Castle had been disqualified because someone had finally realised that the producer behind it, Chris Brann, was actually American and his singer was from Argentina.

I told the Ministry we needed to get a table and they were arguing that we wouldn't win so it wasn't worth it. I told them not to be tight bastards. They gave in and booked us a table. I think it cost them seven or eight grand in the end, but peanuts to them at the time.

Me, Ricky and Fran booked a limo, my dad and Brady came too, and we all headed to Earls Court, dropped my records off in the after-party room when we arrived, then headed to the reception area and got stuck into the champagne. There were some fancy canapes, but I wasn't interested in the food and I was necking the shampoo like there was no tomorrow. Everyone one was shouting "Blocks...Blocko...Brandon...what's happening?" and I was chatting to all the bods I knew, including Norman Cook.

We got to the table and I was already blotto. Ministry CEO Mark Rodel was sitting there, with Matt Jagger, then the managing accountant at Ministry and later head honcho at Universal Records, and there was also three other big hitters from various large companies the Ministry were trying to schmooze. The five of us sat down but everyone was moving around, drinking more and gassing between the tables.

Next to us was the Radio 1 table, including Chris Moyles, Trevor Nelson and Annie Nightingale. It was great hanging out with Trevor for a bit, one of my old sparring partners from the Kiss days. I've also got a lot of time for Moylesy, and massive respect for what he has achieved in his career. I often bumped into him at various functions when he first joined Radio 1, and we've hung out having a few drinks together over the years, also with his partner Comedy Dave too. And I remember myself and Moylesy laughing heartedly that evening at The Brits. I would have loved to see his face after what happened next, though.

The ceremony was under way and I was talking to Dane Bowers and Mark from Another Level at their table, but from this point on I can only remember things vaguely.

Out of the blue, Dane and Mark were saying to me "Brandon, we just heard your name, you've won an award, mate", and I said "what…no…you're joking…really?" And with that, I just got up and walked and headed towards the stage. I didn't even look around to see what was going on. There was an award being given away so at that moment there was no security by the stage. I was marching up towards the stage, had soon passed Norman Cook and Pete Tong, and they were both muttering "Brandon, what are you doing?", and I just carried on and looked at them as if to say, "don't piss on my fire, I'm going to collect my award". I'd made my mind up. I was going to get this award, whatever it fucking was.

Blockster radio plugger Tony Byrne had arrived at Earls Court later than Brandon and co, and was surprised at just how well oiled his client was when the starters were brought out.

Brandon had clearly been drinking all day. We were about to eat our Chinese starter when, with chopsticks in hand, Brandon wandered off to see Dane Bowers and the Another Level boys on one of the 'platinum' tables near the front of the stage. He was definitely pissed by this point and he probably hadn't eaten a thing because the starters were just coming out. He was apparently going on to Dane about how he was nominated for an award, when Dane said "mate, they've just said your name, you've won, you've won".

What ensued next is Brandon Block gold, immortalised forever on various YouTube clips and, at the time, throughout the tabloid press.

So I got up on stage and Ronnie was up there with Davina McCall and Thora Birch and I was stood to the side of them. I leant over and they all looked at me, as if to say, "who the fuck is he?" and at that point I realised that I shouldn't be up there. Then Thora Birch announced "and the award goes to...Notting Hill"...so it was obviously a film category and you can see my face, as if to say, "oh, no...". Davina looked over and said "hello, what's your name?", so I leant into the mic and shouted "Brandon Block".

If I watch it now I think, "mate, you're having a right laugh... what the hell were you thinking?" But everyone in the crowd was going mad, all the people I knew were jumping up and down, pissing themselves, and I forgot how many people were watching on TV because all I could see was familiar faces at the front. At that point I was getting ushered off...when Ronnie said into the mic, "who's that cunt?" so I ran back, but not to kick off, just to carry on the banter. Ronnie threw a drink over me and I threw one back at him.

When I got to the mic, I said "what did you call me?", and he said "the nicest man I ever met".

Turns out that he was worried because George Harrison had been attacked recently and I was staggering about with a set of chopsticks in my hand from the meal they were serving at the table. So I said "thank you very much, you old bastard". At which point I was finally muscled off the stage.

Here's the full transcript of Brandon's one minute, fifteen seconds of Brits fame:-

Thora Birch: And the winner is...hello...and the winner is...OK...confusion...the winner is Notting Hill

Davina: OK...

Ronnie Wood: Oh, it's not him...what the hell's going on here? We have an intruder...

Davina: Fantastic...what's your name mate?

(leaning into the mic): **Brandon:** Brandon Block...oi, oi...

Brandon is escorted off stage by a couple of burly security guards

Davina: Bye mate, bye

Ronnie: Get off stage, you cunt

Brandon was in the process of being escorted off stage by security, but runs back on to the stage, and Ronnie throws his drink over him

Brandon: What did you call me?

Ronnie: The nicest man, I'd ever met

Brandon: Thank you very much, you old bastard

As Brandon is bundled off stage, this time successfully...

Ronnie: You've wasted my drink, now fuck off

Davina: Good on you Ronnie

Thora Birch: Yeah, you rock

Ronnie: I thought it was somebody important...he is now

Davina: OK, now to accept the award from Notting Hill, it's Hugh Grant's annoying sister Emma Chambers

Brandon had drunkenly earned his place in Brits folklore, not so much 15 minutes of fame as a couple minutes of chaos, which would help make him a household name, well certainly for the next week or so anyway. However, a certain friend of his was far from happy.

The twist in the tale was that Jamie Wood, Ronnie's stepson, was Matthew Donegan's business partner in his Outer Sanctum events company, a vital fact not immediately reported at the time. That was the irony. I knew Jamie well and I'd just had a slanging

match with his dad in front of all those people. The security took me down the covered corridor which led to the VIP area, and there were all these paps and they were saying "Blocks, what have you done, mate?" I got to the end, and there was Matthew with his arms crossed, fuming. I've never been so embarrassed about anything in my whole life. Me and Matthew are lifelong friends and to upset him like that was terrible.

Apart from anything else I was so pissed and I was saying "I'm so sorry" and Matthew was glaring at me, shouting "what have you done, you fucking idiot?" and at that point I started crying and my dad was saying "Matt, don't have a go at him" and Matt was screaming "Harve, have you seen what he's done?"…and it was really weird because we were all old family friends. I said "look, I'm sorry, I'll just go in there and play some records", and Matthew was having none of it, saying "you're not going in there, you can't go in there, you nutter, you'll get lynched". Then he ripped my cheque up in front of me and slung me out.

Matthew Donegan had enough on his plate that night.

When I was awarded the 2000 contract I needed to form a company, if I was to get the contract. I just didn't have the infrastructure, though, so I had teamed up with Ronnie's son Jamie Wood, who I had got to know over the last couple of years, and who at that time had a 'furniture for events' hire company. He had an office, a base, staff and phone lines, so we set up Outer Sanctum and took on The Brits contract.

I booked Brandon to DJ, and Jamie was really happy to be involved in the after-party of the Brits. News came in that Mick Jagger was coming down on the night and Jamie's dad was going to be there presenting an award.

On the night I was running around trying to arrange things, and in those days the event and the after-party was for 4,500 music industry guests. We were in Earls Court 1, and the main show was in Earls Court 2. My old mate, Mick Kluczynski, God rest his soul, the Live Event producer for the Brits, who made the Brits what it was, was the guy who prevented Brandon from getting ejected straight away, well, before I got to him anyway. Historically he had been production manager for Pink Floyd, Tina Turner, Elton John, he was a true luminary.

The show had started, Brandon was at his table somewhere and I was getting shit sorted, when Jamie came marching towards me, absolutely livid, shouting "your fucking mate, I'm going to fucking kill him", and I said "which fucking mate, and why are you going to kill him?" He said "your fucking mate Brandon".

I hadn't see any of the drama, but various things were coming over the radio and I was like "oh, fuck!", then I got a bigger picture from some of the security, and I went round to try and find him, because they were saying over the mic that he was going to get ejected. He would have, but Mick was standing there, saying "you can't throw him out, he's playing for Matt later on, you've got to keep him inside".

On the way round I bumped into Bernard Doherty, who was the press officer for The Brits, and coincidently, press officer for the Rolling Stones. And Bernard was grinning from ear to ear, and said "your mate has just made us front page headlines", and I thought "fuck", as I remembered that everybody on The Brits committee knew Brandon was my friend. I was thinking this could be disastrous for me, that it could really get on top.

I told Brandon that he couldn't go into the after party. Vinnie Jones was fuming because he is a big mate of Ronnie's, and with Mick Jagger also inside already, the Stones' security, who were out in force, weren't impressed either. Jamie was saying "Vinnie and the boys are after Brandon and are going to sort him out." Let's just say tempers were frayed, to say the least. There were two reasons he had to get out. One was that they were going to kill him, and second, I was going to fucking kill him. So we got back to the dressing room bit, and I ripped his cheque up, and said get out. I spoke to his dad later, who said, "it's one of those things, and we'll all laugh about it one day", and here we are, finally laughing about it now.

In the end The Brits committee also laughed it off because it was rock and roll, and The Brits needs a bit of controversy each year, and that year, Brandon was it. Bernard was looking for a story, and the Brandon story landed in his lap really.

Vivienne Block remembers receiving a call from a friend, asking: "Have you seen what your Brandon has been up to?", and wryly adds:

All I know is that his father was involved.

Meanwhile, said father had experienced a night when he was not particularly welcome as 'Brandon Block's dad'.

I went to the toilet and he was sitting there with his chopsticks and his champagne glass, very pissed, but there was no particular drama. Then I came out of the khazi, and they're telling me that Brandon's been up on stage and the security have got him, that 'Dave' Bowers had wound him up, and told him he'd won an award. I was pissed off personally, because me and Brady had been up to look at the room for the after-party, and it looked amazing, it was going to be a fantastic night, and we weren't welcome any more.

There were all sorts of stories flying around, that Vinnie Jones was going to put him in a box. The day after Zoe Ball said on Radio One, "well done Brandon, other than that it was a boring show, you were the only entertaining thing there".

Brady, who already had Brandon's fee tucked away in his pocket, had to return to sender.

Before Matt could rip it up, I had to give it back to him, which was comical in itself. After that night, you either loved Brandon or hated him, depending on whether you were a Ronnie Wood fan or not. I think Davina was playing up on stage a bit because I'd pinched her bum at the drinks reception before the show.

The Brits wasn't the first place Brandon had been thrown out of and it wouldn't be the last. But with that big grin of his he shrugged his shoulders and scarpered.

My mates bundled me into a cab and I went straight to Area in Watford, because I was booked to play there later, and by the time I got there the whole club had all heard about The Brits and cheered when I came in.

The scandal made all the national newspapers with that now infamous picture of Brandon with Ronnie Wood's drink all down his green shirt being escorted off the stage. He'd certainly made a Jumping

Jack Splash all right, earning the dubious honour of the front page story of The Daily Star, under the headline "SORRY RON, IT WAS ONE BIG CON", with the accompany strapline "BRANDON'S BRITS SHAME".

Meanwhile, Heat magazine devoted a double page spread to the incident, teasing the piece with a front page picture on their Brits issues and using five more inside. In that feature there was even a fact file with the heading "JUST WHO IS BRANDON BLOCK?", and the following info:-

Brandon Block has been a notorious club character for more than a decade. He used to run a club night called FUBAR, which stands for Fucked Up Beyond All Recognition

He once jumped off the Star Ferry in Hong Kong and had to be dragged out of the water with a big hook

During the height of his mid-'90s drug use, Brandon claimed to get through ten grams of cocaine every day. He went into rehab in 1996

Not surprisingly, Brandon, who had chart success last year with You Should Be Dancing as Blockster, has a large hole in his nose

Brandon's most treasured possession is his fish tank

One caption read "Brandon Block: went completely mental", and so now the readers of Heat magazine were up to speed, but husband and wife TV duo Richard & Judy were still off the pace.

I'd had some gigs booked in Israel, and by then I had actually invested in a bar in Eilat called The C Bar, with a guy called Jeremy Seymour, and had planned to stay for a week in total. I flew out as planned the day after The Brits on the Friday morning, and later that night, with me already out of the country, Richard & Judy were asking on their evening Channel 4 show "where the hell is Brandon Block? We want him on the show". Everyone thought I'd legged it to get out of the spotlight, but the Israel trip was already booked before The Brits, because I needed to spend some time with Jeremy and see how the bar was working out. The Brits thing was the talk of the town for a while. If I'd been in the country I guess I'd have ended up on Richard & Judy too.

THE LIFE & LINES OF BRANDON BLOCK

Darren Emerson had DJd with Brandon since the early '90s and went on to have massive chart and international success with Underworld. He was not surprised to see Brandon up on the Brits stage.

I was chatting to him at The Brits just before he went up on the stage. He was hilarious, and had managed to put his foot through a glass railing in the foyer just moments before the awards started. The next time I saw him he was on the stage with Ronnie Wood. It was genius and typically off the cuff stuff from Brandon.

He's a personality jock and as well as being DJs, I've always looked at him and Alex as a comedy duo, but without the straight man. Those afternoons in Space in the early to mid-'90s were amazing. I was usually playing techno inside in the main room, but could never wait to get outside on the terrace and see what those two were up to. We always had the best fun on the Space terrace at that time.

Our business is certainly better off for having Brandon Block involved in it. I've always had a lot of time for Brandon, and you can't help loving that huge personality of his. Anything is possible with him. I remember once when I was playing for Flying at Soho Theatre Club he came down in a pair of rollerskates...I couldn't believe he'd managed to get down the staircase there in those skates.

Norman Cook adds:-

I remember Brandon had a particularly glazed expression on his face that night, but we hadn't been listening to what was happening on stage any more than he had. In fact, I thought he'd won the award too. I'll never forget his face on his way up to the stage. And poor sod, he really didn't mean to cause anyone any harm. I felt quite sorry for him that night, but I guess he did earn a certain notoriety from it.

Meanwhile, Karen Dunn, back managing Brandon, was rubbing her hands together once more.

* Front page headlines at The Brits (various) (bottom left) * With Simon Jonboy in Hollywood

SORRY RON, IT WAS ONE BIG CON

Brandon BRITs sham

THE DJ who squared up to Rolling Stone Ronnie Wood at the Brits last night hit back saying: "I didn't want to kill Ronnie – I was conned."

The showbiz crowd at

EXCLUSIVE by BEN TODD

became involved in a with rock veteran Wo

SET UP: Brandon Block

SHAKEN UP: Ronnie W

day, March 6, 2000

BRIT OF AGGRO: Brandon comes face to face with Ronnie Wood (above) and the Rolling Stone urges his hardman pal Vinnie Jones (right)

When the Brits thing happened the phone just didn't stop...we got loads of work off the back of that...and it was typical naughty Brandon...you just couldn't pay for that kind of publicity.

Meanwhile, there was a promoter on the Isle Of Wight prepared to pay serious money to get Brandon back from Israel to play at a last-minute booking. Brady suddenly found himself waiting in a hastily chartered chopper, just off the runway at Heathrow airport.

Brandon was due to arrive on a plane back from Israel on the Friday evening, but needed to be on the Isle Of Wight later that night and there just wasn't a connecting flight that would get him there in time. I got a call from Karen Dunn, who told me to go to Denham Aerodrome, just down the road from Ruislip, jump in this helicopter, and somehow because the promoter had a mate who was a big cheese at BAA, we were allowed to land the helicopter and meet Brandon straight off the plane. It was bonkers. There was no customs check and I was told at the time that nobody had landed a helicopter on the tarmac at Heathrow for more than 20 years. Brandon was standing at the top of the stairs, with a big grin on his face, shouting "oi, oi..." and I was in a helicopter pissing myself. He bowled down the stairs of the plane, straight into the helicopter with the customs officials carrying his bags, looked at me and said "fucking hell Brades".

However, with the gig not half as profitable as the promoter had liked, our intrepid duo were left to their own devices to get home, and their mode of transport was slightly less glamorous on the return leg.

We had to check out of the hotel quick sharp, and make a dash to get an early morning ferry, so I could play my Saturday night gigs, but we were struggling to get a cab. There was a young fan of mine hanging around the hotel, who'd been at the party, who said he'd give us a lift, and would drop us back at Denham where we could pick up Brady's car. He had this Ford Escort, so we jumped in that and I guess compared to the way out, we were cattle class on the way home. But me and Brady were laughing as much in this old XR3i as we were in the helicopter. How funny.

There hadn't been much time to think about The Brits, or really appreciate the furore surrounding it, while he was holed away in Eilat, but now Brandon was thrust straight back into Brits-gate, as he headed to the annual Soccer Sixes event at Chelsea's Stamford Bridge ground.

There was no way I was going to hit Ronnie at The Brits. It was like pantomime really up on that stage. Me and Ronnie weren't talking to each other normally, we were leaning forward, taking turns, saying everything into the mic, for maximum effect. Even Davina McCall, who I'd known for years on the club circuit, knew who I was, and, I'm sure only asked who I was to add to the drama. A lot of people actually asked me if it was all staged.

Tony Byrne:-

Brandon had disappeared to Israel for a gig, and I had all these calls, people wanting him on the radio and TV, and because he was away it just made it even better, PR-wise. When he did get back the following Sunday, via the Isle Of Wight, it was the Soccer Sixes at Chelsea that day and there was a lot of anticipation because Vinnie was there and his team were to due to play Brandon's. I was like "we've got a plane to catch tomorrow to LA, go home and get ready for that. It's dead simple, you go out on that pitch, and see what happens, or you get yourself home and we go and have some fun in LA".

I was in a team with Alex P and Ant & Dec, while Vinnie was in the same team as Rod Stewart and Jason Statham. I played for a couple of minutes, kept away from the ball, and then I thought "fuck this," got myself substituted and went home to prepare for the American trip.

Tony Byrne, who was also behind the ingenious BBC documentary From Russia With Spreadlove, which followed Brandon's old mucker Dominic Spreadlove to Sibera for a pioneering gig there, had then come up with a concept for a new show called World Clubbing, which would air on the BBC Choice channel, a forerunner for BBC 3 and 4.

We had different DJs in different territories, with Brandon doing the American leg, which was The RA Club in Las Vegas. We flew into L.A, filmed a load of stuff with a graffiti artist, and then we went out and got pissed. I remember saying those fateful words "we better not get too pissed, Brandon, my life is in your hands" But, sure enough, we went out and got suitably slaughtered. Brandon wanted to go to downtown LA. He was saying "let's go to Compton, let's go to Compton". Fortunately, I managed to get him home, and the next day we met his friend Simon Jonboy, hired a car and drove to Vegas, which was an adventure in itself.

Shortly after I returned from Vegas, Sid Owen asked me to play at his EastEnders leaving party. It was at the Roundhouse in Camden and I went down there with Matthew, who I'd made up with by now and who was involved in organizing the party. Jamie Wood was there, and I apologised to him, so I was a bit sheepish, to say the least. After I'd played Jamie said: "I want you to meet someone". Matthew gave me a knowing look, and I said "no… no…". They led me down a corridor to a private room. Inside and Ronnie was sitting there, with his daughter Leah and then wife Jo (Jamie's mum). They all just stared at me, then Ronnie smirked and said "well, you're the most famous man in British pop now"… I just said "I'm so sorry", and left sharpish.

The Brits Wikipedia page explains: "some time after the incident Block claimed that he had subsequently apologised to Wood, who had merely brushed it off."

Ronnie knows the score. He's rock and roll through and through so I guess he's not that easily shocked. It's true that the notoriety of the whole thing definitely pushed me on again, though, and made me more of a household name as opposed to just within the club industry.

One old friend who saw an opportunity following Brandon's Brits experience was Mark Sloper, director of The 400 Company, in Shepherd's Bush, west London, who was involved in setting up a new television channel Rapture TV.

Mark was a friend of a friend. He was well connected in the film business, to people like Ray Winstone, Jude Law and Sadie Frost, and had this idea about a show called Blocko's Brits. The concept was that I would be studio-based introducing video clips from people around the UK claiming to be the most 'mad for it' in the country.

People would write in and tell us just how mad their town was. They'd send in some of their own footage, and then we picked the best one and sent a crew down there to film them in action so they could show us just how bonkers they were. People would email in and vote for the craziest lot, and the prize would be a trip down to London for a night out with me. But I actually wasn't even drinking at that point. I'd tried to stay off the booze as much as possible after the Brits incident, so there was no way I was going out for a night with any of those nutters.

Instead, I usually got one of my mates to do it, and it wasn't difficult finding someone to take the winners out on an all-expenses-paid piss up. The victors would turn up, dressed up to the nines and we'd splash out on a room for them at the local Travel Lodge too. Ha, ha.

Mark Sloper, who has gone on to make a whole host of leading BBC TV documentaries and consumer programmes, chuckles when looking back at Brandon Block's Brits, explaining:-

I used to live near Brandon, and he was very much the local character when we were growing up. As well as The John Lyon, which was down the road from me in Harrow, he also played regularly at The Victory in Pinner, which was my local. Even then he was completely bonkers. I knew a lot of his friends, entourage, friends of friends, etc.

Rapture was part of the old ITV Digital set-up and I was one of the main contracted producers with regard to content. They asked me to devise some shows, and I came up with Brandon Block's Brits, which was basically a search for Britain's biggest nutters.

I wanted to create an extension of Brandon's and Alex's Kiss radio show, which was mayhem at the best of times. I didn't care much for the music they were playing by then, but I loved the show itself. It seemed that each week either Brandon or Alex were drunk, they seemed to take it in turns. One week, one or the other would be late or wouldn't turn up. I loved the show as a sort of punk rock for the dance music scene, total anarchy. So Brandon Block's Brits, with all its nutty punters, was an extension of Brandon and Alex shouting "oi oi" and generally not giving a shit. But when he did the TV show Brandon was very sensible, and was always on time.

We had a throne built for him to host the show from, and that's currently rotting in my back garden. When the prize-winners came down they were totally in awe of him, and the show was the most popular on the station. It was the only programme that Rapture advertised nationally, in newspapers like The Sun, and such like, and we used to get thousands of entries from people all over the country.

I also did a Channel 4 documentary about Brandon, as part of a series I was commissioned to do called Superstar DJs, the title of which we'd nicked from the Chemical Brothers song. I also did shows on Judge Jules, Tall Paul and, because it was Channel 4 and we needed to have a female, Lisa Loud as well.

I remember driving up to the Midlands with Brandon with him and his mate Brady, and going to a club in Coalville, which was packed and sweaty, and after all the commotion that getting in there with Brandon involved, we then had to go to another club somewhere else in the Midlands, in the back arse of nowhere, and do it all again. I remember thinking that doing this week-in, week-out, for all those years must be very punishing.

As opposed to the Rapture series, which was loads of pissed up kids going clubbing, the Channel 4 one was quite serious and Channel 4 really wanted me to get deep under Brandon's skin. We also went back to the Victory, and reenacted a gig there. If you wander around Ruislip or Pinner or the surrounding areas with him, you'll realise that Brandon is very famous around there, very much the local celebrity. He likes to play the fool, but he's actually very smart. He did become quite aggressive and temperamental around the '95, '96 era, but that was obviously the effects of the cocaine spilling out.

I also went out to Ibiza in 1999 to make a documentary called Ibiza Legends, which focused on Brandon and Alex, plus Alfredo, Danny Rampling and Jeremy Healy. I'd foolishly asked producer Amos and Basics promoter Dave Beer to present it. On the first day of filming Amos disappeared on a session, and didn't come back for four days, so

I was left with Dave Beer, who was so hammered from the night before that he couldn't speak.

The Ibiza Legends documentary itself is hilarious to say the least, featuring an 'in-depth' Dave Beer interview with Alfredo; Brandon and Alex scuffling with a punter at Cafe Mambo who had criticized Brandon's DJing, with Brandon eventually acting as peace-maker and buying the complainant a drink; a cameo from a certain Harvey Block; and Claire Manumission and the Manumission dwarf giving out strawberries at Las Salinas nudist beach as Derek Dahlarge ogles naked Balearic beauties.

As for the Brandon Block episode of Superstar DJ. Well, Brandon's drinking must have been particularly heavy at that time because this is again something he has no recollection of. You would imagine that having a film crew follow you around for two or three weeks may have left some impression.

Brady, Gary 'The Phone' and club boss Leon Lenik are all featured, and Lenik explains in the documentary: *"This superstar DJ thing, it's like film or pop stars. They all start out young and some just fade away, some come, some go. And it's the same with DJs, you can't always put your finger on it, but there's one reason why the ones that last, do last, and it's simple – they're good at what they do."*

Brandon's Rapture TV experience was also another opportunity to hook up again with Jordan (aka Katie Price).

Katie did a little cameo on the Rapture show each week. She used to stand there in a skimpy little outfit and introduce 'Jordan's Clubbing Tips'. And I'd do this little Harry Hill-aside piece to the camera and say… "that's tips!".

I had become quite good friends with Katie a year or so earlier, and there was actually a bit of a hoo-hah when she split up with Dane Bowers, with accusations that I was involved, but nothing went on. I also played at her 23rd birthday party.

Katie said to me that she loved her horses but couldn't find any stables where she was living in Ealing. I suggested she move down to Ruislip because there were loads down near me, and she bought a small flat down on Ruislip Gardens, just down the road from me. She started drinking in the local pubs, and caused a bit of a

sensation round our way at the time, having parties at her flat, and from time to time she'd call me and I'd go down to sit with her in one of the pubs. Obviously she was a young girl then, living her life and she's got kids now and has had a very successful career. I wish her all the best. What's she been able to achieve is amazing so fair play to her.

Looking back the whole Rapture show was completely irresponsible, but I guess I'm hardly one to talk. The irony is that at the time the shows were being made I was probably the cleanest I'd ever been. These 'contestants' were drinking as much neat vodka or other shots as they could, just to try and impress us. It wasn't exactly a good advert for Drinkaware and if the Frank lot had been around then, they would have been up in arms.

I doubt that the panel at Bafta were ever troubled by this particular show. One episode Mark Sloper kindly unearthed for us, however, is priceless. It features Vicky from Swindon, Michael from Perth and Becky from Woking, whose friend Louise explains she is a make-up artist for porn films. Michael downed six individual shots, adding "that was for you, Brandon", while Vicky was "bigging up the beautiful people in Swindon", so an unenviable task for her then. Jordan's groundbreaking Clubbing Tip, meanwhile, was to wear a cowboy hat if you were having a bad hair day (or presumably if you are a cowboy?).

Mark Sloper remembers:-

Brandon and Jordan were already quite close before the show, and I remember that she wouldn't take any money for doing her segments. She said to me at the time, "don't worry, if it's for Brandon, then I'll do it for free".

At the turn of the Millennium, Brandon's boys nights would feature Paul Avery, Ali, Brady and Gary 'The Phone'.

Brandon also took up a monthly residency at Sugar Reef in Soho, one of a new breed of style bars/restaurants in the West End of London, which appealed to fewer and fewer clubbers serious about their DJs and their music.

This midweek session was purely so he could have a regular base to meet up with his boys. Instead of a fee, he was handed a generous bar and restaurant tab, and up to ten of his crew would be out in force each time for a so-called 'catch-up'.

That lasted about five months, until the management worked out the rose Laurent Perrier and the best cigars in the house on top of the most expensive steaks and all the cocktails we were tucking away, even at cost, added up to more than they would have paid me to play.

Brady rarely missed the Tuesday night Sugar Reef session:-

That was our night out, as well as his close friends from over the years, plus the likes of Alex, Tall Paul and Seb Fontaine, DJs he was tight with. We all used to congregate at Sugar Reef on those Tuesdays because we were all grafting Thursday through to Sunday. And that night was Brandon's treat to his mates. There would be a rotation of people coming, but me and 'The Phone' would be there every time.

In April, 2000 'The Phone' cut an unlikely figure in the green room at Channel 4, alongside Mary J Blige, H from Steps and Brandon, when his pal was asked to sit alongside Blige and H on the panel of The Jo Whiley Show, a celebrity chat show set in a dimly lit studio with cameramen dressed in black darting around shooting unusual angles.

It was hilarious. Gary was holding court in the green room, taking the piss out of H from Steps because he used to be a bluecoat at Pontins. Mary J Blige, who had had her own issues with drugs, was asking us what a bluecoat was and what Steps were like, and me and Gary were trying to find the words to describe both, and I ended up saying, "well, Mary, they're both very popular, just not our cup of tea".

Vivienne Block was watching at home with a friend.

I remember Jo Whiley asked all of them what song makes them cry, and I turned to my friend and said, "I bet he says Born Free"...and he did. Brandon's always been one of the most sentimental people I know.

We have often sat watching a weepy film and cried together. I remember we both cried watching a cartoon once.

Meanwhile, on chatroom forum www.dooyoo.co.uk, Mancunia reminisces:-

I've never liked Jo Whiley, but she does know what she's on about and the eclectic mix of guests on that series of shows was great for giving insight into the different genres. I remember in particular a show with Brandon Block, Mary J Blige and H from Steps. The two established and talented guests were discussing fame and the dark side (drugs), etc, while H seemed bewildered to say the least.

By the time we got out to the studio to record the show, we were all bantering and the producers were rubbing their hands together and told me later that me and Gary had helped to relax Mary, and that she really came out of her shell on the show, because she had been apprehensive about talking about her drug addiction up until then.

I'M GETTING 'TROLLIED' IN THE MORNING

The scandal over the Brits was finally beginning to subside, but neither Brandon's fame nor his bookings diary was showing any signs of letting up.

Meanwhile, his typically unconventional take on 'births and marriages' would add two further twists to this tale.

The summer of 2000 saw him continue to ply his trade more and more in the lively party resort of Ayia Napa in Cyprus, and in particular at his Monday night residency at The Castle Club, aptly-titled Pear-shaped.

Brandon was kicking his heels in the business lounge on the way back home from Cyprus one day, when he met someone who would have a profound effect on his life.

I noticed this girl who was gorgeous and I thought "I'm not going to let this one go", so I plucked up the courage to talk to her. She said her name was Sara and that she thought we'd met before. We got chatting on the way home on the plane, and really bonded, and got together soon after.

A few months later Sara told me she was pregnant and I was over the moon. I couldn't believe that I was the father, because I was convinced at that time that the damage I'd done to my body meant that I was never going to be able to produce a baby. Thank God that wasn't the case, because I've got a lovely daughter now, Lily, who was born in 2001 and she is simply beautiful. They say every cloud has a silver lining, and I feel so lucky that I've been able to be a father. Lily's fantastic and me and Sara get on very well. I see Lily every week, and Sara doesn't live far from me so that's great.

Generally, despite my ability to still do stupid things every now and then, and I am only human, I guess, in that respect, I think I have become more responsible because of fatherhood, but then again, it's taken me a lot longer to grow older than most people. The whole era that I've grown up in has been both stifling and

crazy. Even now as a 44-year-old, I don't feel like I thought I'd feel like when I was younger. You look back at when you were ten and the friends of your parents, who were then aged in their 40s, and they seemed ancient. There seemed to be a such a huge age gap back then. Now the kids of 18 and 19 talk the same language as the 40-year-olds and, in many ways, get up to the same things.

With his Blockster work done, Brandon hoped he had another Top 40 hit on his hands, in spring 2000, when he teamed with Bora Bora sparring partner Gee Moore for a pumped-up, jumped-up dance version of the theme music from award-winning film and musical Zorba The Greek.

London Records, through an off-shoot label called Systematic, handed GB United, as they became, a five figure deal, so Brandon quickly enlisted the help of Lock, Stock and Two Smoking Barrels actor Steve Marcus, who played Nick The Greek in Guy Ritchie's critically-acclaimed film.

I knew Gee well by now, and thought he'd be perfect to do the track with. It was an idea I had going backwards and forwards between Ibiza and Cyprus during the summer of 1999, and was obviously tongue in cheek, but I thought it would work at loads of the clubs I was playing at the time. I pitched the idea to someone at London Records and they quickly signed the track. We got some money up front, and they spent a fortune on the video. Steve Marcus was brilliant and what a great man to know. We went out to film it in Ayia Napa. Cue loads of silly attempts at Greek dancing and messing about on the beach.

In the end, there were problems with the release date and the track got lost somewhere along the line. Oh well, we had a great time filming the video, and made a few quid too.

Meanwhile, Brandon would gradually spend more and more time with another female family member over the coming years. Emma Block's mum split from Brandon's dad Harvey when she was nine, but younger 'sis' kept up with her brother on the radio, the TV and, eventually, at huge club events. She adds:-

I didn't see Brandon much between the ages of 12 and 15 because we didn't live together and he was DJing so much. In the mid-to-late '90s I was living in Finchley with my mum and I used to listen to my brother on his Kiss FM show with Alex as much as I could.

When one girl at school found out that Brandon was my brother, she went insane because she was really into dance music.

Then one night I was doing the usual 15-year-old stuff, sitting in the park drinking or something, and I went home to 40 missed calls and loads of texts...."what's Brandon been up to?," etc, etc, etc. It was the night of The Brits, but I hadn't seen any of it.

At my 16th birthday party I remember he turned up and it was a big deal with all my friends, but I didn't realise just how big Brandon was until he got me and six of my mates on the guest list at The Ministry Of Sound New Year's Eve party at the Millennium Dome, 2000/01.

If I'm honest, we all wanted to be in the garage or drum and bass rooms, but I insisted that we push through the crowds in the huge main house room, to the front, so I could see what Brandon was doing. We got to the barriers and the stage and I called a steward over and asked him to tell the DJ his sister is here. A bouncer went and told Brandon, and suddenly me and my friend Katie, who was also 16, were ushered up and the dancers next to him were moved away from this podium, to clear somewhere for us to stand.

We were really high up and at first I stood still, but Katie was saying, "we've got to dance, everyone is looking up at us". Then Brandon played a house mix of Michael Jackson's Billie Jean and the place erupted...so we started dancing in front of 25,000 people. It's funny looking back now, but it was also an amazing introduction to clublife and what my brother did for a living.

And Brandon was making more than a decent living out of the club game still, despite the Millennium signalling, for some, a downward turn in their fortunes. The Ministry party had been his fourth booking that night. He had kicked off at Candy Store in Plymouth, before a private jet flew him back to London for sets at Together at Turnmills, at Freedom at Bagley's and finally The Dome. Earlier that week Brandon had played at three parties on Boxing Day and another two on the Friday (December 29) so a total of nine gigs in the space of six days. A trip to Thailand early in the New Year would be the perfect way to unwind.

After the first half-moon party on the Malibu Beach on Koh Samui in 1997, the next time I was back in Thailand was January 2001, and straight after the hectic New Year's Eve I'd had a week earlier it was a much welcome chance to get some sun on my back.

I had spoken to my friends Korn and Wudh and they were doing the Black Moon Beach Party at Rocky Bay, which was three or four thousand people dancing to what I like to call Thai techno...which is real techno, much more for the connoisseur than Ibiza/Gatecrasher progressive house. I love playing this brand of techno so tracks by Umek, Christian Smith, Adam Beyer, Richie Hawtin, Trevor Rockcliffe and Jeff Mills...very powerful, rhythmic and meaningful music.

Since then I've been out there every January, which I look forward to all year, particularly as I discovered something called 'detox'. During each visit I go to the Spa Samui, where I fast for seven to ten days, have colonic irrigation twice a day and come out feeling fantastic.

There have a been a few blips in Thailand...just drinking, though...like the Ninja 24-hour restaurant where I fell asleep at 3am after a two-day session. My mate couldn't move me so he took all my money off me, my Rolex, my phone, my keys, and I slept for a full 12 hours in the corner, with the odd waiter checking my pulse every now and then.

I'd known Gary Gecko for a few years before Thailand, and by the time I'd got out there again he'd opened his world-famous Gecko Bar, which would be a happy hunting ground, and a great place to hook up with friends over the years, people like Jon Carter, Lisa Loud, Lisa Horan, Johnny and Enzo Orange, Farley, Rampling, Barry Ashworth, Oliver Lang, Jo Mills, Charlie Chester and Charlie The Hat.

A special mention must also go to Samui Steve, Lionel, Andy Vier, Kirk, Johnno, Antonio Atkinson, Kai, Andy Lang, Poker Mickey, Chris, Big Steve, Darren and Matty (Q-Bar, Bangkok), Simon from Dreamers, Cliff Roberts, Thai DJs DJ Longy and DJ A and, last but not least, Essential Samui editor Dave Sambor.

Fresh back from Thailand and in February, 2001, Brandon managed to go from villain to hero when he was approached to be a red carpet reporter for the Brits a year after he stormed the stage at the annual music business jolly. And it was certainly another case of "who you know…".

Seb Fontaine's sister Anouk was working for TV producers Endemol and at that time they were producing The Brits. They wanted to get a bit more edgy, and it was actually her idea to get me involved in the red carpet stuff the following year after my 'incident'.

So there I was, one of the only people allowed THAT side of the ropes as all the stars walked in, and I was actually working for Brits TV, their new online web page. In fact, I was the last one the stars got to, they couldn't avoid me because they had to get past me to get in the door.

I interviewed loads of people…Robbie Williams, Coldplay and Samuel L Jackson. Then one of Eminem's roadies made a beeline for me, and said "I think you're really cool man", and then introduced Mr Slim Shady himself to me. The roadie was saying that he'd seen me with Ronnie Wood on the TV at the last Brits and was telling Eminem that I was so cool and all this shit, and I was saying to Eminem "no man, it's you that's the cool one, it's a real pleasure to meet you". He was great, very gracious and a lovely guy, but the roadie was still going on to him about me as they went inside.

It had been a whirlwind Brits experience for me. I'd DJd at the after-party in 1999, got nominated/thrown off stage in 2000 and now I was a Brits reporter. By 2001, though, I actually felt very comfortable among the whole Brits thing, and Earls Court was beginning to feel like a home from home.

But not as comfortable as Brady and a certain mobile phone entrepreneur.

That next year at The Brits, and somehow we were back in. Brandon was out the front reporting on the red carpet, and he'd got me and 'The Phone' a squeeze. We had a great day, but we were well prepared. We'd had the full breakfast, I'd bought a new Armani mac, and a William Hunt suit, so we were all set up. We'd got the Access All Area passes, and, luckily, we knew the bouncer on the green room door and he said, "if you behave yourselves, you can stay". So we've sat ourselves down on this couch in the corner, and we've had it with loads of them - Donny Osmond and Jamie Oliver, both on the piss with us. Chris Martin - flicking his ears and having a right old laugh with the boy. Huey out of Fun Lovin' Criminals was brilliant too.

Then Eminem came in, with his massive bouncer, who wouldn't let us near him. So we were sitting there, just pulling faces at Eminem, sticking our tongues out, silly stuff. Not being too boisterous, just having a crack.

Everyone seemed to gravitate to us, because the thing is, a lot of celebs are up their arses, but we're not. We're just ourselves, having a laugh, and a lot of them like that when they see it. And the thing is, I don't need nothing off none of them, so I don't give a fuck.

Beyonce, who was with Destiny's Child then, she was great too. I had a little cuddle up with her, when she was sitting with us. Geri Halliwell and Nell McAndrew too, they were both up for the crack as well. Brandon, meanwhile, was out front, stone cold sober, because he was working. By the time he'd finished, though, and we were heading off to the after-party, we'd built up a nice little firm for him, and loads of us cracked on.

Another time we all went to the Kevin & Perry film premiere, and ended up on the piss with Kathy Burke for a day and a half. She was a top laugh, Kathy.

And the TV work was now coming in as thick and fast as the DJ work had at the start of the '90s.

Next up was another jaunt to Vegas, this time as the latest in Sky TV's Uncovered series, a series which had already been immortalised with its debut Ibiza Uncovered, and which starred a certain Danny Gould from Clockwork Orange.

Across six episodes, Vegas Uncovered aimed to *"lift the lid on Vegas' reputation as a gambler's paradise as well as its growing popularity as a destination for clubbers around the world".*

Cue more limos, more helicopters and a harem of lapdancers, several of which landed Brady in some particularly hot water.

My missus at the time had gone up to the school to pick up our daughter, and one of the mum's said she'd seen me in the documentary sitting in the back of this limo with a bird on each arm. My other half hadn't seen the show and I hadn't told her it was on. She was working for Karen Dunn at the time, at Unlimited DJs, so she rang up Sky TV, blagged an uncut version and I come home one day and she's got the limo scene up on freeze frame, and is asking "what's all this about?" A few weeks later I was away in Cardiff with Brandon at an MTV gig. When I got back she'd cleared everything out of the house and left.

Brandon would go on to become a familiar face on British TV screens throughout the noughties, as prime-time television became more and more tabloid.

The so-called Z-list celebrity was born, and yeah I got some stick about it, but it was water off a duck's back for me. My good mate Tamer Hassan, who I've played in loads of celebrity football matches with and who famously starred in the cult 2005 British gangster film The Business with Danny Dyer, once cracked me up when he told me that "Z-list celebrities are right next door to the A-list ones".

Reality television in the United Kingdom can be dated back to the ground-breaking Up series, which set out in 1964 to follow the lives of 14 seven-year-olds every seven years, with the latest instalment due for airing in 2012. But in modern day terms, the summer 2000 British launch of Dutch reality show Big Brother - in which (in case there's anybody left who doesn't know), 12 'housemates' live in a isolated house trying to avoid being evicted by the show's viewers - created a whole new ballgame for the public and celebrities alike.

Big Brother was a huge success, gripping the nation and spawning hundreds of other shows as broadcasters and producers tried to quench the thirst for this new twist on reality TV.

Ironically, the Big Brother theme tune had been co-produced by one Paul Oakenfold, and reflected the big room trance sound Oakey and many of this fellow DJs had now become known for, en route to his relocation in Los Angeles, where he now resides making scores and soundtracks for TV shows and films like Californication and The Bourne Identity.

What can you say about Paul Oakenfold? The man and the legend who has done so much for dance music around the world and who has since risen to such amazing heights in the States, where he's even had a residency on the strip in Las Vegas.

Oakey was someone we all looked up to back in the day and I had the honour of playing at various gigs with Paul in the early days. I used to go to Spectrum and later Rage, as a punter, and he was probably one of the first people who was a real inspiration to me as a DJ. Back in the day he was a regular when I worked at the R & D record shop in Rayners Lane, and it's mad what a few us from those days all went on to achieve, including Rocky with X-Press 2 and his own DJ career.

I continued to play alongside Oakey at various gigs throughout the '90s when he was resident at Cream and still playing at some of the other superclubs in the UK, before he went on to develop his escalating career in America.

Celebrity Big Brother was the natural progression for Channel 4 and producers Endemol, and launched in early 2001, initially as part of the BBC's annual charity-a-thon Comic Relief, a rare dual channel collaboration. In 2002 ITV had developed a winning format of their own, launching jungle endurance test I'm A Celebrity Get Me Out Of Here.

The combination of Brandon's DJ fame, television experience and Brits' notoriety meant he was ripe for such shows, but although the 'big two' would evade him, he would go on to star in a host of other reality shows, but only after narrowly missing out on CBB and I'm A Celeb.

I'd already done lots of interviews for MTV, they had used me and Alex a lot for weird and wonderful stuff, before the days of Jackass and The Osbournes took MTV in a very different direction. MTV had always focused a lot on Ibiza, and then they did their own massive party in 1999 in the quarry. Myself and Alex co-presented some of the Dancefloor Chart shows with a young Russell Brand too around 2000, in the UK and Ibiza, and after Off Yer Med, the Rapture show and my dalliance with The Brits, I was in a good position for all this reality TV stuff.

I had auditions for both those flagship shows at one point. I came very close to getting on the 2005 Celebrity Big Brother, but it was the year Bez from Happy Mondays was on it. Once he'd been signed up I guess that meant there was no place for me in the Bez/music/clubby role, so to speak.

Then with I'm A Celeb I actually knew one of the producers, because she had worked on the MTV Ibiza '99 event, when me and Alex were tearing the place up and she told me she had thought "let's try and get that nutter on the show". However, after reaching the second stage of interviews a couple of times that famous trip to Australia has also evaded me. I'm still holding out for another call...and I even mentioned it to Ant & Dec when I saw them last...you know where I am boys...hint hint.

But Brandon was perfect for a handful of other reality shows, which ranged from single episode appearances on Never Mind The Buzzcocks, a music special of The Weakest Link and Celebrity Fear Factor; a cameo in Bo Selecta, plus more lengthy "residential" stints in Extreme Celebrity Detox, based in Thailand; Trust Me, I'm A Holiday Rep, set in Crete, and Celebrity Scissorhands, closer to home in central London.

Commentary involvement in other shows like Shameful Secrets Of the 80s (...and 90s), and, fittingly, It Shouldn't Happen On A TV Awards Show and The Most Annoying Pop Songs...We Love To Hate, followed, as well as a string of appearances in celebrity poker shows.

I appeared on Bo Selecta in 2003, when I was taking part in the Charity Soccer Sixes tournament at West Ham's Upton Park football ground. The genius that is Leigh Francis was playing his hilarious Avid Merion character and, among other things, was trying to swap football shirts with Jordan and winding up Rod Stewart and his missus Penny. At one point he ran on the pitch and grabbed me and Perry Fenwick, who plays Billy Mitchell in EastEnders, and it was great to be featured, albeit briefly, in a comedy show I've always loved.

Sky TV's hilarious Saturday morning show Soccer AM always had a strong team at Soccer Sixes, and the presenter then, Tim Lovejoy, was someone I'd known for years, since I met him at a house party in the mid-'80s with Birchey. Tim's from Rickmansworth, near Watford, and he's been down to Area in Watford when I've been playing. I was on Soccer AM a few times with Alex, talking about Tottenham, so it was always good to hook up with that lot at the Soccer Sixes.

Next up, a year later, I was on the panel in an episode of BBC2's Never Mind The Buzzcocks, when Mark Lamarr was the host. Phill Jupitus and Bill Bailey were the captains, all great comedians in their own rights. My fellow panellists were Specials frontman Terry Hall, comedian Dave Fulton and Kwame Kwei-Armah from Casualty, who has since gone on to become a very successful playwright. It was great hanging out with Terry Hall in the green room before and after the show. I'm often referred to as a 'legend', but I've got nothing on this guy. The word legend gets bandied about too much, but really is deserved in Terry Hall's case.

Lamarr, as deadpan as ever, introduced Brandon with the following quip: *"He is the Ibizan tourist board's greatest asset that doesn't begin with an E, superstar DJ Brandon Block. He's a notorious party animal and has been linked with Jordan…the rumour is, it was a good night for both of them. She was seen on the arm of a top DJ, and he was her one millionth customer."*

Shortly after that it was a music special of The Weakest Link, which was a bizarre experience to say the least. After my mum and dad had divorced, it seemed that one of them was always playing Tony Christie's album, with the two favourites Amarillo and Avenues And Alleyways blasting out of the stereo. It brings back memories of them not getting on for me, and then suddenly I was on The Weakest Link with Tony Christie, and not only that, standing bloody well next to him as well. I spoke to him in the green room and told him that my mum still has an autograph he gave her at a concert 30 years earlier, and he was great, and gave me a signed copy of his latest CD for her.

But Tony was the first to go, and I was standing there thinking "you can't vote him off, what's my mum going to say?". I was next, though, after Matt Willis from Busted colluded to get me voted off. It was great fun to be involved in shows like this, though. Bonnie Langford, Darren Day and Harvey from So Solid Crew were also on that one, so we were a funny old bunch. And host Anne Robinson is actually pretty scary when you're standing there, getting the first degree from her.

Also, in 2004, the film It's All Gone Pete Tong was released. Set in Ibiza, the movie's title played on the now accepted modern-day 'cockney rhyming slang' for something going wrong. Lead character Frankie Wilde, played by Paul Kaye, was a leading DJ who had gone completely deaf and locations used for the film included Pacha, Amnesia, Privilege, DC10 and Pikes hotel. Given the fictional DJ's 'caner' lifestyle and problems with tinnitus it would be easy to draw parallels with Brandon's life, and particularly as producers called him and Alex in to talk to them when the film was in pre-production stages.

We went to talk to them, and they made it pretty clear that the film was loosely based on a combination of me and Derek Dahlarge. I didn't hear much about it after that, and then the film came out with cameos from people like Carl Cox, Tiesto, Paul Van Dyk and, of course, Pete himself. They did ring up and invite me to the premiere, which I attended, but it would have been nice to have had a bit more of an input if my life had been an inspiration for the lead character.

Meanwhile, Brandon was unaware he was about to 'star' on Sky One stitch-up show Celebrity Snatch... thanks to a certain character called 'The Phone'.

I was off for a couple of weeks doing a loads of gigs around the Med, and 'The Phone' had been on my case while I was away about organising our latest day of listening to the tunes I'd been sent. Gary was well into his music and often sat with me while I sorted through my records, but he was particularly keen to sort this one out, and kept texting me about it. The backdrop to all this was the local paper in Ruislip recently running a story about irate residents in and around my cul-de-sac complaining about some parties I'd been having. The paper had run an article about the possibility of me selling-up and moving to Thailand...yes, that old chestnut... and the local 'action group' had welcomed the news.

'The Phone' had picked me up from the airport from my trip away, and driven me straight home, insisting we start listening to some records immediately. He was in the record room and I was unpacking and opening post, etc, and he was blaring out tunes on my Funktion One speakers, and I was saying "yeah, that's not bad", etc, etc, when there was a knock at the door. And it's these two geezers asking for "Mr Black", which they repeated throughout, so that wound me up no end. They were saying they're from the council, that they've had complaints, that there's been an article in the paper, that it's the middle of the afternoon and they can hear loud music.

They said they had a warrant to confiscate my equipment and I'm standing there saying "look guys, there's no need for all this". In the end, I did a deal with them to take away a couple of old Technics I had in my attic, and the guys said that was all good if I give them a little sweetener. So I got some cash and helped them out to their van with the decks. Of course, when they opened the door there was a film crew inside, "surprise, surprise, " etc, etc. It had all been filmed by secret cameras. 'The Phone' and my neighbours were in on it all and I'd been got...hook, line and sinker!

Brandon's first television poker appearance came in 2004 too, and if he enjoyed being on the other TV shows, then, playing one of his great passions, poker, on the box really was an offer too good to turn down. He would appear in several more shows until 2008.

Poker has been an indulgence of mine for ages. I used to play with my mum's ex-boyfriend, when I wasn't chasing him around the kitchen. That was one thing we did connect with, seven card stud poker, and chess, which I also played with him. He's dead now, God rest his soul.

Then around 2005 in my continual search for new addictions, I started playing online a lot. And while gambling is obviously not the best of addictions, I've fortunately never been interested in playing for big money, or doing it to make money, it's always been about keeping myself occupied. I've had my poker room with a red bay poker table, which seats eight people, for five years or so, and my little poker crew come round regularly. There's Terry The Cod,

so named not because he owns a chippie, but because he's always 'fishing' for bets, plus Big B, Den, Rich, Wes, Anil, Rob, Damon, Dangerous Dave and Shaky, who is actually Steve Long. He got that tag because when he gets a good hand his hands start shaking uncontrollably. A lot of the boys are mates from the gym I go to, people I play badminton or squash with. We put £20 each in a hat, and you can buy more chips at a certain time, but nobody ever stretches themselves that much. It's a good social night, but we never go mad with what we bet.

Cable channel Challenge TV were the first to screen the poker, and I was invited to take part in a tournament being held at West End style bar and club Pangaea. I was there playing with Colin Murray from Radio One, plus Norman Pace from Hale & Pace, and, of all people, Nick Leeson, the trader who brought down Barings Bank.

There was also a guy there called Roland De Wolfe, who used to write for a poker magazine, and I played on the same table as him that night. He's from London and went on to be one of the top runners in Vegas, winning millions of dollars.

The Pangaea event was my first introduction to poker circles, and I kept in contact with people I met, and was asked to play in a few other events by Eddie Hearn, who is the son of boxing and snooker promoter Barry Hearn. Together with his old man, he runs the Partypoker.com site. Suddenly as the poker got more and more popular, internet sites were springing up all over the place, and all the big betting shops got involved too.

I played on a few televised games with people like Tom Parker-Bowles, darts' world champion Phil Taylor, footballer Teddy Sheringham and racing pundit John McCririck. I also went into the Sky studios a couple of times as a celebrity that punters could play against at home through their Sky remote controls, which was always good fun.

Celebrity Fear Factor on Sky One provided Brandon with another trip of a lifetime, and unusually, some unchartered territory.

I'd never been to Argentina, so when an all-expenses paid trip to Buenos Aires, plus a few grand in my pocket, was on the table I said "let's do it". I turned up at the airport, not really knowing who was going to be involved and, once more, some familiar faces were on board too. First was Terry Christian, who I'd never really known before, but The Word had obviously been very big for him, and he knew exactly who I was, so we got one very well. Then there was Adele Silva, the Emmerdale actress, a lovely girl and we became very close. Then Lisa I'Anson turned up, and another old pal, presenter Toby Anstis, and it was particularly nice to see him. I'd known both Toby and Lisa for years from Ibiza and the club scene in general.

The whole thing about the dance scene is that, chances are, most people who made anything of themselves post 1990, in the media industry, were involved in the acid house or following club scene at some point, as a punter, because it gripped everyone of a certain age then, and particularly most creative and media-linked people. So when I did the reality stuff I bumped into loads of people that I'd come across in the past.

We were flown to Argentina by business class, which was a touch, and then spent our first night in a lovely hotel in Buenos Aires, and got pampered nicely before any of the 'fear' was introduced. The next morning we were blindfolded and driven away from the hotel. It took a good hour to get to our destination, and the whole time I was trying to inch my blindfold up a little bit by a series of tactical blinks and twitches. I managed that a little bit, and could see this imposing building in the distance and I knew straight away that's where we were heading. We got there, and it turned out to be a very tall old watchtower, and we were bundled into a lift, and up we went.

When we reached the top floor our blindfolds were taken off. We were 600ft up and could see across the whole of Buenos Aires. There was a window, with a 15ft pole coming out of it, and the task was to crawl out across the pole, to a little ledge, stand on the ledge and then jump up in the air and catch a flag. We were all

(clockwise) * On the panel of Never Mind The Buzzcocks
*'Papped' out on the town with Katie (and Jessie)
* With Wudh, Lisa Loud and Lisa Horan in Thailand
* With sister Emma * Sara and Lily Block
* Charlie Chester and partner Jo Mills (right) with Justine at Gary Gecko's wedding in Thailand, 2004

THE BUZZCOCKS

NO BLOCKHEAD: Jordan with lucky B

JORDAN'S

HOME TIME: Smiling Jessie leaves with DJ Brandon Block

We're Jess

harnessed in, and wearing helmet-cams, and I actually did it in the fastest time, but it was bloody harrowing, to say the least. So I won the task and was deemed to be the biggest threat to the rival team on the show and I was voted off by them, so that was a weird format.

Fortunately for me it meant that I was unable to take part in the next task, which was absolutely disgusting. It basically involved lots of rubbish from a local abattoir that they couldn't use anymore, so intestines, pigs' arseholes, bull's penises, fish eyes, really horrible stuff, thrown at the celebs from a height. Among all this stuff were some strawberries, and as it was coming down off this elevator-type contraption the others had to catch some strawberries in their mouths, while trying to avoid the crap. The stench was unbearable.

But the stink at Celebrity Fear Factor out in Argentina was nothing compared to that in Thailand over the New Year of 2004/5 at Brandon's surprise wedding.

The unlikely marriage had all started with an innocuous snog in Koh Samui the year before.

His love affair with the Thai island was much longer-standing than that of his latest love interest. After his 1997 debut there, Brandon returned to Thailand in the January of 2001 and every year since has spent January out there, recuperating, detoxing and enjoying nights out with friends. But that one defining trip and kiss in January, 2004 nearly changed his life forever.

Kicking the year off in Thailand soon became a must for me, hanging out with like-minded people I knew from Ibiza, party people who wanted some winter sun and something a bit more chilled. However, in true Blocko style, it could never be completely chilled.

One evening at the start of '04, after a fantastic night at Gecko, with Justine, Dominic Spreadlove and Sarah Tuke, and after a fair few Tiger beers, we ended up at Bophut Hills at our good friend Danny's mountain-top villa, which at the time was the best one on the island, certainly before the influx of property developers. For some reason I decided to climb inside a huge poolside flower pot,

and wedged myself so my shoulders were under the rim, with just my head poking out. It was a modern take on Michael Bentine's Potty Time and Bill & Ben all rolled into one, but now I was well and truly stuck. I tried to tip the pot over, by rocking from side to side, with the hope that I would roll into the pool, freeing myself as I swam to safety, but unfortunately Thai ceramics just aren't Block proof, so as I tipped over the pot split completely in half, ripping through my leg to the bone. Luckily it was only my leg that needed 14 stitches, and once again, for me, it could have been so much more serious. I was accompanied to hospital by James Mitchell, and nursed at my apartment by the ever trusty Justine, and told to stay in bed for four days.

During the same trip, I met this girl out there. Our paths had crossed before in Ayia Napa, and we had the most amazing kiss outside The Reggae Pub. It must have lasted for about an hour, and everyone was asking me what I was up to. A mini holiday romance followed for a few weeks, but I had to get back to the UK, and she was staying out in Thailand.

We carried on talking on the phone when I got home, and then I got booked for this big party, an Emmys event in Vietnam, and it meant that I could fly back out to the Far East and also take in Gary Gecko's wedding, which otherwise I would have missed.

So I flew out to Thailand, headed straight to Koh Samui, just making it in time for Gary's nuptials, at which I played I'm Into Something Good by Herman's Hermits as Gary and his wife rode down the beach towards the bar on an elephant (as you do...). In fact, I DJd all day at his wedding, literally around eight hours, getting well oiled in the process.

It was great hanging out with my lady friend again, and we also ended up at Danny's villa that night, another fun-packed party with more poolside frolics and the highlight our mate Kevin riding a moped into the deep end of the pool. Like you do...

That next morning I had to be thrown out of the villa so I could catch my flight to Vietnam, with the worst hangover in the world.

Brandon was soon back in Ruislip and his new love, a secretary from Essex who worked in the city, was back in London too. The romance rumbled on into the summer, but was about to take a turn for the worst.

That summer I was booked to play at the Player's Pool Party in Marbella. She was already going with her friends, and I said "no worries, I'll go with the boys...you go with the girls", but she took it the wrong way, and we split up shortly before the trip.

When I got to Marbella, I begged her to come back with me, but she was having none of it, so, true to form, I went out on a big bender for a couple of days. She eventually agreed to give it another go, but I said for this to work you'll have to move in with me, and when we got back from Marbella she did exactly that. I'd fallen in love with her, so it all made sense to me, well at least it did, then.

Shortly after she moved in, I was booked to play in Tel Aviv, so I took her with me to Israel, proposed to her when we were out there and splashed out on a diamond ring worth four grand at the airport on the way home. We quickly started planning a wedding in Thailand, which seemed the obvious place to do it, and around the same time, at the start of the next year. I spoke to Gary Gecko and we started to make the arrangements to get married on New Year's Eve.

The next thing I knew, she was moving things around in the house, and my mates were ribbing me and then I started to get cold feet. But everybody had booked to go out to Thailand for the wedding. My mum, my next door neighbours, Paul Avery, who was the best man, Lisa and Lisa, and loads of mates. I told myself it was only pre-wedding nerves, but then on the morning we were meant to fly out there, December 27, 2004, we woke up to discover that there had been the massive tsunami in Thailand and that the country was in chaos. She was saying "it's a sign, we can't go", but I said "we're going, we have to", and so off we went.

Before the wedding party hit Koh Samui, the plan was for Brandon, his fiancée, and some close friends to meet up in Bangkok, where Brandon needed to stop off to collect his wedding licence. He had secured a DJ booking at the Metropolitan Hotel in the city centre in return for a free room or two, but the flight out already appeared doomed.

The plane was stopping off in Dubai, where we were actually meeting some other friends, but we argued all the way to the airport, through customs and ended up sitting in different rows on the plane. When we got to Dubai we met up with my mate Tony Wheelchair and Kevin Andrews, and that broke the ice and we started talking again. Everyone was asking us if we were all right because they could tell something was up. Then when we got to Bangkok, she wanted to go out, and I was knackered and wanted to stay in. In the end, Aves took her and her sister out in a tuk tuk, and they all got back at about 6.30am. I was furious.

But if Brandon was angry at that one night in Bangkok then his fiancée was more than entitled to be a little bit peeved at what was to follow.
On a much more serious and immeasurable note, the sheer tragedy created by the tsunami - which ravaged coastlines bordering the Indian Ocean, killing 230,000 people in fourteen countries - wasn't helping Brandon's cause where his marriage licence was concerned.

We still needed to get our paperwork from the embassy in Bangkok, but thousands of people had congregated there to find out whether their loved ones were safe. As we approached the embassy we saw hundreds of people comforting each other outside. It was only then that we realised the enormity of the situation. I tried to explain that I had come to collect my wedding licence and in not so many words we were told to go away, and quite understandably so too. So with no paperwork, and seemingly no wedding, we headed out of Bangkok to Koh Samui.
Gecko got on the case and sorted out a Baptist priest, but with me Jewish and her Catholic, and no papers, the whole thing was looking decidedly dodgy. The actual wedding day went quite well. In fact, if I ever did it again, I'd like it to be very similar.
I DJd for a bit, and the reception party carried on into the early hours as the wedding merged into the annual and world-famous Gecko New Year's Eve beach party.
Loads of us ended up, yet again, back at Danny's villa. At around 8am on New Year's Day, my new wife and her sister decided they'd had enough and the pair of them went back to our

room. That was obviously my cue to leave too, but, oh no, I couldn't make it easy for myself. There was no way I was going to leave my own wedding after-party, so I did the old "I'll be back in a bit, love", but actually turned up back at the room some time in the afternoon on the third of January!

Not the best start to married life, and I spent the rest of the trip trying to make up for it. We did go on a three-day detox in a nearby retreat and things were starting to seem OK, but then we got back to our room the day before we were flying home, and I believed I had earned enough brownie points to meet up with Simon Jonboy for a few farewell beers.

The plan was that I'd hook up with her at Bar Solo a few hours later for our last night, but I turned up two hours after that, half-cut, and it kicked off big time. She stormed off back to the hotel, while I continued, out on the piss.

By the time I'd got back the next morning, she'd packed up and left for the airport. I missed the flight, but that flight, to compound her misery, got delayed in Dubai for nine hours and the plane I did manage to get on later that night was on time, and we ended up getting back to London within minutes of each other.

That night we were back at my place, lying in bed, wondering what the hell we had done, and what the hell we were going to do. We actually had a registry office wedding booked for the next week because we'd been worried before about the authenticity of a Thai wedding, but we decided it was best we go our separate ways.

The wedding we did have in Thailand literally wasn't worth the paper it was written on, so it was the world's easiest 'divorce' ever. And at least she had seen at first hand what an idiot I can be. She left a few hours later and that was that. Amazingly, we're still good friends to this day.

So it was back to the drawing board for Brandon.

Back home in London, Tony Truman - Brandon's one-time business partner in Linekers in Ibiza - was in a relationship with EastEnders actress Charlie Brooks and planning a joint birthday party with another Albert Square star, Dean Gaffney.

Tony remembers:-

Me and Dean were having a birthday bash and I saw Tamsin Outhwaite at the EastEnders studios and invited her to the party. She said, "well I might come, because I quite like your mate Brandon". I said, "you sure you got the right fella?", and she said "yeah, but I've heard he's a bit wild". I said "to be honest, he's sorted himself right out, he hasn't done any gear for years, and he's off the booze at the moment as well. So, yeah, why don't you come along and I'll introduce you to him". So Tamsin turned up at the party, I got her a drink, and said "come in the other room and see Brandon, who is DJing". We walked through and Brandon was behind the decks, absolutely lagging...with his headphones all over his face, almost sliding down the wall, as he tried to stand up. And he was so pissed that he thought Kacey Ainsworth, who played Little Mo Butcher in EastEnders, and who was with Tamsin, was actually Tamsin, and started trying to chat her up instead. So that was that, another potential Blocko relationship bit the dust.

Haha...I guess some things are either meant to be or not.

In those days I got to know various people on 'the circuit' and would get asked all the time about certain friendships - the likes of Jessie Wallace and Katie Price. I was in the papers a few times, but it was all purely platonic. Press coverage has been part and parcel of my life since I can remember.

Here's what the tabloids had to say about both 'relationships'.

Daily Mirror, Thursday September 19, 2002...*Only last week EastEnders star Jessie Wallace declared that this year had been the "worst" of her life.*

But funny how a few beers and good male company in the form of DJ Brandon Block can put a smile on a girl's face.

The pair enjoyed a lively night on the tiles with Jessie's EastEnders co-star Charlie Brooks and her boyfriend Tony Truman at London's Elysium nightclub.

When it came to calling it a night, Jessie, 30, shared a cab with her new best friend.

The Sun, Thursday September 19, 2002...*EastEnders star Jessie Wallace has been on a date with hell-raising DJ Brandon Block.*

They were spotted enjoying dinner at a London restaurant. An onlooker said: "Jessie seemed a bit coy at first, but soon they were both laughing and joking.

Last night Brandon told us: Jessie is very attractive. I'd like to see her again.

Daily Star, Monday October 19, 2000... *Gorgeous model Jordan scored with the Daily Star's very own Brandon Block at the opening of a trendy nightspot. Club guru Brandon was powerless to stop Jordan as she moved in on him.*

Blockster won the day as Jordan gave him a rose and they headed to another club before slipping away in a taxi together.

Brandon said yesterday: "Myself and Jordan are good friends".

However, Brandon's scattergun approach to romance has often paid huge dividends. As well as Brazilian millionairesses passing through in the Ibiza glory days, and female fans prepared to swallow their pride throughout the '90s, he did manage to impress the odd dancer along the way too.

Jason Bye chuckles as he explains:-

I remember when Brandon went out with a Spanish dancer from Amnesia called Monica. It has to be said, she was amazing. Roger Sanchez went out with her afterwards, and he didn't know she'd been with Brandon. He wasn't best pleased when he was told, and was saying "what? Brandon, went out with Monica? Sheeeeeeeet...".

Monica used to say to me.... "you know Brandon....I luuuuurrrvvve Brandon'. So I said to Brandon, there's this bird in Amnesia, she's fit as anything, and she likes you. She was head of the dancers. I think she's settled down with someone now.

My oh my, Monica was indeed lovely. She was Spanish, with a little bit of Italian in her and, not long after I found out she liked me, she had a tiny bit of Jewish in her too! Boom boom. She used to dance on the podium just above me at Amnesia and there would be thousands of people on the dancefloor below, but I'd be playing to just her, really.

A WHOLE NEW BALL GAME

Although I had been appearing more and more on reality TV shows, my day job was still that of a DJ and the noughties provided some memorable clubbing moments in Ibiza, the UK and beyond.

When I'd got myself clean of cocaine, and in the years after that, I really started enjoying playing out in Ibiza. Myself and Alex had been long-time residents there at various places and, as well as significant involvement with clubs, promoters and brands other than Space, we had also started to get involved with some big holiday tour companies, like 18-30, with John Davis - for whom author Colin Butts, who wrote Is Harry On The Boat, then worked - and Chris Brown, who went on to work with John.

And with the tour companies, and also the likes of Clockwork Orange at Es Paradis, or Tonic at Eden, we were getting paid great money, as opposed to the £200 here and there we got for Space and other places in the early days. And we were playing every day so it soon adds up and, of course, in my case, none of my money was going on coke.

At the same time, the hotels we were staying in, because the tour companies or the individual clubs were putting us up for two or three days at a time, were a big improvement too, certainly as opposed to the apartments we used to rent ourselves for the whole season.

We stayed at Pikes consecutively for a few seasons, just outside San Antonio, so a massive big up to Tony Pike... THE true Ibiza legend. This was in the days when the likes of Carl Cox and Erick Morillo stayed there too, before they bought their own places out there. I'm honoured to have been inducted into the photo hall of fame in the Pikes reception, and they even named a cocktail after me called the Bloxie, a vodka and water melon shake.

Our friends also opened the now world-famous Es Vive hotel in Figueretas, near Ibiza Town, in 2001, so big respect, thanks (and well done) to owners Jason Bull, Max Leverett and Nick. And you can't mention that crew without their boys, Big Shane, Tony Baloney and Howard Boyle, the infamous Elvis impersonator.

And in the latter years I started to spend a lot more time in Ibiza Town, particularly if staying at Es Vive, which gave me time to spend with my long-time friends at The Rock Bar, now situated at the front of the port, so Nick and Sid, Hippy Sid and one of the founder members of the Extreme Team in Andorra, Uncle Kev.

It was amazing being clean and enjoying Ibiza at a higher level, so to speak, but then I guess I couldn't have got much lower. I was still drinking, and enjoying myself, and occasionally, when I was coming to grips with first substituting cocaine with alcohol, I can vaguely remember being tempted to do a line, but I was actually really scared to go back. Petrified. I was still, largely, in a mental war zone.

Now, however, there was finally light at the end of the tunnel, and although I was still getting pissed up for two or three days at a time, invariably I made it home each night. The sheer fear of cocaine and what I was capable of doing with it would never let me go back to it, and it never has.

Nights like Tonic at Es Paradis on a Thursday evening, which had its own 'carry on' session on Space terrace on the Friday morning, between 2002 and 2005, were good to Brandon.

Tonic promoter Chris Brown first met Brandon when he booked him and Alex to play at one of his massive United Dance parties in Stevenage in 1992, and then, when he was part of the hugely successful production outfit Ruff Drivers, at the huge 18-30 Sundance parties at the Zoo Project, just outside San Antonio. As one of the live acts, Brown would perform alongside Sundance resident Brandon in the summers of '97, '98 and '99 and remembers:-

At that time being as unprofessional as you could was positively encouraged in some DJ and club circles and Brandon and Alex were like Olympic gold medallists in that department. They'd thrown the rulebook out the window and the crowd loved it. There was even that club in Coalville, Passion, who actually had optics installed in the DJ booth for Brandon.

I had six Top 40 hits as Ruff Drivers, but then I got sucked back into promoting again, and started Tonic at Eden when that club opened in 2000. I had no hesitation in making Brandon and Alex my residents and we ran every Thursday there for four years. In fact, it was so popular that from 2002 to 2005, after I approached Fritz at Space, we did the Tonic carry on party there every Friday morning too, from 9am onwards, three hours after we'd shut at Eden on the Thursday night. The boys were naturally my residents there as well.

After that, I became the booker for the Big Reunion Parties which are held each November, across two weekends, at a holiday camp in Skegness. And I have the dubious honour of being the first promoter to bring infamous Bora Bora 'dancer' Spiderman over to the UK, booked especially to dance at The Big Reunion. He wasn't paid, but let's just say his rider was spectacular. The guy is a legend and is actually a performance arts teacher from Portugal, but with millions of hits on YouTube, he's also now a global legend. He would come and dance at Space too, but was always getting thrown out by the security for stripping off completely naked.

There have been many weird and wonderful characters in Ibiza, who have gone on to earn legendary status, and who have all added to the fun and games. Spiderman was just one in a long line of people like Nino, the 'Argentinian Captain Birdseye', who was always at Pacha, or Pippi, who is also Argentinian, and who was famed for her white outfits and cuddly bear. All these people just added to the flavour of Ibiza, and many can still be found knocking around after all these years.

After a decade of fun by the sea, Brandon was invited to play at the inaugural Party On The Piste on the slopes of Andorra in the Pyrenees mountains bordering Spain and France.

With the ski season from December to April, in the years ahead it would be a chance to combine work and pleasure before his annual pilgrimage to Thailand, and then a couple more times upon his return in the run-up to the summer.

The first Party On The Piste was at The Panorama Bar in Arinsal, Andorra, 2002 which had a big terrace, and myself and Alex were invited out there. At this point I'd never tried any snow

sports, apart from the obvious one, but fortunately I'd long given up taking mountains of that stuff.

I quickly succumbed to snowboarding, and so opened another chapter of extreme clubbing...no expensive drugs needed, just pricey equipment and extortionate lift passes. I had found another new niche, for which I could spend unnecessary amounts of cash on equipment and board-wear which, as any enthusiast knows, has to be updated annually or, in my case, being as impulsive as I am, a new ensemble is needed for almost every descent.

After that fantastic first introduction to winter sports, I've been invited back to Andorra to play several times each season every year since. I now play at Surf for my friends Jose and Roberto, who also own an Argentinian steak house in Ibiza.

And I quickly discovered many workers from the Spanish summer resorts could be found doing exactly the same in the winter ski resorts, for them a case of 'Benidorm On Ice'.

On that first trip I befriended two of my original 'Extreme Team' members. Kelvin Batt is a surf-master extraordinaire and one of the maddest snowboarders out there. He later owned a bar in Andorra, which was as mad as him, and also opened a surf school in Cornwall. Ski-master extraordinaire Adrian Kay was next up and both Kelvin and Adrian were quickly enrolled to the 'Extreme Team', due to their joint love of drinking, party antics and rolling down hills at great speed.

Later members included Tigger, Lee John and, of course, Uncle Kev, who when not running The Rock Bar in Ibiza, runs one of Arinsal's most popular pubs, Quo Vadis. Now that's what I call a job share!

Back at home a long-time friend of mine, Wardy, jumped on my new snowboard buzz too, and has been on every trip with me since. Wardy became the wing commander of our 'Extreme Team', and helped me pick up various other lieutenants along the way too.

Snowboarding had quickly become a recognised sport, and is now part of the Winter Olympics and, as with the DJ world, the snowboard fraternity had its heroes. I had the good fortune to meet many of them, but not without my good friend at Oakley,

Stuart Morgan, who quickly employed me to play at all of the Oakley-sponsored events, which was most of them in those days.

I met 'Brits' champion Jamie Baker at an X-Box party at Gumby's Big Day Out in Val d'Isere in France in 2003 and I've gone on to produce tracks with Jamie and his brother Bobby (aka the Fabulous Baker Brothers). Jamie is also my partner in DJ luggage range Blox Box.

Other snowboard stars I've met along the way include Gary Greenshields, Elliott Neave, Martin Ward, Danny Wheeler and Hamish Duncan.

Meanwhile, snowboarding took me to other places like Verbier and Saas Fee in Switzerland and French resorts Chamonix and the Trois Vallees (Meribel, Courchevel and Val Thorens).

I was actually amazed that there was so much fun to be had in in a ski resort, and it was a nice alternative to nightclubs, where the emphasis was still on hedonism and wild parties.

Apres ski is world renowned so, sure, people party in the evenings in the resorts, but most are skiing the next morning, so it's more of a traditional old school party vibe - heavy drinking and hangovers the next morning. For me, being out in the fresh air with an aim for the day, rather than being holed away somewhere chasing the night before, is always a good thing.

That said, I did actually play at an Ibiza beach party out in Meribel with DJ friend of mine Tim Lyall, Kevin Andrews (Hoxton Whores) and Alex P. It came complete with sand on the terrace, and mulled wine flowing like sangria!

And just like Ibiza, MTV were quick to jump on the snowboarding phenomenon too, hosting their annual Snowball event, which I have also been part of.

Today dance music has crossed over to every sphere of popular culture and both the Snowbombing and the Altitude comedy festival, which I have been happy to play at, are testament to that.

Meanwhile, many of the reality TV shows Brandon had taken part in may have seemed as futile as his coke-fuelled take on clubland, or indeed his brief marriage, but one particular show was poignant to say the least

And it's Channel 5's Extreme Celebrity Detox in 2005, which still tickles Brandon, and he certainly had plenty of 'tickling' to do on this show!

It wasn't masturbation as such, but we did, for some length of time, have to play with our perineum, which is basically, without being too crude, the area in between your arse and your balls, well for us guys at least. Both sexes have it, though, and massaging it in the correct way is meant to give this amazing release of pleasure, and there we were doing it on national TV.

see YouTube link, 'Extreme Celebrity Detox - 4oD - Channel 4'

One of Brandon's colleagues on this show was Rebecca Loos, allegedly a mistress of David Beckham and by now a reality show veteran herself, who was no stranger to televised masturbation after performing that very task on a pig so its semen could be collected on Channel 5's The Farm a year earlier.

A few months after Extreme Celebrity Detox, Loos was a dinner guest at Brandon's house.

Back in Thailand, though, and 1980s "yoof" TV presenter Normski and EastEnders' actress Carol Harrison completed Brandon's group, which was specialising in Taoism, the ancient Chinese philosophy and study of the natural order of the world.

Dotted around various outposts around the world were three more groups, including a tai chi one with Jack Osbourne and a Shamanism one with Factory Records legend Tony Wilson.

We were on a remote Thai island known for its extreme rock climbing. There was this weird geezer running our group and he was unreal. He had a retreat somewhere in Cornwall, and had these two women with him who he called his "angels". He also had this sidekick, who was a strange bod to say the least. He stood there and did everything his master asked of him, bowing to him at every occasion.

The "weird geezer" in question was Kris Deva North, a Taoist Master Trainer, who had been "practising Chinese Taoist philosophies for over 20 years".

The show's narrator explained: *"This group is heading for a course that will fully awaken their sexual powers and are about to experience the biggest culture clash of their entire lives."*

Quite ironic considering Brandon's dip in "sexual powers" in the late '90s!

As the four celebs landed on the island, Kris Deva North laid out his mantra, stressing: *"We believe that the most powerful part of human energy is sexual"*, then explaining that the group will be focusing on *"meditation, tai chi and advanced masturbation practices"*, before adding *"there's also the little matter of a mock execution"*.

But as the group prepared to *"get to know themselves internally and master their sexual energy"*, Normski quipped: *"I didn't realise the course was actually going to involve wanking! I was just hoping to go away and chill out a little bit."*

Kris Deva North, with one of his angels in tow, was keen to demonstrate the Taoist art of genital weightlifting, much to the amusement of Brandon and co, and strapped a cloth, which had a five litre bottle of water attached to the other end, to his scrotum. He began swinging it strenuously between his legs, while standing next to him, the angel explained that, in preparation, she had already "inserted a jade egg", before going on to talk to the female members of the group about the ins and outs of her own weightlifting technique.

We were not privy to how many litres the angel was swinging, but Kris Deva North quickly gathered momentum and, quite poignantly in Brandon's case, added *"by reflecting on the experience of death I encourage people to get out of their box. I do try to induce a pleasant feeling before doing something nasty. Self-discovery can almost be harrowing sometimes. Everybody finds their cut-off point. We don't actually kill people, but we do help them have an inner death so they can have an inner rebirth"*.

All of which just about sums up Brandon's dealings with cocaine.

Blindfolded stroking followed, then slow-dancing to romantic music. Brandon was paired with a female angel, but couldn't face it, and walked off the 'dancefloor'. Normski, meanwhile, was cheek to cheek with Kris Deva North himself, and later pointed out: *"That's weird, I've never danced with a geezer before"*. Next up was "taoist hugs", and Brandon was up close with the male "angel of death" while Ronan Keating's When You Say Nothing At All played, a more bizarre scene you'd be hard-pushed to find!

Meanwhile the 'breathing out of your testicle' task next was a whole different ball game. Literally!

The final task involved twelve hours of meditation, billed as a death ceremony, and which was meant to take you back to either near birth or near death. I told the producers "I've done near death already thank you very much, so I'm a celebrity, well sort of, anyway, please get me the fuck out of here and away from this bread and butter."

I'd also worked out that if I got off the island then, I could get back to Krabbe by boat and fly to Koh Samui to spend a couple of days with Gecko and his lot, and still meet up two days later in Bangkok for the business class flight home with the rest of the cast and the crew.

However, I'd just got in this long boat, and was about to set sail, when this massive storm started. They told me we'd have to wait until the morning, so I was stuck in my tent overnight on my own because everybody else was doing the mock execution.

One of the producers Charlie Colsten-Hayter, sister of Tony thought it was hilarious so filmed me at one point in the naughty tent, and it went out on the show.

I was all right, though. We were meant to have given our phones in, and I did give in my British phone, but kept my usual Thai one with me, and Gary had been sending me top-ups throughout the whole trip so I could keep in touch with everyone. I never made it to Samui, but Gecko met me in Bangkok anyway.

Brandon was back on his travels again in 2006, when he took part in Trust Me I'm A Holiday Rep, another gem from the creative folk at Channel 5.

If anyone knew by then how to entertain the package holiday massive, it was Brandon, and this time his co-stars were Emma Jones, not so famous for her kiss and tell tales on Princess Diana's boyfriend

James Hewitt; celebrity chef Nancy Lam; TV presenter Rowland Rivron; Noel Sullivan from Hear'say and (Mr Popular...NOT!) Paul Burrell, another link to Princess Di, after his notorious stint as her butler.

Another year and another memorably-titled reality show, but this time all in the name of charity, and the BBC's Children In Need campaign - namely Celebrity Scissorhands.

I was absolutely useless at the hairdressing, but I did earn a place in the Guinness Book of World Records for the most spray tans in an hour. One more dubious honour to add to the list.

Another motley crew had been assembled for this, with Javine, the singer who just missed out on a place in Girls Aloud in Pop Stars: The Rivals; teen rocker Lil Chris, baseball cap and all; comedienne Ninia Benjamin; Star Wars star Warwick Davis; socialite Tamara Beckwith, and the salon's assistant manager, '80s pop icon Steve Strange, all casted too.

But at least this show was being screened on prime-time BBC1. And the show would allow me to catch up and have some quality time with my old friend, the beauty salon's boss and renowned British hairdresser Lee Stafford. Lee's originally from Southend and we've got mutual friends down there. Since the show we've aimed to be in Thailand each year at the same time, and detox together.

Celebrity Scissorhands was the last reality show I did, as such, and I think that when your time has gone your time has gone. I had a specific agent who looked after my TV work, initially Sue Rider, then Jo Gurnett Management, who were looking after the likes of Tony Blackburn and Terry Wogan at the time, and then Mike Leigh, who handled me at Jo Gurnett, but then set up his own company.

I wouldn't say no to another reality show, as there still seems to be lots of legs in them. Producers, you know where I am!

At the end of the day I did those shows because I enjoyed them, not for financial reasons. I met and worked with some amazing people.

THE LIFE & LINES OF BRANDON BLOCK

Away from the world of reality TV, Brandon had another business venture in mind, and during a trip to Marbella pitched his idea to Wayne Lineker, famed for his string of successful bars throughout the Mediterranean, and brother of football legend Gary.

Another sunshine destination where I made my mark in the noughties was Puerto Banus, Marbella. In summer 2007, promoter Tony Wheelchair and I got chatting at a party there to Wayne, and suggested a Linekers Bar in Ibiza, and that preferably somewhere situated in my spiritual home of San Antonio would be ideal. With Wayne's know-how and mine and Tony's club connections the whole thing sounded well worth exploring.

I've known Tony Wheelchair for many years, first playing in Puerto Banus for him and Loughton-based promoter George D some years earlier and also at Tony and Tony Truman's Players Pool Parties out there.

One such series of events in Marbella in 2007 were called Dusk Till Dawn, and during one week in July of that year parties were held at Nikki Beach, Ocean Club, Tivo, Pangea, Sky Lounge, Plaza Beach, Glam, News Cafe and Prive Beach.

Promoted by Two Tone Promotions, DJs included Brandon, Luvlee, DJ Marie, Hoxton Whores, Marble and Tristan. Tickets were priced at £125, but gained you VIP entrance to all eight events, and priority bookings on tables, free sun beds and loungers at all beach parties.

Tony Wheelchair remembers the Puerto Banus years with Brandon fondly:-

*(clockwise) * At the South Africa World Cup, 2010, with 'the lads', including my neighbour Craig, left*
* On the slopes in Chamonix king with Wardy, 2004/5
* Rebecca Loos and Normski at Extreme Detox, Thailand
* With The Es Vive boys (left to right) Chris Christofi, Jason Bull, Max Leverett and old pal Steve Lee
* dressed in uniform for Trust Me I'm A Holiday Rep
* With Harvey and Alex P on Space Terrace
* Extreme Team action with Wardy (right)

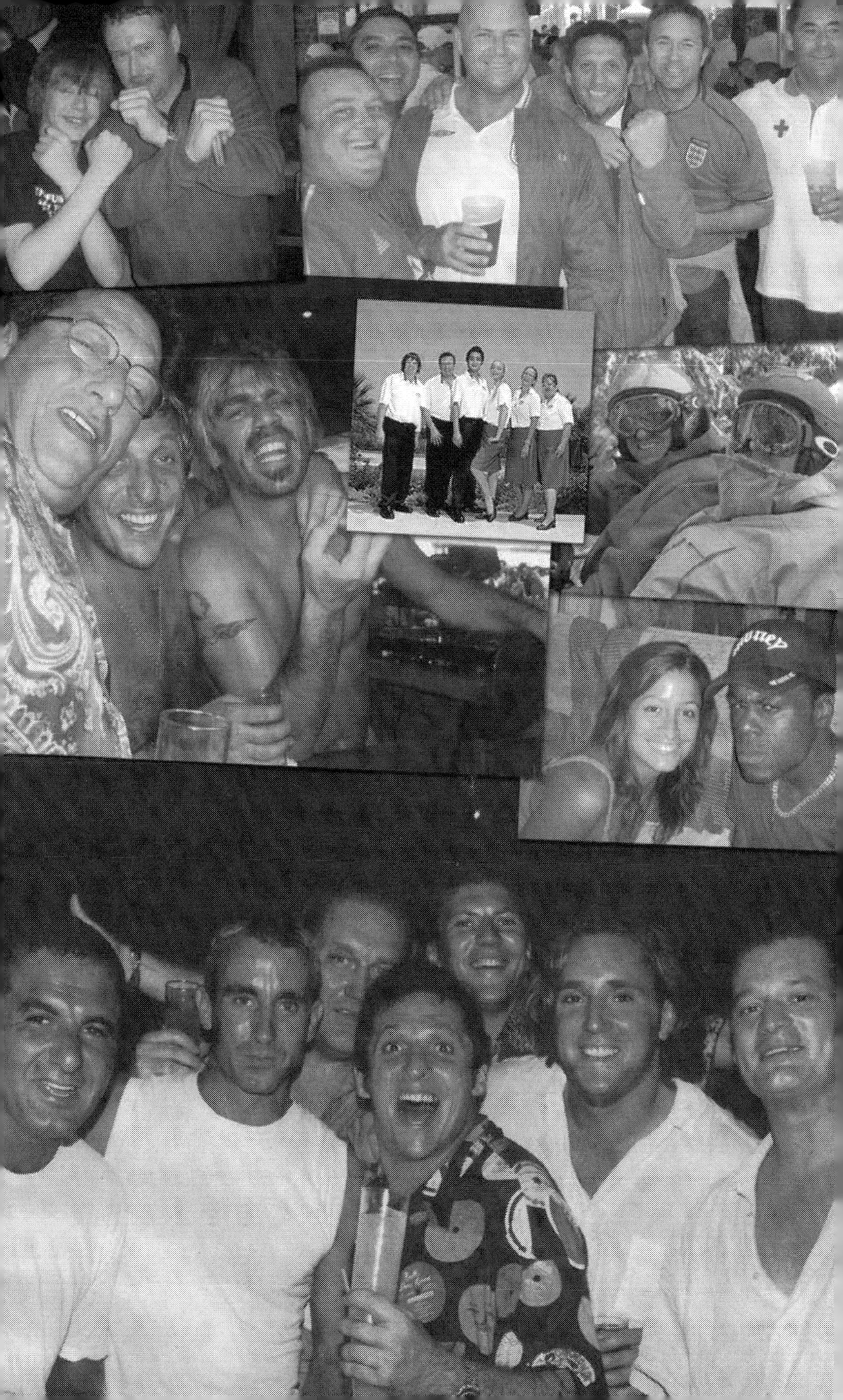

THE LIFE & LINES OF BRANDON BLOCK

I was out in Marbella with George D in February, 2001, looking to hook something up, and we managed to do a deal with this guy who owned a club called Scream, which had previously been owned by racing driver James Hunt.

He wanted to know our unique selling point, what we were going to do different, and we explained that we were going to be the first club in Puerto Banus to charge on the door, and we used Brandon as our bargaining tool. We said we were going to bring him out to be our resident. We signed the deal and did four seasons at Scream, a weekly night called Back To The Old School.

Towards the end of that run myself and Tony Truman launched the Players Pool Party week, and we went to town on it. We hired this villa worth £60m for the main event and chartered EasyJet planes to get everyone out there, selling the flights, accommodation and passes to all the events.

Brandon was headlining the Players Pool Party each year too, and any time he was on the plane we did our deposit with EasyJet on damages. There was always a party on that plane, the bar would be drunk dry and one time Brandon staggered off the flight with a life jacket on.

We'd been told that he needed to keep off the booze, and one year, after he'd got carried away one night, we left him locked in our apartment, which was on the seventh floor of a plush eight-storey apartment block, and went out for something to eat. We got back and he was nowhere to be seen, but the front door was still locked. So thinking he must have got out through the balcony, we asked both the people below if they knew anything and they said they'd seen a strange person on their terraces, but hadn't let him in. Turns out that after having no success going down, he climbed back up, and up again, and on to the balcony of the penthouse at the top. The place we were renting was worth £800,000, but this gaff at the top was £1.5m. We later heard from the guy who owned it, that just after midnight he was in bed with his missus, when Brandon comes through the balcony, into the master bedroom, said "good evening" to the shocked couple and let himself out the front door.

That was another time we got a call from Brandon in Fuengirola, 45 minutes away, once more with Kevin Andrews from the Hoxton Whores, asking if someone could come and get them.

One of his party tricks was pouring beer into a carrier bag, doing a handstand and then drinking the contents upside down.

Another year we were doing a party at News Bar, which is a lovely place and there were VIP tables with people drinking Crystal rose, really premium stuff. Brandon was DJing, and suddenly left the booth, leapt onto the top of a sofa, jumped up and was hanging off the ceiling fan, another of his party pieces. He managed one and half spins before the fan ripped out of the ceiling and smashed up ten grands worth of booze on one of the VIP tables. It was quite a spectacle and, amazingly, the club eventually asked us and Brandon back.

But that was Brandon, he really helped us liven up Puerto Banus. They weren't used to people like that at the start of our time there, but after a few years, everyone knew Brandon and he could walk into any bar and drink for free. They all loved him.

After a great few seasons out in Marbella, myself and Tony were explaining to Wayne Lineker that we felt San Antonio in Ibiza was on the way up again, after being shunned as the rubbish of the island for large periods by the so-called trendier people out there. I always thought that was bollocks because I have had the best fun in San An, and probably got up to the most mischief there.

After all, San An was the first place me and the boys and me and Baggy went on those initial trips to Ibiza in '90 and '91. San An always will have a special place in my heart, way back to Tommy Mac and Alan Warman's after hours nights at La Passion, on the road in between Amnesia and San An, etc.

For the Linekers Ibiza project Wayne suggested we got Tony Truman involved. The pair of them got the whole thing rolling and went over to Ibiza to look at a few venues, quickly falling in love with the space that we eventually opened. It's an excellent spot with a great terrace and view, and capacity of around 200 and we really couldn't have asked for anything better.

During my involvement in Linekers, Wayne's son Duane ran the place, and myself and the two Tonys were silent partners, not

involved in the day to day running of the bar. We really hit the ground running in 2008, and each summer was better each time. We would open around 8pm, and by 10pm it was usually chocka.

Season-wise, we opened from late April until October and I would go out there every other week during that period. I DJd there when I could or when they wanted me to, but to be honest, the resident jocks we had, Sam Dungate and Grant Collins, always did a great job, and knew exactly what they were doing. They were originally the residents at the flagship Tenerife venue, but thankfully we managed to poach them.

Brandon still clearly has the same affection for the island which helped shaped his career so much. The Linekers link topped the whole experience off nicely for him, but in early 2011 he decided to opt out of the project.

Let's just say Linekers was a nice little investment for me at that time, and for a couple of years it felt good to own a very small part of an island I've been so involved in.

Tony Wheelchair's new venture, with Linekers Bar partners Wayne and Duane Lineker, and Tony Truman, which will also involve Javier Anadon from Mambo, is the Ocean Club, Ibiza, a sprawling 3,000-capacity beach club in San Antonio, so look out for a brand new Players Pool Party week of events there and appearances by Brandon throughout summer 2012.

I was asked back to play at Space in 2011 at the closing party, which was great, but I haven't really DJd at any of the bigger clubs in Ibiza for the last few seasons so Linekers did give me a reason to keep going back to Ibiza and to catch up with all my friends there. However, these days I'm happier spending longer periods of time chilling out in Thailand.

Sure Ibiza is still an amazing island, and will always be popular with party people, but it's changed so much since I first made my mark there. I've never followed the trends really anyway, I've always been my own entity, I suppose. I've never wanted to be in

the coolest or hippest bars or clubs. Wherever I am in the world, I've always just been after the best party and the best laugh.

At the end of the day, Space terrace was the coolest club in the world for years, and they can't take that away from me. If someone gets my flights and hotel sorted, and I get paid for the gig in Ibiza or wherever in the world, even at my tender age, I still appreciate that, and there really is no better place in the world to DJ than Ibiza. And even more so now, it's nice to go abroad with a clear head and chill-out, check out some nice beaches and restaurants, or witness different aspects of that particular part of the world, rather than running around off my chops all the time, causing havoc.

In 2010 I turned down several Ibiza bookings over one fortnight, instead gratefully accepting a gig in Cape Town at a friend's club, which included tickets to the England vs Algeria World Cup group game.

I'm a passionate Tottenham fan, and on a trip to Dubai in 2007 I bumped into an old friend John Juniper, who owns The Bill Nicholson pub behind the East Stand at White Hart Lane. The pub has a large garden and is a favourite with staunch Spurs fans. Since meeting John in Dubai, myself, Alex P and Andrew Galea have played each year at an end of season party on the last home game of each season, which are always great days out, with Keiran Cassidy, Terry Mordecai and Ricky. A special thanks to Harry Redknapp for bringing us back!

My love of football and my natural patriotism, meant that the chance to have a crack at recording a World Cup anthem for the England football team was, again, something I wasn't going to pass up. Myself and Kevin Andrews from the Hoxton Whores had produced a couple of tracks over the last few years, one called Don't You Feel The Love, which sampled Gladys Knight's Taste A Bitter Love, and a few other bits, and we got together to record something in time for the 2006 World Cup. I'd always loved the classic film The Italian Job. It's widely regarded as THE greatest British film. I just the loved chirpy cockneys abroad angle, with the legend that is Michael Caine, and it still cracks me up every time I watch it.

I had the idea of using the classic Self Preservation Society track from the film, which is actually called Getta Bloomin' Move

On and was produced by Quincy Jones, along with most of the rest of the soundtrack…and not a lot of people know that…ha, ha.

We needed to clear the sample, but me and Kevin buggered around with the track for a bit, and it does what it says on the tin. The chorus originally said "We Are The England World Cup Society", and we just missed out on getting it on a football compilation for the 2006 tournament. For the 2010 World Cup in South Africa we changed it to We Are The England Football Society and we got actor Danny Dyer involved. Me, Danny and Kevin all chanted and whistled on it. We did the song for charity McMillan Cancer, because I'm a big supporter of the work they do, and also the Hopscotch Children's Charity, which arranges holidays for disadvantaged kids.

Projects like the football song are welcome distractions for Brandon, who as the second decade of this Millennium unfolds is constantly evaluating his life and soul-searching about exactly what he's going to do with the rest of it. His battle with drugs was won a long time ago, and now he appears to have conquered cigarettes and alcohol too.

Many people will argue that the longer you're off the gear, the easier it is, which is true to a certain extent, but don't forget that the nature is in the beast, and if you've ever been addicted to any form of drugs, any slip you have will allow that little monster to rear its ugly head again. And no matter how strong you are or think you are, you really don't want to be putting yourself under that sort of pressure again.

The same thing applies to alcohol and cigarettes, and any other addiction, be it bad or good. I've steadily drunk less and less over the years, and go weeks without a drink, but, due to my constitution being what it is, I am able to indulge in prolonged and abnormal drinking and, of course, as I get older, it's all so much more difficult to recover from.

One such session in spring 2010 started when the sun came out on a Saturday afternoon, and a few old family friends popped over for a BBQ. This extended to the local pub, for a 50th birthday party, where I was DJing for a pal, and which allowed me to delve in to the archives of real jazz funk. At this point, with a few drinks inside me, I'm never happier, and in true soul funkster form this led to various spirits in tiny glasses - shots, as I believe the youngsters call them!

Back home around 1am, with the hordes from the pub, and, of course, waking up the whole cul de sac (apologies to my ever understanding neighbours), the party then continued until the early hours, with my new complimentary Funktion One monitor speakers (thanks Tony and Christine) blaring at full pelt.

We finally sneaked in a few hours kip between 4am – midday (approx!), to be awoken by the sound of a clattering glass and a pint of Magners, as opposed to the sensible option of clattering plates and cutlery and the smell of a good old fry up. This started the ball rolling again for another instalment of that long-running soap opera, the 'Sunday Session', at various locations.

Come the Monday, after a torrid night's sleep, my head was all over the gaff, and I was soon smoking heavily, literally to get through the week, and all after numerous attempts to stop…three weeks off, three weeks on, etc.

I highly recommend that if you're undertaking a recovery of any type, please, please try and do it by the book. As referred to earlier, my choice to go it alone with the coke, without the recommended support, was, in my opinion, a hindrance to my recovery. Ho-hum, there's no telling me, and never has been. The longer you're off it, the easier it is to slip back in, and to kid yourself that it's been so long now that you would be able to control it, is like a recovering alcoholic thinking he could get back to having just a couple of pints or glasses of wine each night.

Smoking has always been another bane of my life, and it's largely brought on by drinking binges, which in turn creates the addiction once more, again having a continued negative effect on my persona.

As I finish this book in December 2011, my drinking is in check, and has been good for a while now, and I haven't smoked a cigarette for a couple of months (Thanks Alan Carr...)

BACK TO BLOCK

With the summer of 2011 starting to hot up finally, I took to the road with Brandon for a stint as bag man. Tour manager/minder Brady had long retired, the fees on offer now not always stretching as far as a driver, and the need for protection from narcotics a distant memory.

Three Saturday bookings were on the agenda - a 5pm - 7pm set for a Corona BBQ session on the courtyard at The Vibe Bar in Brick Lane for his old friend Norris Da Boss Windross; a 10pm - 11.30pm stint at a Worthing club night called Sitting Pretty; with a 00.30am - 2am set at Coalition in Brighton, just down the sea road, wrapping up the night.

A trio of bookings, with all due respect, not in the realms of a textbook Golden/Progress/Godskitchen combo of the late '90s, but then this wasn't the late '90s, and there's not many DJs who were big in that era still out there getting three bookings on a Saturday night.

As Brandon finished his set at The Vibe Bar tragic news filtered through that Amy Winehouse had been found dead a few miles down the road at her Camden home. It struck a chord with many dancing and seated around the decks, and Brandon fittingly wrapped up his set with a dance mix of Amy's anthem Tears Dry On Their Own.

It was long before details of the iconic 27-year-old singer's death were confirmed, when a coroner's verdict of misadventure was later recorded, but I could not help making immediate comparisons to Brandon's recovery. Just how close had he been to pushing it too far the hundreds of times he tested his body to the limits.

Not a drop of alcohol passed Brandon's lips on this particular Saturday, as he snoozed and snored loudly in my car between each club. A bottle of water at each gig was all he needed. It was a far cry from the madcap, coke and vodka-fuelled roadtrips of yesteryear.

At each venue he was greeted by welcoming promoters and eager punters, posing for dozens of photos with the paying public at each party, before, during and after his set. And I can safely say 'the boy' has still got it. Great tunes and anthems all the way, not a beat missed, arms in the air throughout (as well as the crowd!) - all concerned happy and an example of professionalism all round.

For the trainspotters out there, here's a selection of what Brandon played the night before.

5pm - 7pm: CORONA SUMMER PARTY @ VIBE BAR, BRICK LANE, including:-

Backfired (Joey Negro Mix, Grant Nelson special edit) - Masters At Work
Feeling The Light (Grant Nelson re-edit) - Soulsearcher vs Michelle Weeks
If We Can Fly (Dennis Ferrer Getaway Mix) - Soul Dhamma feat Donni
Make My Dreams (Wicked Massive Edit) - Mischief
Another Star (Soulful Mix) - Pagany feat Myles Sanko
Let's Groove (Brandon Block, Karl G & Jamesie Mix) - Turncoats
Off (Original Mix) - Ministry Of Funk
Sinfonia Della Notte (Gel Abril Remix) - Dennis Ferrer
Making Love Till Sundown - Funkagenda
Night At The Dogs - Jesse Rose
Tears Dry On Their Own (Alex Alvarez Remix) - Amy Winehouse

10pm - 11.30pm: SITTING PRETTY @ TANGERINE BAR, WORTHING, including:-

Billie The King - DJ Pippi
Cerveza - Matt McLarrie
Do What You Wanna - DJ Mes & Sonny Fodera
You Stopped Loving Me - Burns & Fred Falke
That's How Good Your Love Is - Richard Earnshaw & Giles vs Jocelyn Brown
Let's Groove (Brandon Block, Karl G & Jamesie Mix) - Turncoats
Between Two Worlds - DJ EQ
Life / Run Run Run (Coyu & Edu Imbernon Remix) - Butch
Off (Original Mix) - Ministry Of Funk
If You Could Read My Mind - Amber
Let The Music Spill - M&S feat Starview

12.30am - 2am: COALITION, BRIGHTON, including:-

The Bag (Castelli Ipanema) - Ministry Of Funk
Dholak (Original Mix) - Rampus
DJ, You've Got My Love - Richard Dinsdale

Spanish Lick (Original Mix) - David Herrero
Superstylin' (Ant Brooks Mix) - Groove Armada
Umbungo - The BeatThiefs
Downpipe - Mark Knight v. Underworld
Everybody Dance Now - Kevin Andrews
Deep Inside (Harry Choo Choo Romero Dirty Piano Mix) - Hardrive
4 U (2001 Remix) - Fourth Measure Men
Cry (Just A Little) - Bingo Players

Behind the scenes, Brandon has been devoting a day and a half of his week working in the drug rehabilitation sector, studying towards a possible NVQ (National Vocational Qualification). He is reluctant to go into full details, because of confidentiality issues, but explains:-

I've been helping out in the drugs field, but this isn't an afternoon picking poppies. I was sitting in my office at home in 2010 after many weeks of not being very constructive with my time, and I was feeling down, getting confused about what I was going to do with my life in the future. I was becoming more and more disillusioned with the new music that I was being sent or that was coming out, and, I guess, mentally, I was feeling a bit scarred and needed some new motivation in my life. I was wondering what I could do, so I googled 'drug counselling services' locally, and I saw the name Blenheim CDP, which struck a chord, as I attended my first ever CA meeting with them in 1996.

I saw some options to volunteer, which also gives you the training that you need. Importantly you didn't need qualifications at all to start so I rang them up and I was invited in for a chat.

A lot of good drug counsellors have been addicts themselves, and I think the hands-on experience gives them a great insight into addiction and recovery, although this is only my humble opinion. I don't have academic experience, but I have hands-on or, I guess, nose-on experience. My admiration goes out to all involved.

I started as a volunteer in November 2010, and I go there one or two days a week, or when required, helping out with group therapy, assessments and the day-to-day running. And, to be honest, it's very therapeutic for me.

Later through that project I was asked if I wanted to go to a class where I could study towards a qualification in drug rehabilitation. And after six months of doing that every week I passed and was given a certificate. I received a certain amount of units and if you amass more units you can get an NVQ, or progress further to a diploma. It was a great satisfaction to know that I had actually passed something after all this time, and I'm going to seriously think about taking those studies further.

Who would have thought that a man who spent so much time with a key or note up his nose would end up making 'keynote' speeches about cocaine addiction.

Meanwhile, Brandon is out there DJing every week, bookings which come through old associates, friends and various agents, and which still earn him a regular living.

And you sense there will be a steady trickle of bookings for many years to come. Brandon has played and worked with so many promoters in the UK and all over the world, and you only have to spend one day with him to see how many contact him each week, prospecting about his availability for existing or forthcoming projects.

The odd celebrity appearance at a function, which may find its way on to the pages of Hello or OK Magazine, helps generate more bookings on 'the circuit', including playing at the weddings of soap star pals like EastEnders stars Scott Maslen (Jack Branning) and Laurie Brett (Jane Beale), Alex Walkinshaw, aka Smithy from The Bill, and also birthday parties for celebrities like Jamie Oliver.

Then there are the reunion parties, which gathered pace in 2009, when many old promotions were celebrated by promoters and punters alike, often via Facebook groups set up by old regulars.

Twenty Years Of Acid House reunion events included Full Circle at Winkers Farm Country Club in Chalfont St Mary in August, and a

*(clockwise) * From the 'Bloxbox' DJ luggage range*
* With Ant & Dec after DJing backstage at the Robbie Williams, Knebworth gig, 2003
* Promo for Abu Dhabi gig, December, 2011
* With EastEnders' star Scott Maslen, 2009
* With Gary The Phone and Carlton Leach, 2009
* DJing for Jamie Oliver at his birthday, 2006

STARLIGHT

Al Maya Island & Resorts in association with Starlight events presents

AL MAYA

UK DJ Legends
BRANDON BLOCK
TALL PAUL

FRIDAY 02 DECEMBER

BORA BORA
al maya island

STARLIGHT
CHRIS DELA

BORA BORA
MIDDLE EAST

AL MAYA ISLAND & RESORT - ABU DHABI
Tickets available from the Resort or ADCC - VIP Reservations
0503 174 696 or 0508 174

month before, a joint Flying & Shakavara party in Vauxhall, south London, where old foes Charlie Chester and Brandon were pictured in the DJ booth together.

Meanwhile, at the time of going to press in December 2011, Brandon was approaching a festive period which would see him play in Abu Dhabi, Monte Carlo, Verbier in Switzerland and Guernsey, as well as whole host of UK-based bookings.

I still get asked to play at a lot of midweek corporate events and functions too. For one Apple Christmas party my fee consisted of a fully-loaded 27 inch iMac computer. I'm a massive Mac fan so that was ideal for me.

Just before Christmas each year I jet out to Hong Kong for my annual Christmas Eve booking at Drop Club, and then, as usual, travel on to Thailand, where I party and DJ a little bit, chill-out a lot more, and also manage to fully detox again until the end of January.

Then February and March can often be filled with midweek residencies at various ski resorts.

The DJ bookings still seem to be coming through on a regular basis, but there is a lot less lead up time than before. They used to come in months, even a year in advance, now it's more often than not a few weeks before. But I'm still playing out loads so in the words of Chas & Dave - "mustn't grumble".

As well as the club bookings, I do a lot of birthday parties for friends, for which I'm never without my very good pal and DJ Chris Mills, who has the best knowledge of music for a young'un. Millsy is also my online personal trainer, as he's too lazy to get out of bed to do the personal bit...only joking son!

I've also been playing around with production again. I think as I get older, my musical preferences tend to stick to the old school, which for making new music means I can tap into a wide range of classics. Although technology moves so fast these days, I'm pretty much up to date with it all. However, in my advancing years, the younger fraternity seem to thrive on that stuff just that little bit more, and good luck to them. It still astounds me the amount of music being uploaded, downloaded and side-loaded per day.

My most recent studio projects have included working with The Fabulous Baker Brothers (aka snowboard champ Jamie and his brother Bobby), with James Hockley as The Teeleafs, with Tall Paul as The Grifters and also with my pal from The Bodyrockers, Jon Fitz, while other re-edits and remixes I've been playing around with include a cover of Paul Rutherford's Get Real, which Paul has agreed to re-vocal for me.

And as well as the production, I've also been promoting again, with my old mucker Ali, which has been fun after all these years... 25 in fact, since we started DJing together at The John Lyon. Our new party is called Sweet Sensation, and the first was a multi-roomed event with a huge marquee attached to one of our local pubs in Ruislip, and was a 700-capacity sell-out. More events over Christmas/New Year and on Bank Holidays will hopefully follow, and the great thing about this party is that it brings so many of our old friends together, more than 20 years after we all started going out.

Another of my long-terms projects/business ideas will hopefully come to fruition soon too - my Bloxbox range of lifestyle luggage, with DJs in mind, is being manufactured in China and should be in the shops in 2012. After carrying so much baggage (nudge, wink, wink...) around for the last three decades, to see my own range of bags on sale will be particularly satisfying.

LIVING ON A PRAYER

Brandon still goes to see Bill Shanahan at the clinic several times each year and Shanahan never had any doubt his star pupil would pull through.

Despite his battle with cocaine, alcohol and cigarettes, Brandon really is an inspiration to others. The booze and fags will always be a concern, but he is well aware of that. I'm glad that his drinking is limited now, though, and that he is at least constantly trying to give up cigarettes, because that gives his lungs a chance to rebuild each time.

I suppose you could say I gave up cocaine my way. I didn't go to the meetings a lot, and do the whole recovery process as suggested. I didn't do the '12 Steps' programme, as such, and I did carry on drinking. I had two slip-ups with cocaine very early doors, in the first few months, and on the last occasion it was just one line, a single nose, and didn't lead to a whole gram or a big session. For someone who was taking the amount I was taking that was good.

Once I'd got through the clinic, my head had turned, it had gone completely the other way. I was too frightened to even to attempt to fuck about with that shit again. I just didn't want to go back to that place.

My demeanour still when I'm out, often with my arms in the air, when I'm DJing, may give the impression that I have indulged, but that is the way I am. I've always been like that, before drugs and since drugs. I have such a love of music that I can't stop being that way. I always get involved with the crowd, I like to feel the music.

People may have seen me drunk, which I get from time to time - and I still have the capability of drinking you all under the table.

Many people come up to me at the end of the night still and say "c'mon, let's get on a sesh", and I say, "yeah, course we can, not tonight, though, I'm driving, I'm not drinking", and they're like "but you said that last time"... and all they really want is to have a laugh with me, and that's fair enough, because I am good fun, and was probably great fun when I was out of my nut.

The fact that some people can still do that on occasion, is up to them, but I can't, I'm not that person. I'm the guy who goes way over the top. And will end up having a heart attack if I attempted to go back on it. I just have no desire to risk that. I'm just too good being clean to go down that rocky road again.

Brandon's contemporaries all have their own take on the cause and effect of recreational drugs.

Up Yer Ronson promoter Tony Hannan points out:-

I don't touch drugs any more, but my take on the whole thing is that the so-called acid house scene was a social and musical revolution. For instance, before acid house and ecstasy came along white and black people didn't really mix socially in Leeds, and you wouldn't get large groups of people travelling to, say, Manchester, for a night out. Yet before you knew it there were 200 Leeds United fans in the Hacienda partying with the Man Utd and Man City fans.

It's well documented that ecstasy sorted out a lot of problems with football hooliganism, not just in the north, but in London as well. With ecstasy the last thing on anyone's mind was a fight. History always repeats itself and I always think that punk rock wiped out cheesy disco and acid house wiped out cheesy rock and pop. Then after ecstasy revolutionised boozy clubs in the late '80s and early '90s, cocaine came along and made it all moody again.

Hannan has benefited from the multi-cultural nightlife that the acid house generation produced, and, like Brandon, ventured into the bar business himself. He owns Leeds City Centre venue The Rock Bar, which is both inspired by and twinned with the well-known Ibiza bar of the same name. He continues:-

I've been through my ups-and-downs, like Brandon or anyone else, I guess. With business partners, I opened an Ibiza-style boutique bar in Leeds. It's nice to still be involved in the social side of things, but a few scares that I've had recently with my health have helped keep things in perspective.

Life is never a straight road, you have to live the lows to enjoy the highs and I personally have no regrets. Like many involved in our scene, I'm just happy to have come out the other side. They say youth is wasted on the youth, and we certainly got wasted. Sure, we all did some stupid things, but you're only on this planet once.

I haven't been well recently, and while waiting for some prostate cancer and leukemia tests to come back, everything really hit home to me. Brandon was great, ringing me up at all times of the night, cheering me up by talking nonsense.

And Brandon always gave us the best laughs and got into the best scrapes. I remember he'd played for us in Leeds once in the early '90s and we were back at someone's house cracking on, when we suddenly realised we'd lost Brandon. It was 9am and someone called up and said he'd been spotted, sitting on top of an advertising billboard, with a yellow marigold washing up glove on his head waving at all the traffic. Classic Brandon. Another time, when we were at his mate Del's flat in London, always sticks out in my mind. It was a posh apartment which had a lift in it, which opened up into the actual flat. We were all partying one night, and Harvey Block was there too. Brandon and his dad suddenly disappeared down in the lift, and when they came back up and the doors opened, they were wearing each other's clothes. Priceless!

Swainy points out:-

The thing about the cracks we used to have, was that it was one big great laugh. There was no nastiness to it. No punch-ups at the end of the night. It's a bit of a cliche now, but it was all about love and peace, and having a giggle. We did lots of silly things, but the main thing I remember was the laughs we had. And the next time we were all out, we just seemed to pick up from where we'd left off. Are people still that crazy? Maybe, although I just don't think people are as hedonistic these days.

Vivienne Block concludes:-

I feel very proud of what Brandon has done. I love him to death, and if there was any part of my body that he needed, that wasn't worn out, he could have it. He is one of the nicest, kindest, most generous people I know. He's not always the most thoughtful, and there's been a lot of drama, but lots of good times and fun all the same. And within it all, I've enjoyed so many amazing family days with Brandon. And that's what I love about Brandon, he has always spent a lot of time with his family, no matter what's he's gone through.

Meanwhile, Emma Block reasons:-

As I got older I noticed that people were introducing me as 'Brandon Block's sister', and I think fame within your family can have its downfalls. At its height, I remember family meals out being disrupted a lot because people wanted to talk to Brandon all the time, but he took it all in his stride, like he always does.

I've met some really random people through Brandon, like getting drunk at one party with both Jason Donovan and Tony Hadley from Spandau Ballet. Over the years me and Brandon have got gradually closer and closer, so that's great.

I was always very proud he was my brother, but I wasn't always aware of his achievements, and I'm so proud of what he's doing now, especially with the drug counselling.

Harvey Block believes Brandon deserves any praise that comes his way for keeping off cocaine.

When you consider the quantities of drugs that he was doing, and the money he was spending on it, the fact that he continued to work within that environment, when people were literally throwing it at him, and yet he managed to stay clear of it, that's an amazing accolade for him, and shows the willpower that he had and has.

I think he deserves an award for that. Unlike Amy Winehouse - and our hearts go out to her family - Brandon was very lucky, and thankfully he has survived.

(clockwise) * The Ruislip Funk Patrol (with Brandon, Brady and Aves) at Caister Weekender, 2008
* Out for dinner with mum Vivienne, 2010
* (centre) At Shoreditch House, 2011, images by JaxEtta
* With Aves, Derek Dahlarge and Matt Trollope at Sancho Panza, Notting Hill Carnival, 2011, image by JaxEtta

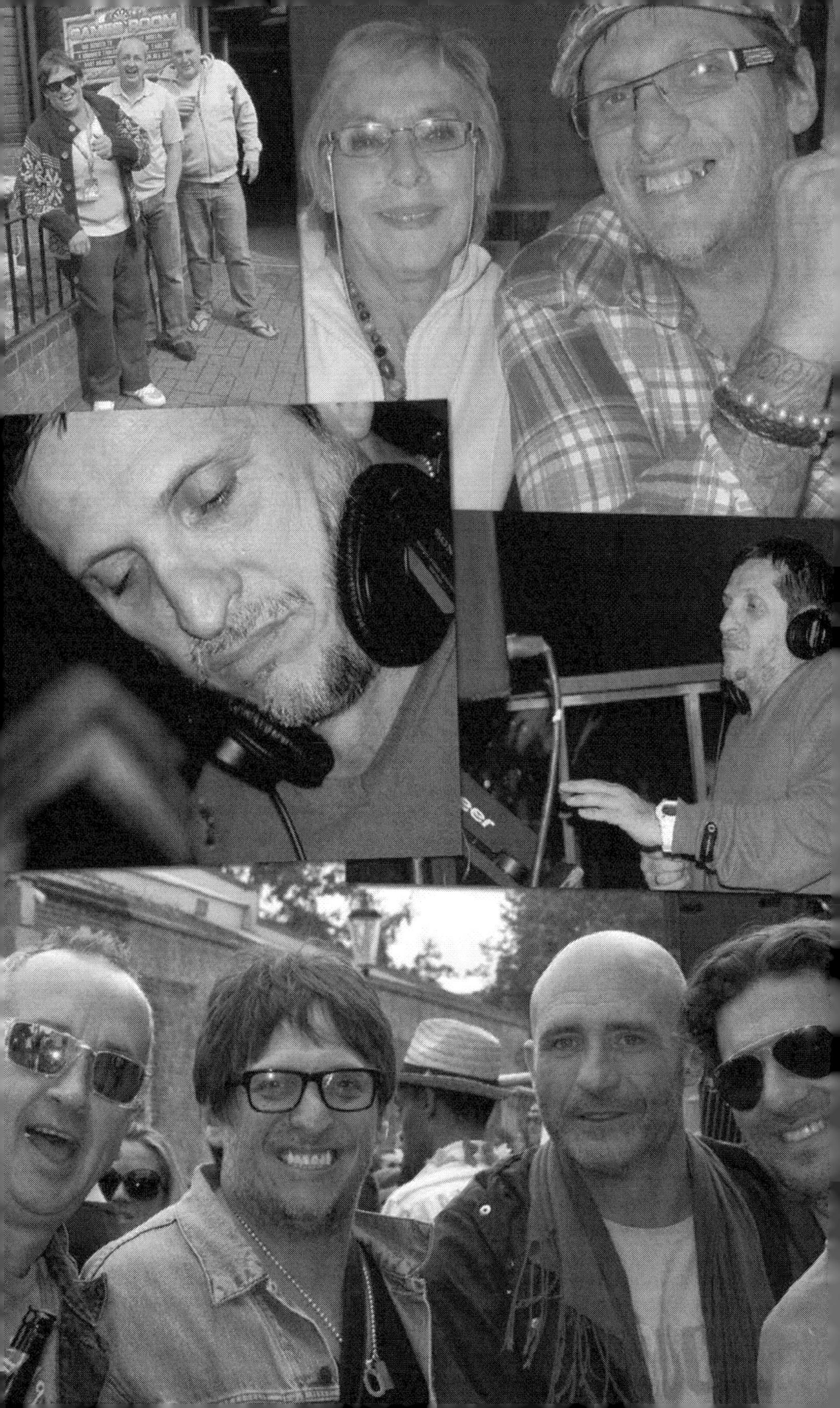

I don't know if a lot of Brandon's anger in the early days was anything to do with me and his mum splitting up. I know that he's got a lot of love for me, and I have a lot of love for him, but, as father and son, you often find it hard to show or demonstrate that.

He's made me very, very proud for many many years. I think there's still a lot for him to achieve, with his understanding of music, maybe on TV and radio again, and you never know what he could go on to do. I think he could be the ideal vehicle for many music-related projects. If he'd had a management team that looked after him 24-7, and that's an impossible task, maybe he could have gone on to even greater success.

Creation Records boss Alan McGee, who managed both Primal Scream and The Libertines, summed up that issue of management succinctly in the days after Amy Winehouse's death, when he told The Sun Newspaper:-

There is nothing a manager, friend or family member can do to help someone who is addicted to drugs. It is completely down to the individual to help themselves. The buck stops with the person doing drugs.

I've managed some of the worst drug addicts in rock 'n' roll. You step in to do what you can but some want help and others don't. Managers are there to manage careers. You can't go to the toilet with the artists every time.

Unlike the various members of the notorious '27 Club', Brandon did make it through to his 30s, although only just. He was living with his mum until he was 29, which is unusual for a successful media personality.

Although he did during that time develop and maintain a cocaine addiction of gargantuan proportions, maybe spending those years at the family home did eventually encourage him to kick his habit once and for all.

His mum being on hand to sit with him during the depths of his addiction in familiar surroundings surely provided a vital comfort blanket when push came to shove.

Interestingly, Brandon only tried to give up once and that one time he was successful. He wasn't in and out of rehab all the time, he was in, and then he was out.

Harvey Block continues:-

One thing I suppose I've always been envious of Brandon, is this unbelievable circle of friends that he has. I haven't necessarily approved of all of them over the years, but he is still very very good friends with many of them, lots of them kids I used to take to football when he was at cubs, or wherever, and that's a great testimony to his character, and a tremendous achievement in itself. In today's world, there's so much else going on, people don't seem to hang on to their old friends.

Brandon, when you consider the lifespan of a DJ, and that he started in the mid-'80s, and has been DJing more than 25 years now, he's still playing out loads, and he can still put together and play a great set. The money is not as good as it used to be, but that's the economic world that we live in today.

Brady admits handling a post-cocaine Brandon was testing at times:-

When he came off the gear he was hard work. But he did keep off it, and I wouldn't have had it any other way. For the first two years I was virtually with him 24-7, and the next five years, we were together Thursday through to Sunday all week. I lost several relationships over that time because I was never home.

We used to drive to Liverpool, to Cream, and then do two or three clubs on the way back. We'd be out the house 12 - 15 hours. We'd always do two or three on a Saturday, and that was solid for about four or five years. In all honesty, we had a great run. There isn't a gaff I haven't been in I don't think. To be fair, we had it right off.

I hadn't been to a nightclub for about three years, but I went out with Brandon recently, and I thought "I don't miss this". At one stage I'd go to the opening of an envelope. I've been clubbing all my life, but as punters we're too old for it now.

The old days were unbelievable. We're two-bob geezers really. We work the streets, as such, to get a pound, but everywhere we went it was VIP. We went to bashes that you wouldn't even think we'd get a tap in, but we got in everywhere.

There wasn't a night that we couldn't go out somewhere and have it, proper, red carpet all the way.

As a crowd pleaser, there was no better DJ than Brandon. I noticed that we always had more record boxes than the other DJs. He'd have two boxes, I'd have another two, and we'd both be fighting through thousands of people to get to the DJ booth. He'd get in there, eye it up, see what's what, and go from there. A lot of DJs would turn up with one bag, and they might have had three gigs that night, and they would have played the same set at each. Brandon's sets were never the same from club to club, and that made it a lot more interesting for me too.

Me and him, we just sparked off each other. When other people don't find things funny, me and him are on FM...we used to say everyone else was on medium wave. I can look at him, and know what he's thinking. It was like a love affair, or what they call these days, a 'bromance'.

And the significance of everything that happened, or the good fortune bestowed upon many of the leading DJs, is not lost on Lisa Loud either.

I feel completely blessed to have been surrounded by so many talented people. When I left school, started going out and developed my public persona as I started DJing I suddenly felt the luckiest person alive and I naturally embraced it, and it turned into a massive amount of creativity. The fact that I was working as a DJ and working for record companies, and running my own promo firm was never lost on me. I did feel privileged and being around the eclectic and magic group of people that was the acid house scene was simply amazing. It hasn't been bettered since, and probably won't be. There was the '60s, there was punk and there was acid house, that's how it reads. We did acid house, that was us, we did that.

Quite early on I realised that we were part of something that was probably never going to happen again and feeling that I was part of something relevant, and the feeling of being involved in something special just cannot be beaten. The whole DJ experience was always fun, never hard to explain. We weren't 'Billy Bigtune' DJs. I'd like to think that our little crew, Brandon, me and the others, were always about being an extension of the crowd more than anything else.

Brandon concludes:-

Our generation has so far come off relatively unscathed, in the scheme of things.

There are numerous people who have died of drug-related deaths and many families who have lost loved ones. I send my deepest sympathies to them all. Looking back, many of us were so lucky to scrape through such an experimental era.

Cocaine is a big killer, but millions of people who have taken pills or use coke regularly on a recreational basis are still luckily alive. Who knows what effects on them there will be in ten or twenty years time.

Considering what I've got up to during my life, I'm overjoyed to still be alive, and now I have the opportunity to prolong my life even further, for the sake of my daughter, the rest of my family and obviously myself.

It's taken me so long to catch up where growing up is concerned, and I don't think I will ever really catch up. I've done serious damage, I know I have. The last time I saw Bill Shanahan, I asked him if I had done permanent damage, because I still have times when I feel really shit, and he said, "well, I'll be honest, you have done permanent damage, because you took so much of that stuff. It kills brain cells, and there's no way that you could come out of that unscathed".

When I started doing drugs in the early days it ran alongside the music, and with ecstasy it was, of course, because of the music initially. Obviously I took drug-taking to all sorts of extremes, particularly with cocaine. The whole thing about the recreational use of drugs then was that it was meant to be fun, but nowadays there is so much crack and heroin on the streets...drugs less associated with club culture. Also, people are taking prescribed drugs more and more on a supposedly recreational level too.

In fact, I'm amazed what a problem drugs are in this country now. I know the government are very serious about rehabilitation and everyone has the capacity to change. Help is there if people want it.

When I was growing up I didn't know what an alcoholic was, but at the time I think my drinking would have been classed as binge-drinking, and when you're younger, that's actually looked upon as normal behaviour for someone growing up in the UK. Most people grow out of that, though.

I became addicted to cocaine because I took so much of the stuff. Obviously my DJ fees meant I could afford it, at least for a while, and there was always a dealer around, so that made it easier.

I didn't have a 'normal job' to go to the next day or any day, in fact, and who can say whether things would have been different for me if I had had what you would call a 'normal job'. I certainly wouldn't have had such easy access to coke. Maybe it would have been different if I'd got involved in a serious relationship in my early 20s too, got married, had kids the conventional way, etc.

All things considered, for me, taking cocaine was all about the buzz, let's make no mistake about that. Yes, I had the money, yes, I enjoyed the escapism and yes, I enjoyed the buzz, but at the end of the day I had one of the best jobs in the world, so quite why I needed any other buzz than that, I don't know.

At that time for glamour and rubbing shoulders with the rich and famous, you couldn't beat it, and, well, I guess for a while we were the rich and famous too.

As I approach my 45th birthday I'm currently very contented, still in touch with many of my old friends, and, on a weekly basis, with all my closest pals, which means that my life has been so far, so good. Albeit, a little hairy at times.

My friends to this day, have always been my friends. The people who I am close to today, are, by and large, the same people I started out with. More and more I feel I just want my old friends around me.

If I was ever in trouble, it would be those old friends who I'd call. I'd probably have to get a cab to wherever they were...haha... but they would be there for me when I got there.

When I look back on the last 25 years I believe, however the music business or club industry progresses, that our generation had the best of it – the music, the fun, the parties and Ibiza at its very best too. I know the times we had were risky and reckless, and I nearly lost my life, but I have no regrets, and often refer back to the famous Serenity Prayer, always quoted to people going through rehab, recovery or counselling...

...God, grant me the serenity to accept the things I cannot change; Courage to change the things I can; And the wisdom to know the difference.

YOUR STORIES

Thanks to everybody who responded to our online request for Blocko memories. A selection of them have been included, as supplied.

Michelle Barr
All the stories people have about you, maybe you should consider writing your book(s) in volumes????
Good luck babe... xx

Matt Crane
Random night in Es Vive, guy standing on a chair reaches up and tries to hang off the lowered ceiling around the bar. Lasts about a second before the whole ceiling falls down, he lands on his arse still holding some ceiling saying "it wasn't me"

Niall Mongan
Too many to mention...where do we start...lol !!

Heidi Morgan
You getting hit by a car in Ibiza

Roy Jackson
You on new years day, 2005, drinking shots of tequila through snorkel and mask ha ha

Rob 'Doc' Taylor
Finding and delivering your records to Pacha Mallorca, 2 minutes before you were meant to start DJing!

Mac Mcintyre
You being thrown out of News Cafe, Banus, for trying to hang onto the ceiling fan and fly round the room....doorman didn't realise you were on the decks....piss funny

Shellie Rooney
Lol sounds like u've had many a laugh!! Wicked bet u can't remember any of these !!! Haha x

Daniel Ashley Yantin
The mong out song in Diamond club, Dubai...........! In the fountain outside planet hollywood you me and gary! The 3 day bender in the bunker, you me tim, gary, george and pete!

Danielle Moss
You were my DJ for my 21st at the Sudbury Arms ! It was feb 23 years ago ! Omg ! I've got pics somewhere x you of course went on to much bigger things but you can't take the boy out of wembley can you xx we are all grown up now x

Scott Moran
After party with the lads after the manor born at the ramside hotel in durham. A few of us and you and Alex, you did a 'magic' trick but actually really smashed some kids cartier watch! I laughed for weeks!!! Legend!x

Danny Weltman
i can rember doing a gig and brandon took on carl cox on 2 decks 1st then 3 decks think it was perception or fantazia. what a battle....or could of been energy or mythology good few years ago hahhahaha

Paul Wilson
are you avin a fuckin laugh, how many books do you want

Emma Newton
Playing hide and seek with the spanish police on plaza beach after rearranging the beach!! Xxx

Nicki Davidson
Bubba where do you want me to start

Niki Waldegrave-Clark
Most times I rang you to do your weekly daily star column, i'd wake you up and you'd missed your flights. I remember one time you were asleep on the toilet floor at Ibiza airport, and were gibbering so much, it sounded like you were talking Swahili! We had to make the column up that week as kept trying to get at least a few words out of you before deadline but it wasn't happening!! X

Nicki Davidson
Haven Stables !! Anyone except Paul Gorgeous Wilson remember then?

Antony Antonio Atkinson
me and you doing 100kph racing andy vier home...hitting a speed bump and nearly getting grazed knees

Aj England
pretending to be a gnome in wigan you in drag

Steve Altman
You at the milk bar with both legs in the milk urns they used to have there, being rolled round the place screaming and shouting off your cakehole :))

Simone Barclay
no but i have an old mix tape of yours from the 90s and i listen to it every day in my car!!!!! its faultless!! xx

Steve Altman
You still have a tape player in your car??

Simone Barclay
i do get players in my car though too!!

Rhian Evans
I have a cheesy chips/ airport check in story which included you telling a plane full of people that you were a lama trainer

Clara Da Costa
How about sheets being put together to climb down from the balcony ha ha ha :o) xx

Jeni Swan
Nope! Was always as twatted as you! ;) lol

Sam Dungate
me u n Grant going to Space in there 1 min b4 the doorman tried frog marching u out for trying to rugby tackle kryoman hahha funny as fook.

Chris Christofi
I could fill up a book just about your escapades in ibiza

James Collins
I have Brandon but I don't know if you want me to remind you. Just remember Honeyclub a few years ago & Alex having to hold you up. It was nothing to do with me m8! Well not much!!

Nikki Miller-Mccall
Erm...finding you under a palm tree next to sands after DC10 seems to hit the spot Brandon.....!!!! lol xxxx

Darren Bird-Braddick
Where do I start FUBAR, Club For Life, Hollywoods, Sugar Reef, Oscars in Clacton, Club UK...might do my own book with all the stories mate, see you next Saturday Brand D x

Richard Elliott
would all those people who can't remember a good story, leeaaave the roooom now please. ;-)

Ian Bullock
Decadence Wednesday nights..Bakers Birmingham. VIP toilet ..you me, yan, alex, chris millard, just chatting!

Jon White
There's a few from our Sunday's at Klute mate... You went AWOL before the gig, only to be found on the roof - only knew you were there coz we could see ya legs in the air! Drinking the water from a vase of flowers on the bar... will mail the others :)

Millsy
That wedding we were playing at, for a mate of yours...the band was going on so long that you bundled the singer off the stage and dropped Martha Reeves and the Vandella's Nowhere To Run.

Samantha Jane Devenny
The Cross, circa 1998, you were in the booth and I came in with you and people were calling us Barbie and Ken...don't ask me why...perhaps because we were both in the same 'state'???

Samantha Jane Devenny
Mambo, circa 1996, one afternoon/early evening - you and Alex had just run in off the beach as the Spanish filth had done a 'comb' across the beach looking for illegal 'things'...you were both barely able to stand, let alone speak

Dizzi
where would i start...shower curtain pole in hotel trying to see if it works same as straw, or manager standing below as we try to force a chest of drawers out the window to follow the .t.v ...or the electric parrot on beach screaching at you...

Lynne McDermott
memories of u... lol, yeah loads!! Letterkenny at the M8 night, where u chucked the decks into the crowd at the end of the night...:) x

Rob Sugarfree Solari
One of my faves was you DJing in the Loft, Meribel and trying to jump on the decks... all you succeeded in doing was putting a big cut in your nose, blood pissing out... my ex Rhian was giving you first aid (pressure) while I was putting in CDs, and cueing them up. All this

after you appeared on stage (uninvited) a few hours earlier in the middle of KT Tunstall's set... she saw you, introduced you to the 1000 people in the crowd then you got thrown off by the bouncers, I came to rescue you at the side door, you were stumbling everywhere, lost your footing, went to grab me... but all you succeeded in doing was grabbing my full pint of beer and falling over backwards tipping the whole pint all over you. Nice!

AW
When Aves got nicked for d & d in watford and the o/bill asked us to drive the car to the station following them (pissed and mangled) when we got there waiting for his realease we racked a few up on the sergeants counter in the foyer haha have that!

Neil M English
brandon, oi oi, what about in 92 in ibiza, you walking around in a made up nappy and punk wig, off your trolley, mental mate, not seen you since south africa last year, there were 10 german bombers..., space how low can you go, space how low you go, x

Lisa Horan
haven't you got enough yet!!?? Blocko !!! xxx

Cheryl Roberts
Got a funny story involving a certain footballer and the news of the world, remember you and Alex chasing the reporters up the street for me and kicking their car. They absolutely shit themselves. Got dates and other incidents involving that and even solicitors statements. Xx funny!!

Susan Neal
Don't even go there too many things to tell !

AW
Blocko, what about me and you gettin miami-viced round the back of the astoria ? Old bill chored you and i done one into the night, that copper tryin to search 3 of us at the same time....er ,dont think so! Ta ta

Phil Drummond

I remember quite a few of these mate. The Es Vive was classic, so was huge new year that lasted 4 days and ended up with the JD and snorkel incident, the Brits, driving the TT into the pub, i could be here all day.

Steve Bryant

Inside Space in Ibiza in the early 90s....me and loads of Europeans, it was so dark you couldnt see your hand......walked outside and Brandon was playing September/EWF, what a contrast !!!!.....got followed by a 6' 4" stocking wearing tranny who kept blowing me kisses.......while my mates Judge and Carver sat there pissing themselves...

Steve Bryant

Sunday nights at FUBAR......u need a book about that..!!!!

Howard 'Helvis' Boyle

So it was my 21st birthday smash up. Been to Manumission all night... Where i used to die on a toilet in front of 10,000 people every week Dressed as the King. eating a cheese burger....Then roll into Garden of Evil (Eden) Where i meet Brandon for the first time. He was wearing a Arab mask on his head and was holding court with a few girls...... Straight away it was 500mph banter between us and he was intrigued that I was with my Dad who had done more little fellas then anyone, and was chewing his face off at the bar. After 4 hours of madness we all head off to Bora Bora where Brandon, Alex and johnny the dwarf have a light sabre fight on the beach. The force was strong with them. Legendary!

Mark

I remember one night we drove down from hatch end to bournemouth where you were DJing with boy george at the academy and we did 10 grammes between us, most of it on the way down there, many a night was spent in the hatch end sin bin where you got too off your nut to turn up to your gigs. another night at hatch end i was in bed with some bird and my mate let you in and you sat on the end of the bed whilst me and her were at it and wouldnt move till you got some bugle!

Wayne Anthony

In 1995 I was promoting the Havin'It in Ibiza compilation series and a night at Pacha called Love It so I was on the island and late one night I bumped into a drunken Brandon and Alex P sitting outside a bar knocking back shots. I joined them as we knocked back around 20 shots, as a group of lads and girls sat on the table next to us, each with a poster from one of the island's club nights, talking excitedly about the DJs playing there. And in particular about Brandon and Alex, who they clearly had never seen before because they were sat right next to them. After ten minutes of going on about how good the lads were, I decided to butt in, introducing them to Brandon and Alex. The group laughed it off, and because Alex and Brandon had been out for three days and were in no mood to chat with them, they had no reason to believe me. I on the other hand found it extremely funny and continued my banter with the group who insisted that I was lying. In the end I suggested they let Brandon and Alex sign the posters because they'd be gutted when they found out it was true. They handed over the posters, Brandon wrote 'fuck off , you cunts' and Alex scribbled 'bollocks'. Priceless.

Sarah Sharples

I was working in Tipis Bar in Magaluf in 1997 and after I'd finished work at around 2am one night I went out for drinks and ended up at KOs Bar chatting to Brandon and he invited me over to Ibiza that morning. He was leaving at around 11am, so I went off back to my apartment and picked up a bag of clothes and headed to Ibiza to Space for the day, and on to outside event later that night where Brandon was also playing. The next morning I got a flight back to Majorca and was promptly sacked for missing a night's work. Little did they know that I was dancing about in Ibiza to Brandon, and I would have stayed if I'd known I was going to get sacked! I just want to thank Brandon and his friends for that great memory.

Catford D

When i first arrived in ibiza in 1995 i had never taken an e, done a line or been to a rave. That all changed quick but my abiding memory of 1995 was of you and Alex DJing at Space and of meeting up with you in the Star Cafe and Oacha, and our football matches with Juan, Ozzy and the crew on Friday afternoons. Cut forward to 96 and I was living in apartment No 1 behind Mambos with Mel and the girls and knocking out enough bugle to feed the 5000, most of it being taken by the pair of us. DJing wise you was running the show in 96, what with the Up Yer Ronson residency and Space there was no one to even come close to you that summer. It was always a proper laugh hanging round with you then, the highlight, the day of the electric storm and blackout no question. Me, you, Marcus, Blond Simon and the West End flooding, followed by mas nose at my apartment in the pitch black.

Unfortunately the bugle took a hold of me, as you will be aware of and be able to understand, it ruined everything for me, I think. I had tons of brilliant times but in 98 and 99 but even though i was resident at the New Star and Clockwork and DJing at Amnesia and Chic I had a cloud over me. I was fucked for pound notes due to the gear and couldn't recover. I owed everyone wedge and was taking so much shit it was impossible to get in front. You did so much for me in those times, most of which is not quantifiable in dollar because I just couldn't tell you how much you looked after me, except for £500 you gave me in one lump that I have always intended to return to you (more of that in a minute), but it wasn't just dough. You looked after me like a brother and even though I'm not around anymore that doesn't mean I don't remember those things.

Drugs fucked my life up bad and it has taken me years of graft with no raving or Ibiza to sort it but I am on top of my life finally at the age of 35. No matter how many Steve Angellos or David Guettas come along they are all playing catch up to you and Peezy in the achievement stakes because the pair of you privatised the sunday rave, that is your legacy even if it is not acknowledged. Every person who set foot in Ibiza in the 90s wanted to see you play but even though the music has changed, when you was rocking the terrace in them days no one has come close to that vibe since, it was the very definition of the word party, no fashion consciousness, no bad feeling, just friends and brilliant music and sunshine and the good memories you have left so many people have to be respected on the highest level.

I always idolised you and its nobody's fault I went off the rails except my own. I have dealt with all my shit through years in the wilderness, and next summer I am coming to see people I have not seen in a long long time and you are top of the list, monkey in hand, thanks for always being such a brilliant friend. I will see you next summer, and the first drink is on me, your main man always.

Selina

Although Blocko's book will be a huge success & make all those that read it roar with laughter, some of his escapades for those that love him dearly are hard to relive. There are still chapters of his life I don't like talking to him about, there are pictures I hate to see, memories I wish I didn't have, hospital visit's I wish I hadn't had to make, BUT he's still here, still the same old Brandon, still the same kid he was when I met him nearly 30 years ago. So good luck with everything to come & sorry for not giving any stories, but even the title The Life & Lines of Brandon Block makes my face smile but my stomach tighten. Fondest wishes.

DEDICATIONS by Brandon Block

Anyone name-checked in the main body of this book was mentioned because they touched my life at some point. The following people also made a lasting impression on me. Apologies for anyone I've forgotten...the memory is not what it used to be!

Dear friends who have been lost over the years, but not forgotten...
Caroline Canning (Flo), Patrick Ranger, Elsie Bees, Big Ian Norgate, Breeze, Herman, Denton, Henry Spurgeon, Billy Hudson, Math Artimati, Lloydy, Jason Farr.

The early years...
Toady Norgate, Carl Norgate, Nugget, Adrian, Hornet, Terry Shepherd, Ali Sham, Mitch and Rob (wonderful memories of your wedding in Thailand), Janet Bees, The Mullins, Russell and Dawn, Jane Chappell, Alison Holder, Lisa Mania, Sam Goldie, Steve & Louise Arts, JK and Norma Keane, Michelle Jobe, J'O B - The Under The Pool Table Club, Tom and Karen, Keiran, Anthony Lol, Chris Winters, Tony Brown, Trevor and Roy, Dean Delaney, Jimmy Woodley, John, Rob and Dennis Hutchinson, Rossi, Todd and Jason Axton, Andy Lee, Andy Hobbs, Paul and Wayne Pinto, Mick Bastien, Nick Williamson, Debbie Williamson, Joe Sidoli, Jill and Blue Jeans, Mark Ruston, Milkshake, Bullet, Phil Jenkins, Nick, Liggie, Gwan Fey, Sandy Redhead, Gabby, Rob Marks, Brad Barnes, Tony Neir, Lesley Thompson, Andy Barracliffe, Henry and Wendy Mac, Macky, Henry Weatherly, Red Lester, Noel and Pat Purcell, Dean Paul, Buzzard, Dean Long, Jason Long, Jim Teelan.

DJs, friends and clubland figures who I've had fun with...
Pat Bones, John Kelly, Shovel, Clifton, Roy the Roach & Rachel, Pete Marsh, Des Mitchell, Chris Good, John Grainger, Jimmy 'P' Prentice, Nancy Noise and Jimmy, Gerry Drew, Simon Baldwin, Ginger Mick, Greek Chris, Craig Walsh, Charlie the Hat, Tony 'Balearic' Wilson, Andy Nicholls, Steve Bicknall, Smokin Jo, Mark Haggerty, Noel Watson, Bobby & Steve, Chrissy T, Rude Boy Rupert, Benji

THE LIFE & LINES OF BRANDON BLOCK

Candelerio, Paul Jackson, Gareth Cooke, Paul Harris, Steve Smith, Gary Dillon, Steve Butler, John Adamson (To the Manor Born), Canny Bag a Chooda, Mark Rowell, John Shaw (South Sheilds), Ya Fanny Smells a Coconuts in a Jordy Accent, ee, why its bountee!!!, Alex Lowes (Southport Weekender), Andy Curry, Enzo, Johnny Orange, Luke Neville, Barry and Barry Faulkner and Ashley (Sugarshack Empire), Ricky McGowan, Jon Mancini (Colours), Zammo (Rhumba Club), Stuart Macmillan and Orde Meikel (Slam Soma Records), Bumper, Nagger, Bongo Clive, Andy Harkin, Jon (Pleased), Dave Pearce, Little John Manumission, Tyrone & Chris Griffin (Godsckitchen), Marion Stone, The Cuban Brothers, Matt Swan, Plug, Nikki from Maidenhead, Jackie from Walton, Charlie Blau, Bryn, Andy Swallow, The Captain, Simon Bentley, Andy Harkin, Ollie Lang, Damon, Jon Fitz and Frankie Barbados (Castle Club, Ayia Napa), Johnny and Andy (Temptation, Cambridge), Danny, Scott and Tracey Mac, Simon Gavin, Graham Ball, Rob Manley, Dylan, Andy Savva (Exeter Pavilion), Darren Stokes, Micky Brookes, Beero, Judge Jules, Fergie, Billy Nasty, Al Mackenzie, Jon Carter, MYNC Project, Rob Wilder, Steve Lawler, Pete Gooding, Andy Baxter, Alex Wolvenden, all at MOS, Hed Kandi - The Originals, Mark Doyle, Andy Norman, John Jones, Paul Wilkins, Gordon Mac and everyone at Kiss - thanks for the great years....DJ Suzy, Nicola Stapleton, Chris Butler and Gina, Slipmatt, Vanessa P, Vanessa F, Carpet Face and Audible, Clifton, Brett and Keiran Hayes, Brad and Kirsty (Sugar), Brad Martin, Alison Cook, Cymon Eckles, Jon Rocka, Jon Dickens, Jonny O, Gary Haisman, John Dennis, Carl, Splurge, Evette Spurgeon, Mitzy, Steve and Simon Hanson, Lawrence and Jonny Nelson, Leo and Russ (Sitting Pretty), Howie (Coaltion), Simon Coggin, Fitz, Trevor, Tanner, Danny Miller, Markus Peck, Danny Harrison, Gilley, George and Mike at The Villa, Mark Otis Reading, Jaffa, Badger, Elliot, Paul Payne, Richard and Paul Bamford, Simon Lincoln, Mark Spear, Elias, Steve Dobson, Matt Hutch, Ian Ellis, Maria and Michael Lopez, Stacy and Brian Tough, Mark Abery, Russell Cleaver, Lisa Nash, Denzel, The Sharp Boys, Mark Fuller, Carl Pearsall, Russell Clements, Catford Dan, John Davies the Priest, Eddie Lock, Hippy Sid (even with his haircut), Vaughan (Flower Power Pacha), Charlie Parker, Tony Garvey, Ginger Dean, Little Simon, DJ Pippi, Jim Bond, Nick & Sid (Rock Bar),

Ceasar de Morello, Giovanni (Es Paradis), Tony Onetto, Jason Cooker, Stuart Patterson, Dave Jarvis, Danny Tenaglia, Frankie Knuckles, Tony Humphries, David Morales, Josh Wink, Ralph Lawson, Nick Tan, Alex Miles, Mike & Claire, Andy & Dawn, Stuart, Griff and Jay, Elliot and all from Manumission, Mo and all the Bartons from Cream, Alex Ellinger (alubias cocidas con heilo!!!), Keith Robinson, Martin, Paul and Jodi Shoer, Phil The Golf, Jimmy, Dave and Laura Low, Jesse James, Jeremy B, Jem J, Jeff Jefferson, Jeff at Gigamesh, Jason Lorimer, Carlton and Jason M, Big Joe Egan, Adam Saint, Jason Heard, Pete Walsh, Paul Taylor, Matt Playford, Matt Frost, Matt Earley, Martin, Luke and Simon (Luke 1997), Adam Kate (464), Danny (Red Alert Agency), DJ Kiddo, Kevin Mac, Kie and Sarah Guy, Josh Roberts, Phat Phil Cooper, Tank and Troy, Jaran, Jamesy, Mark Walker, Tony Grimley, Tony Nicholls, Howard Donald, Twiggy, Wayne and Gary (Honey Club, Brighton), Yousef, Ziggy, Tomislav, Stixx, Steph Chanlder, Spencer, Fenton, Slim, Steve, Russ and Barry Prestige, Roy Fulbrook, Ronnie Trainer, Debbie Chappel, Debbie Birch, Deano (Imaculate), Mark Squirrell, Barney, Billy Dunseath, Rob Burton, Richie Malone, Richard Dinsdale, Eddie Temple-Morris, Ed Kurno, Hardy, Boy George, Gaz White, Fat Tony, Darren Braddock, Daniella Westbrook, James Parker, Andy Thompson, Kerry J, Kerry, Tony Petchell, James Byford, Ilka, James Bronson, Howard Marks, Greg Stainer, Mark Sampson, Spencer Baldwin, Mark Knight, Nick Turner, Nick Bridges, Lucy Saunderson, Damo Walsh, Dan Montila, Danae Gooch, Danny Foster, Danny Francis, Danny Hutch, Craig Egan, Louisa Demarco, Gary Dedman, Steve Walker, Leroy Fornhill, Nick Breton, Grant Halder, Alsy Rosenthal, Dirty Sanchez, Sasha Levy, Steve Altman, Maria & Michael Lopez, Johnny Press, Adam O'Dowd, Sam Fitsch, Nick Rafferty, Neil (Candy Club), Owen (Area), Steve Harvey, Wayne Eldridge, Mete...and all at Dance Aid!

Ruislip Massive...
Spence, Sherry, Ollie, Andy Campbell, Matty Wright, Mark, Darren, Clive, Glenn and Darren, Carly, Lisa, Maria and Cayley, Paul Kelly, Ryan, Rob Kentish, Paul Winter and my fantastic neighbours LOVE ALWAYS! - Jane, Terry, Craig and Keith.

Agents...
Cath Mckenzie and Brian Merchant, Paul at Pure DJs and Barry at Fresh DJs. Thanks for all the hard work over the last few years.

Pubs...
The Woodman: Chris Teresa, Paul Burley, Tony Bean, Dave Bean, Faz, Chelsea Chris, Rangers Chris, Spurs Doug, Big Pete, Dennis.
The Six Bells: Mark and Sarah.
The Clubhouse: Hapz, Jags and Gee.

Other friends I've made on my travels...
Dubai: Tim, Dai, Matt, Sara, Buff.
Greece: DJ Romylos...my Greek brother, DJ Petros.
Ayia Napa: Michaelis, Charlie, Dassos, Andreas, Bambos.
Mallorca: Sam, Ricardo, Gordon Phillips, Damon Jay, Doc.
Skiing: Scotty, Rob Sawyer, Warren Smith, Laurence Fuchs, Latte, John White, Darren BCM.
Thailand: Aaron Jesson, Marco Saltzman, Army Paul, Joe Chablis, Cliff Tuck, Matty Sunset, Simon (Dream Girls), Nick, Des and Chim, Dean Lambert, Big Ian and Bobby.

To all my new friends at Blenheim CDP - thanks for everything, looking forward to some new projects.

Very special mentions to Samantha Webb - thanks for your inspiration and knowledge...and to Selina and Justine for your unfaltering friendship and support!

All it leaves me to say is...hold tight you nutbags, cod'n'tater, on goes ya boot off...I'll be the judge of that!, Top Of The Pops...let's 'ave it! (not too much, though). LOL xxx

Blocko x

ACKNOWLEDGEMENTS by Matt Trollope

My partner in rhyme Jax for the belief to take on this project initially and her support throughout.

Mum and Dad...if Carlsberg did parents...

To Brandon for this unique opportunity...and the hundreds of kebabs, dinners and random gifts along the way.

Millsy! What can I say? My rock on the Ibiza field trip and my Blocko confidant ever since. Your 'assange' over the last few months was vital.

Jimmy P for his sterling work with all things imagery, and for putting up with all my emails. Seriously!

Lindsay Jones for the proof in the pudding. An amazing job!

To all the people who have contributed during the project...and especially the interviewees...Vivienne Block, Harvey Block, Emma Block, Ali, Aves, Brady, Matthew Donegan, Dean Thatcher, Swainy, Jon Jules, Lisa Loud, Lisa Horan, Dizzi, Karen Dunn, Mark Sloper, Tony Hannan, Jenny Rampling, Danny Gould, Andy Manston, Chris Brown, Tony Byrne, Dominic Spreadlove, Carlos Diaz, Pepe Rosello, Javier and Christian Anadon, Ernesto Zenith, Gee Moore, Tony Truman, Norman Cook, Darren Emerson and Jeremy Healy...thank-you one and all...and a special mention to Jason Bye, whose prompt and extensive photo selection was also hugely appreciated.

Much gratitude to Bill Shanahan for his expertise. Respect sir.

Stuart Patterson for the pep talk at the start...and the beano to Nice.

To Peter Marshall for his 'professional view'.

James Desborough for his brainstorming and vision.

Bill Brewster for his advice. Rob Blake for the Space terrace poster.

Suz Willems for her sheer enthusiasm!

I'd also like to thank those friends who offered continual encouragement along the way... Andy Constantinou, Nicky Holt, Mem Mousa, Cheryl Robinson, Jackie Ross, Ash Sheldrick, Matty Wilkins, Jane Adams, Ronnie Turner (and his bottle of JD!!!) and Jose De Oliveria.

To my journalism heritage... Roy Mills for my big break at the Romford Recorder all those years ago, thus securing my place in the 'Golden Lion All Stars' alongside Roy Bridge, Sheelagh Bree, Dave Kidd, Dave Warriner and Roy Weal... and not forgetting, down the road in Ilford, my loyal editor Chris Carter.

And last, but not least - Bill from Impressions for the light at the end of the tunnel!

ABOUT THE AUTHOR

Matt Trollope completed his NCTJ journalism degree at Harlow College in 1991 and blagged a job on his local paper, The Romford Recorder. His dance music journey began a decade earlier on a family trip to New York when, at the age of ten, his spends secured a seven inch copy of I'm In Love by Evelyn 'Champagne' King. He had the beat in his young Essex bones and his east London background helped school him in jazz funk, before acid house exploded in the late '80s during his late teens. As Matthew James, Matt freelanced for DJ Magazine and M8 throughout the '90s and flirted with the national tabloids too. Dance music-related projects have included record shop Izit Dance ('94 - '96), a spin-off DJ agency ('96 - '03) and co-ownership of lovable rave den The Lodge in London, NW10 ('04 - '08). Matt lives in Ladbroke Grove with partner Jax.

For full biography go to www.matttrollope.com.

* Matt is also the author of One More - A Definitive History Of UK Clubbing, 1988 - 2008.

Printed in Great Britain
by Amazon.co.uk, Ltd.,
Marston Gate.